# IFIP Advances in Information and Communication Technology 511

## Editor-in-Chief

*Kai Rannenberg, Goethe University Frankfurt, Germany*

## Editorial Board

## IFIP – The International Federation for Information Processing

IFIP was founded in 1960 under the auspices of UNESCO, following the first World Computer Congress held in Paris the previous year. A federation for societies working in information processing, IFIP's aim is two-fold: to support information processing in the countries of its members and to encourage technology transfer to developing nations. As its mission statement clearly states:

> IFIP is the global non-profit federation of societies of ICT professionals that aims at achieving a worldwide professional and socially responsible development and application of information and communication technologies.

IFIP is a non-profit-making organization, run almost solely by 2500 volunteers. It operates through a number of technical committees and working groups, which organize events and publications. IFIP's events range from large international open conferences to working conferences and local seminars.

The flagship event is the IFIP World Computer Congress, at which both invited and contributed papers are presented. Contributed papers are rigorously refereed and the rejection rate is high.

As with the Congress, participation in the open conferences is open to all and papers may be invited or submitted. Again, submitted papers are stringently refereed.

The working conferences are structured differently. They are usually run by a working group and attendance is generally smaller and occasionally by invitation only. Their purpose is to create an atmosphere conducive to innovation and development. Refereeing is also rigorous and papers are subjected to extensive group discussion.

Publications arising from IFIP events vary. The papers presented at the IFIP World Computer Congress and at open conferences are published as conference proceedings, while the results of the working conferences are often published as collections of selected and edited papers.

IFIP distinguishes three types of institutional membership: Country Representative Members, Members at Large, and Associate Members. The type of organization that can apply for membership is a wide variety and includes national or international societies of individual computer scientists/ICT professionals, associations or federations of such societies, government institutions/government related organizations, national or international research institutes or consortia, universities, academies of sciences, companies, national or international associations or federations of companies.

More information about this series at http://www.springer.com/series/6102

Gilbert Peterson · Sujeet Shenoi (Eds.)

# Advances in Digital Forensics XIII

13th IFIP WG 11.9 International Conference
Orlando, FL, USA, January 30 – February 1, 2017
Revised Selected Papers

 Springer

*Editors*
Gilbert Peterson
Department of Electrical and Computer
  Engineering
Air Force Institute of Technology
Wright-Patterson AFB
USA

Sujeet Shenoi
Tandy School of Computer Science
University of Tulsa
Tulsa
USA

ISSN 1868-4238          ISSN 1868-422X  (electronic)
IFIP Advances in Information and Communication Technology
ISBN 978-3-319-88396-0     ISBN 978-3-319-67208-3  (eBook)
DOI 10.1007/978-3-319-67208-3

Printed on acid-free paper

This Springer imprint is published by Springer Nature
The registered company is Springer International Publishing AG
The registered company address is: Gewerbestrasse 11, 6330 Cham, Switzerland

# Contents

# Contributing Authors

**Sudhir Aggarwal** is a Professor of Computer Science at Florida State University, Tallahassee, Florida. His research interests include password cracking, information security and building software tools and systems for digital forensics.

**Albert Antwi-Boasiako** is the Principal Consultant at e-Crime Bureau, Accra, Ghana and Cyber Security Advisor to the Government of Ghana, Accra, Ghana; he is also a Ph.D. student in Computer Science at the University of Pretoria, Pretoria, South Africa. His research interests are in the area of digital forensics, with a focus on digital forensic process standardization.

**Stefan Axelsson** is an Associate Professor of Computer Science at the Norwegian University of Science and Technology, Gjovik, Norway; and an Associate Professor with the Norwegian National Criminal Police, Oslo, Norway. His research interests include digital forensics, intrusion and fraud detection, visualization and digital surveillance.

**Nicole Beebe** is an Associate Professor of Cyber Security at the University of Texas at San Antonio, San Antonio, Texas. Her research interests include digital forensics, cyber security and advanced analytics.

**Saheb Chhabra** is a Ph.D. student in Computer Science and Engineering at Indraprastha Institute of Information Technology, Delhi, India. His research interests include image processing and computer vision and their applications to document fraud detection

**Tommy Chin** is an M.S. student in Computing Security at Rochester Institute of Technology, Rochester, New York. His research interests include cyber security and digital forensics.

**Kam-Pui Chow** is an Associate Professor of Computer Science at the University of Hong Kong, Hong Kong, China. His research interests include information security, digital forensics, live system forensics and digital surveillance.

**Junbin Fang** is an Associate Professor of Optoelectronic Engineering at Jinan University, Guangzhou, China; and a Visiting Professor in the Edward S. Rogers Sr. Department of Electrical and Computer Engineering, University of Toronto, Toronto, Canada. His research interests include digital forensics, quantum cryptography and visible light communications.

**Ryan Good** is an M.S. student in Computer Science at the Air Force Institute of Technology, Wright-Patterson Air Force Base, Ohio. His research interests include digital forensics and network security.

**Zachary Grimmett** recently received his Ph.D. degree in Computer Engineering from the University of Tulsa, Tulsa, Oklahoma. His research interests include mobile communications devices, digital forensics and malware analysis.

**Garima Gupta** is a Post Doctoral Researcher in Computer Science and Engineering at Indraprastha Institute of Information Technology, Delhi, India. Her research interests include image processing and computer vision and their applications to document fraud detection

**Gaurav Gupta** is a Scientist D in the Ministry of Information Technology, New Delhi, India. His research interests include mobile device security, digital forensics, web application security, Internet of Things security and security in emerging technologies.

**Monika Gupta** recently received her Ph.D. degree in Physics from the National Institutes of Technology, Kurukshetra, India. Her research interests include image processing and computer vision and their applications to document fraud detection

**Qi Han** is an Associate Professor of Computer Science and Technology at Harbin Institute of Technology, Harbin, China. His research interests include digital video forensics, hiding communications and digital watermarking.

**Bruno Hoelz** is a Computer Forensics Expert at the National Institute of Criminalistics, Brazilian Federal Police, Brasilia, Brazil. His research interests include multiagent systems and artificial intelligence applications in digital forensics.

**Shiva Houshmand** is an Assistant Professor of Computer Science at Southern Illinois University, Carbondale, Illinois. Her research interests include computer and network security, authentication, digital forensics and usable security.

**Zoe Jiang** is an Assistant Professor of Computer Science and Technology at the Shenzhen Graduate School, Harbin Institute of Technology, Shenzhen, China. Her research interests include cryptography and digital forensics.

**Qiong Li** is a Professor of Computer Science and Technology at Harbin Institute of Technology, Harbin, China. Her research interests include quantum cryptography, multimedia security and biometrics.

**Rui Li** is a Visiting Assistant Professor in the Golisano College of Computing and Information Sciences at Rochester Institute of Technology, Rochester, New York. His research attempts to address multidisciplinary data analytics challenges by developing scalable statistical procedures and efficient learning algorithms.

**Sijin Li** is a B.S. student in Information Engineering at Jinan University, Guangzhou, China. His research interests include digital forensics, computer vision and deep learning.

**Changwei Liu** is a Postdoctoral Researcher in the Department of Computer Science, George Mason University, Fairfax, Virginia. Her research interests include network security, cloud computing security and digital forensics.

**Lishu Liu** is a Machine Learning Engineer at RetailMeNot, Austin, Texas. Her research interests involve the application of machine learning algorithms to locate, extract and present relevant information from massive data sets.

**Marcelo Maues** is a Computer Forensics Expert at the Renato Chaves Center of Forensic Sciences, Belem/Para, Brazil. His research interests include computer and network forensics.

**Logan Morrison** is a Computer Scientist with the U.S. Department of Defense in Washington, DC. His research interests include digital forensics, computer security and data recovery.

**Rayan Mosli** is a Ph.D. student in Computing and Information Sciences at Rochester Institute of Technology, Rochester, New York. His research interests include memory-based malware detection and digital forensics.

**Mariusz Nowostawski** is an Associate Professor of Computer Science at the Norwegian University of Science and Technology, Gjovik, Norway. His research interests include machine learning, code generation, autonomous and biology-inspired computing, blockchain and distributed ledger technology, and mobile and heterogeneous peer-to-peer computing.

**Martin Olivier** is a Professor of Computer Science at the University of Pretoria, Pretoria, South Africa. His research focuses on digital forensics – in particular the science of digital forensics and database forensics.

**Oluwasayo Oyelami** is an M.Sc. student in Computer Science at the University of Pretoria, Pretoria, South Africa; and an Information Security Analyst at Performanta, Midrand, South Africa. His research interests include digital forensics, information security and threat intelligence.

**Yin Pan** is a Professor of Computing Security at Rochester Institute of Technology, Rochester, New York. Her research interests include game-based digital forensics and memory-based malware detection.

**Gilbert Peterson**, Chair, IFIP Working Group 11.9 on Digital Forensics, is a Professor of Computer Science at the Air Force Institute of Technology, Wright-Patterson Air Force Base, Ohio. His research interests include digital forensics, artificial intelligence and statistical machine learning.

**Dmytro Piatkivskyi** is a Ph.D. student in Cyber and Information Security at the Norwegian University of Science and Technology, Gjovik, Norway. His research focuses on the analysis of off-chain scalability solutions for Bitcoin and other crypto-currencies with an emphasis on security.

**Heloise Pieterse** is a Senior Researcher at the Council for Scientific and Industrial Research, Pretoria, South Africa; and a Ph.D. student in Computer Science at the University of Pretoria, Pretoria South Africa. Her research interests include digital forensics and mobile device security.

**Huw Read** is an Associate Professor of Digital Forensics and Director of the Center for Advanced Computing and Digital Forensics at Norwich University, Northfield, Vermont. His research interests include digital forensics and computer security.

**Sujeet Shenoi** is the F.P. Walter Professor of Computer Science and a Professor of Chemical Engineering at the University of Tulsa, Tulsa, Oklahoma. His research interests include critical infrastructure protection, industrial control systems and digital forensics.

**Anoop Singhal** is a Senior Computer Scientist in the Computer Security Division at the National Institute of Standards and Technology, Gaithersburg, Maryland. His research interests include network security, network forensics, web services security and data mining.

**Jason Staggs** recently received his Ph.D. degree in Computer Science from the University of Tulsa, Tulsa, Oklahoma. His research interests include telecommunications networks, industrial control systems, critical infrastructure protection, security engineering and digital forensics.

**Iain Sutherland** is a Professor of Digital Forensics at Noroff University College, Kristiansand, Norway. His research interests include digital forensics and data recovery.

**Renier van Heerden** is a Principal Researcher at the Council for Scientific and Industrial Research, Pretoria, South Africa. His research interests include network security, password security and network attacks.

**Hein Venter** is a Professor of Computer Science at the University of Pretoria, Pretoria, South Africa. His research interests are in the area of digital forensics, with a focus on digital forensic process standardization.

**Xuan Wang** is a Professor and Ph.D. Supervisor in the Computer Application Research Center at the Shenzhen Graduate School, Harbin Institute of Technology, Shenzhen, China. His research interests include artificial intelligence, computer vision, computer security and computational linguistics.

**Duminda Wijesekera** is a Professor of Computer Science at George Mason University, Fairfax, Virginia. His research interests include systems security, digital forensics and transportation systems.

**Guikai Xi** is a B.S. student in Information Engineering at Jinan University, Guangzhou, China. His research interests include digital forensics, deep learning and machine intelligence.

**Kaiqi Xiong** is an Associate Professor of Cybersecurity, Mathematics and Electrical Engineering at the University of South Florida, Tampa, Florida. His research interests include computer and network security.

**Konstantinos Xynos** is a Senior Researcher and Senior Manager at DarkMatter LLC, Dubai, United Arab Emirates. His research interests include digital forensics and computer security.

**Ken Yau** is an M.Phil. student in Computer Science at the University of Hong Kong, Hong Kong, China. His research interests are in the area of digital forensics, with an emphasis on industrial control system forensics.

**Zi Ye** is a Data Analyst at Andorra Life in Los Angeles, California. Her research interests include the application of machine learning algorithms to locate, extract and present relevant information from massive data sets.

**Siu-Ming Yiu** is an Associate Professor of Computer Science at the University of Hong Kong, Hong Kong, China. His research interests include security, cryptography, digital forensics and bioinformatics.

**Liyang Yu** is a Lecturer of Software and Microelectronics at Harbin University of Science and Technology, Harbin, China. His research interests include digital image and video forensics.

**Bo Yuan** is a Professor and Chair of Computing Security at Rochester Institute of Technology, Rochester, New York. His research focuses on applications of computational intelligence in cyber security.

# Preface

Digital forensics deals with the acquisition, preservation, examination, analysis and presentation of electronic evidence. Networked computing, wireless communications and portable electronic devices have expanded the role of digital forensics beyond traditional computer crime investigations. Practically every type of crime now involves some aspect of digital evidence; digital forensics provides the techniques and tools to articulate this evidence in legal proceedings. Digital forensics also has myriad intelligence applications; furthermore, it has a vital role in information assurance – investigations of security breaches yield valuable information that can be used to design more secure and resilient systems.

This book, *Advances in Digital Forensics XIII*, is the thirteenth volume in the annual series produced by the IFIP Working Group 11.9 on Digital Forensics, an international community of scientists, engineers and practitioners dedicated to advancing the state of the art of research and practice in digital forensics. The book presents original research results and innovative applications in digital forensics. Also, it highlights some of the major technical and legal issues related to digital evidence and electronic crime investigations.

This volume contains sixteen revised and edited chapters based on papers presented at the Thirteenth IFIP WG 11.9 International Conference on Digital Forensics, held in Orlando, Florida on January 30 to February 1, 2017. The papers were refereed by members of IFIP Working Group 11.9 and other internationally-recognized experts in digital forensics. The post-conference manuscripts submitted by the authors were rewritten to accommodate the suggestions provided by the conference attendees. They were subsequently revised by the editors to produce the final chapters published in this volume.

The chapters are organized into seven sections: Themes and Issues, Mobile and Embedded Device Forensics, Network and Cloud Forensics, Threat Detection and Mitigation, Malware Forensics, Image Forensics and Forensic Techniques. The coverage of topics highlights the richness and vitality of the discipline, and offers promising avenues for future research in digital forensics.

This book is the result of the combined efforts of several individuals. In particular, we thank Mark Pollitt and Jane Pollitt for their tireless work on behalf of IFIP Working Group 11.9. We also acknowledge the support provided by the U.S. National Science Foundation, U.S. National Security Agency and U.S. Secret Service.

GILBERT PETERSON AND SUJEET SHENOI

# I

# THEMES AND ISSUES

# Chapter 1

# ESTABLISHING FINDINGS IN DIGITAL FORENSIC EXAMINATIONS: A CASE STUDY METHOD

Oluwasayo Oyelami and Martin Olivier

**Abstract**    In digital forensics, examinations are carried out to explain events and demonstrate the root cause from a number of plausible causes. Yin's approach to case study research offers a systematic process for investigating occurrences in their real-world contexts. The approach is well suited to examining isolated events and also addresses questions about causality and the reliability of findings. The techniques that make Yin's approach suitable for research also apply to digital forensic examinations. The merits of case study research are highlighted in previous work that established the suitability of the case study research method for conducting digital forensic examinations. This research extends the previous work by demonstrating the practicality of Yin's case study method in examining digital events. The research examines the relationship between digital evidence – the effect – and its plausible causes, and how patterns can be identified and applied to explain the events. Establishing these patterns supports the findings of a forensic examination. Analytic strategies and techniques inherent in Yin's case study method are applied to identify and analyze patterns in order to establish the findings of a digital forensic examination.

**Keywords:** Digital forensic examinations, Yin's method, establishing findings

## 1.    Introduction

Causality is about drawing relationships between an observed phenomenon – the effect – and its plausible cause(s) [4, 6, 7, 10, 19, 23]. Establishing these relationships supports the findings of a forensic examination. In establishing cause and effect relationships, a forensic examiner identifies patterns in the evidence that may be used to establish findings and also to attribute the source. Understanding these patterns and how

© IFIP International Federation for Information Processing 2017

Published by Springer International Publishing AG 2017. All Rights Reserved

G. Peterson and S. Shenoi (Eds.): Advances in Digital Forensics XIII, IFIP AICT 511, pp. 3–21, 2017.

DOI: 10.1007/978-3-319-67208-3_1

they can be applied to test hypotheses are central to establishing the findings of a forensic examination.

In order to demonstrate causality, a forensic examiner searches for patterns that support a hypothesis. The more supporting patterns that are found, the more compelling are the causal findings. These supporting patterns ultimately form a web of consistency that provides support for the findings of the forensic examination. The use of a web of consistency is supported by Casey's certainty scale [3], which notes that evidence supported by multiple independent sources has a higher certainty value than information obtained from a single source.

The case study research method proposed by Yin [25] offers a systematic process for investigating occurrences in their real-world contexts. This research method is very popular in the social sciences, where it has a definite focus; in fact, Yin's seminal book on the topic is currently in its fifth edition [25]. An analysis of Yin's approach reveals that it is particularly appropriate for examining isolated events; moreover, it addresses questions on causality and the reliability of findings. The merits of case study research are discussed in earlier work [18], which established the suitability of the case study research method for conducting digital forensic examinations. This research extends the earlier work by demonstrating how the case study method can be applied in digital forensic examinations.

## 2.     Causality and Digital Systems

A digital system contains a complex set of software programs that are executed within the system. The control logic of a program executes and controls the operations of the program. It receives input commands from a user and executes the commands on the computing system. It also controls and executes automated operations that have been structured in the software program.

The execution of input commands and/or automated operations by the control logic causes effects in a digital system. This implies that the control logic is the cause of the effects in the system. An effect triggered by the control logic may be a passive effect or an active effect. A passive effect occurs when control logic execution causes traces or side effects in the digital system; thus, passive effects are referred to as traces or side effects in the system. On the other hand, an active effect occurs when control logic execution triggers further control logic executions in the system; these further executions of control logic correspond to active effects in the system. Active effects may also leave traces that are passive.

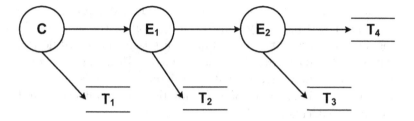

*Figure 1.* Cause and effect in a digital system.

Figure 1 illustrates a cause and effect in a digital system. A cause $C$ leaves a passive effect or trace $T_1$ and its execution triggers an active effect $E_1$. The initiation of the active effect $E_1$ leaves a trace $T_2$ and its execution triggers another active effect $E_2$. The initiation of the active effect $E_2$ leaves a trace $T_3$ and the execution of the active effect $E_2$ leaves a trace $T_4$. As illustrated in Figure 1, an effect can be an active effect or a passive effect, which is a trace in the system. The active effects – namely, the control logic executions – are transient in the system. In other words, active effects are not observable because the execution of a command itself is invisible in the system. It is the traces that are observed in the system.

The following examples clarify the concepts of cause and effect in a digital system:

- **bash Shell Command Execution:** An example of cause and effect in a digital system is the execution of a **bash** shell command initiated when a certain input is provided by a user. The input to the **bash** shell is stored in the **bash** history and execution is initiated by the control logic. A forensic examiner knows that the control logic initiated the **bash** shell command because of the traces of the command initiation left in the **bash** history. However, the execution of the **bash** command itself is invisible. Therefore, it is not possible to know if the command did execute. It is also possible that environmental variables may have been configured to disable the **bash** history. However, programs that execute may leave traces and a forensic examiner may conclude that the program caused the traces.

- **crontab File Execution:** A second example is the execution of a **crontab** file. A **crontab** is a system service that causes commands to be executed at specified times. The execution of **crontab** is controlled by the **cron** daemon, whose control logic executes the commands in the system background. When the specified time for a command execution is met, the `cron` daemon initiates the command and passively logs the initiation of the command. The logging of the `crontab` command is a passive effect while the execution of the command is an active effect. However, the command may or may not have executed and may not leave any traces in the system. There may or may not be passive effects to indicate execution success or failure.

- **Database Trigger Execution:** A third example is the execution of a database trigger. A database trigger executes a sequence of commands when a logical condition is met. The initiation of the database trigger may create a log entry (passive effect) and its execution may create another log entry and may also initiate another trigger (active effect) that may, in turn, cause a log entry.

- **Email Arrival at a Mail Transfer Agent:** A fourth example is the arrival of email at a mail transfer agent. Email is forwarded from one mail transfer agent to the next until it is delivered to the recipient's inbox. The arrival of an email at a mail transfer agent causes a log of the email communication to be written, which is a passive effect. The email is then routed to the next mail transfer agent in the delivery path or is delivered to the recipient's inbox. The routing of email is an active effect while the delivery to the recipient's inbox is a passive effect.

Drawing inferences from the above examples, the arrival of an email at a mail transfer agent is similar to a `bash` shell interface waiting for a command from the user. It is also similar to a `cron` daemon waiting until the time arrives to execute a command from `crontab`. It is also similar to a database watching data and waiting for a condition to be met in order to execute an operation. From these examples, it is possible to conclude that a `bash` shell command entered by a user, the logical conditions satisfied in the `crontab` and database trigger examples and the arrival of an email at a mail transfer agent are all forms of input to a system executed by the control logic that causes effects to occur in the system.

A digital system operates in a pre-set mode of execution and system configuration; additionally, as illustrated above, it is programmed to accept certain inputs. Depending on the input that is received, the control logic executes the expected sequence of commands that are predefined by the system. Depending on the system configuration, certain traces are typically left in the system. This implies that, by analyzing the system configuration and the known inputs, a forensic examiner may be able to predict the traces that will be in the system. This can be viewed

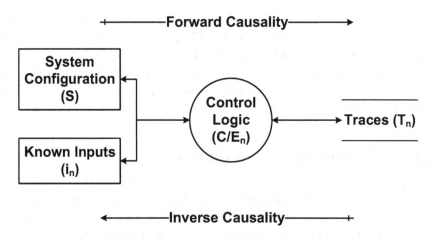

*Figure 2.* Causality in a digital system.

as "forward causality." On the other hand, a forensic examiner may also be able to use the traces found in a system to predict the system configuration and system inputs at the time; this can be described as "inverse causality."

Figure 2 illustrates the notions of causality in a digital system. Forward causality enables a forensic examiner to predict the traces that are expected based on the system configuration and program input. Inverse causality enables an examiner to predict the plausible causes in the system. Based on the predictions made from the traces by applying inverse causality, an examiner can test the predictions made about the plausible causes by applying forward causality to demonstrate the observed side effects or traces.

## 3.     Using Yin's Method

This section reviews the application of Yin's case study approach as a scientific method for conceptualizing digital forensic examinations [18]. The case study method as described by Yin [25] is suitable for examining isolated occurrences. The process of carrying out a forensic examination involves three main aspects: (i) understanding the body of knowledge in the field; (ii) formulating hypotheses in the examination; and (iii) testing the hypotheses (empirical testing).

### 3.1     Body of Knowledge

A forensic examiner must have scientific knowledge and experience in the forensic field in order to practice in the field. An understanding of the body of knowledge in the field is a necessary requirement for all forensic science disciplines [9, 13, 15, 17]. An examiner must have expert knowledge in the field in which the examination is intended to be carried out. Without expert knowledge in the field, an examiner cannot consistently make valid claims nor will the hypotheses be based on the body of knowledge and experience gained from scientific practice within the profession.

## 3.2 Hypotheses Formulation

Hypotheses formulation is driven by the questions that are asked about the evidence [22, 26]. The formulation plays an important role in the examination of evidence [1, 2, 5]. The process of formulating hypotheses also guides the examination phase. Hypotheses formulation typically yields multiple hypotheses, one is the main hypothesis and the others are alternative hypotheses. The main hypothesis reflects what the examiner expects to observe and demonstrate in the context of the examination. The alternative hypotheses are plausible explanations that oppose the main hypothesis and must be disproved.

In forming a hypothesis, an examiner typically would seek to answer one or two main forms of questions during the examination of the evidence. In its first form, the examiner may be required to address a decision problem [14]. In its second form, the requirement is to address a narrative problem [20, 21].

The decision problem addresses the examination of evidence in terms of the narrative. For example, a generic decision problem in digital forensics may be stated as "Does this sequence occur on the disk?" where the sequence may refer to a software signature, execution of malicious software, downloaded software or evidence of a network intrusion or compromise. A decision problem is usually answered by a yes, no or inconclusive.

The narrative problem, on the other hand, addresses the examination in terms of causality. An example is "What caused this sequence to occur on the disk?" where the sequence is as illustrated above. The narrative problem requires an examiner to examine and explain the facts that support the conclusions that are made. Interested readers are referred to [14, 20, 21] to explore the use of decision problems and narratives in digital forensics.

Hypotheses formulation takes one of the two forms discussed above. While a narrative problem may also be interpreted in the form of a decision problem, both forms serve different purposes, but also achieve the same goal of explaining the findings made from the evidence examination. Hypotheses formulation should be done before examining the evidence to ensure that the examination is free from bias [8, 9, 13, 16].

It is important to note that, depending on the nature of the examination, it may not be necessary to formulate hypotheses. For example, when measurements are required to determine an outcome, the formulation of hypotheses is not a requirement.

## 3.3    Hypotheses Testing

The main purpose of the evidence analysis phase is to test the hypotheses. In testing a hypothesis, a forensic examiner has to consider the likelihood of a particular occurrence reaching a definite conclusion. In the example above, which asks the question "Does this sequence occur on the disk?" the examiner may seek to demonstrate the occurrence of the sequence on the disk. The result is usually a yes or no based on the weight of the supporting patterns found in the evidence. The result may also be inconclusive, indicating that what is observed does not provide sufficient proof to confirm or deny the plausibility of the occurrence of the sequence. This may occur in situations involving file deletion, evidence tampering or insufficient evidence.

The question "What caused this sequence to occur on the disk?" examines the occurrence in terms of causality. A forensic examiner may seek to demonstrate that the sequence is attributable to a certain cause and confirm the hypothesis. However in doing this, the examiner must also actively identify evidence that refutes the hypothesis. An examiner may successfully prove that an observed effect is attributable to a cause, but in order to strengthen the finding, the examiner must refute other plausible rival explanations.

A methodical approach must be applied to prove the hypothesis, analyze the evidence, establish causal relationships and demonstrate a web of consistency between the evidence and its plausible causes. A number of techniques proposed by Yin may be applied. The techniques include pattern matching, explanation building, time-series analysis and logic models [18, 24, 25]. Also, when examining complex digital evidence, an examiner may use the cross-case synthesis technique, which applies the logic of replication, namely literal replication and theoretical replication.

The pattern matching technique enables an examiner to compare patterns predicted before an examination against the observed patterns. Predicted patterns are expected findings based on the body of knowledge and apply forward causality [18, 24, 25]. Using the pattern matching technique, an examiner can demonstrate that a set of hypotheses or explanations $E$ explains a set of observed patterns or observations $O$, while knowing $E$ but not having observed $O$ at the time.

The explanation building technique enables an examiner to develop a narrative of a case by specifying a set of causal relationships about the occurrence, or explaining how and why the occurrence happened [18, 24, 25]. This involves stating an initial hypothesis or explanation about the case and then testing the hypothesis. If the hypothesis is found to be inconsistent, it is revised to reflect the new findings. The revised hypothesis or explanation is then tested again as more observations are made in an iterative manner until an explanation is made that fully reflects the final findings of the case. Using the explanation building technique, an examiner can demonstrate how, from an initial set of hypotheses or explanations $E_1$, an examiner can iteratively revise and create new explanations $E_i$ that are consistent as the observed patterns $O_i$ are examined.

The time-series analysis technique enables an examiner to bring together key aspects of an occurrence in chronological order. The chronology also reflects the case as a set of causal relationships, showing which key aspects may have caused or contributed to the existence of other aspects [18, 24, 25]. The time-series analysis technique enables an examiner to determine that the observed patterns $O_i$ are not causal effects of other patterns based on their occurrence times.

A logic model enables an examiner to break down a complex occurrence into repeated cause and effect patterns and to demonstrate how the final findings are obtained from intermediate findings [18, 24, 25]. Analysis of the logic model identifies the observed patterns $O_i$ that may have contributed to the occurrence of other observed patterns.

Another important technique is cross-case synthesis, which is mainly applied in multiple case examinations. The cross-case synthesis technique involves multiple case studies that help determine whether the findings from selected cases support any broader or particular conclusions. This technique applies the logic of replication, which has two components, literal replication and theoretical replication. In literal replication, an examiner selects a number of cases with the goal of demonstrating similar findings; this provides a web of consistency. Theoretical replication enables an examiner to select and examine another set of cases while predicting opposing results with the goal of invalidating the opposing results [18, 24, 25].

Whatever the technique or combination of techniques employed in a case, a forensic examiner must consider and address the observed patterns that point to alternative explanations. In doing so, the examiner collects data on alternative explanations and examines them in order to demonstrate their suitability or unsuitability. Demonstrating the un-suitability of rival explanations can be very helpful in explaining the case.

## 4. Causal Relationships in Digital Forensics

This section discusses causal relationships in digital forensics and how these relationships can be established.

### 4.1 Understanding Causal Relationships

Drawing relationships between a cause and its effect requires the iden-tification of patterns during the analysis of evidence. The patterns that are found can be applied to establish and demonstrate various relation-ships. These relationships include correlations, data consistency and plausible causes. Relationships that form correlations are discerned from patterns that reflect matching data. Consistency relationships are de-rived from patterns that posit a cause or plausible causes on an effect. Plausible causes are a number of likely mechanisms or actions that can initiate an effect or may have initiated an effect.

A valid user name and its corresponding password are matching data that have a correlation as a login credential. A relationship that demon-strates consistency could be a successful login attempt to a website, which reflects a valid user name and that the corresponding entry in the password database was applied. A successful login attempt to a website may also be achieved via an SQL injection mechanism captured in a database log (that enabled access to login information) or via a brute force attack. Plausible causes of the successful login to the site are the use of an SQL injection mechanism, brute force attack and valid login credentials. By identifying patterns in the evidence, a forensic examiner can posit that an action was taken that caused an effect to occur. Corre-lating patterns from matching data support the claim of consistency and consistency patterns can be applied to demonstrate causal relationships.

### 4.2 Establishing Causal Relationships

Establishing causal relationships supports the findings of a forensic examination. It also strengthens the claims of causal inferences made by the examiner. The three main concepts that help establish causal relationships are: (i) specification of the necessary and sufficient con-ditions for causality; (ii) establishment of a web of consistency in the evidence; and (iii) refutation of alternative hypotheses or explanations.

**Necessary and Sufficient Conditions for Causality.** An effect may occur under certain conditions and a number of conditions may be necessary for an effect to occur. The existence of a number of causes may not indicate that all the plausible causes contributed to the effect. A cause may be considered to be sufficient to initiate an effect without the participation of other conditions or causes. Thus, a forensic examiner may be required to determine the cause(s) that contributed to the effect observed from two or more plausible causes. The examiner may further determine the conditions under which the effect would be rendered implausible. A condition $X$ is deemed to be necessary for an effect $B$ to occur if and only if the falsification of the condition $X$ guarantees the falsification of $B$. A condition $X$ is deemed to be sufficient if its occurrence guarantees that the effect $B$ will occur. Necessary conditions are the conditions without which an event cannot occur whereas sufficient conditions are the conditions that guarantee an expected outcome.

Consider a simple example where $X$ implies visiting a web page and the side effects $B_i$ of $X$ may be the HTML file displayed on the screen, followed by subsequent connections to retrieve images for the page, followed by requests to retrieve the linked web pages. The action of $X$ may also cause the source IP address to be logged on the server, the web page to be logged in the browser web history, the file to be cached at the source system, and so on.

Suppose that $X$ and $Y$ are two events where a web page was visited and assume that a defendant has acknowledged $X$ and denied $Y$. It is sufficient to prove that $Y$ occurred if the forensic examiner can show that the conditions necessary for $Y$ to have occurred are observed and the effects that can be attributed to the occurrence of $Y$ are also observed. The demonstration of these conditions establishes a web of consistency in the evidence, which shows that the claim is backed by multiple sources of evidence that support the findings. A finding made in an examination without the necessary conditions of the hypothesis being met refutes the validity of a hypothesis.

**Web of Consistency.** A web of consistency is established when evidence from various sources are found to corroborate and, therefore, create a convincing argument for the findings. The specification of the necessary and sufficient conditions of a case supports the establishment of a web of consistency. The more tightly coupled the evidence, the less likely that there will be several plausible causes.

In the case of the example above, where the defendant denied that a web page $Y$ was visited, establishing a web of consistency requires that devices such as a firewall, proxy server and/or intrusion detection system in the network have activity logs that validate the fact that the web page was visited. Examining the defendant's computing device may also provide evidence from the browser web history, web cache, search history, cookies and web beacons that stored information about the defendant's online activities. It is also possible that the defendant may have cleared the cache and deleted web history records. The examiner may then have to show that deletions occurred. In essence, the examiner expects to see traces or signs of deletion in order to make justified inferences about the case. When there are limited or no traces, justified inferences cannot be made about the case.

**Alternative Hypothesis and Explanations.** As stated above, plausible alternative explanations may be found that explain an occurrence. These explanations may be eliminated or at least considered doubtful by showing that one or more conditions necessary for the effect to be considered attributable to the alternative cause were not found. A statement by Campbell [24, 25] demonstrates the significance of alternative rival explanations in the examination of occurrences: "More and more I have come to the conclusion that the core of the scientific method is not experimentation *per se*, but rather the strategy connoted by the phrase 'plausible rival hypothesis'."

The refutation of rival explanations can be used as a criterion for interpreting the findings of an examination. When rival alternative hypotheses are refuted, the findings of an examination are strengthened. The forensic examiner must demonstrate that a certain rival cause does not fully address the conditions present in the case and, therefore, cannot be an attributable cause. This provides a more convincing argument for the findings. The greater the number of rival explanations that are addressed and excluded, the stronger the findings of the case.

In summary, when establishing causal relationships, the specification of the necessary and sufficient conditions, the creation of a web of consistency and the examination of alternative explanations enable a forensic examiner to demonstrate sufficient proof of the hypothesis and to strengthen the findings of the examination.

## 5.     Lottery Terminal Hacking Incident

This section illustrates the application of the case study method to demonstrate causality in a lottery terminal hacking incident [11]. The incident involved the manipulation of a lottery game system known as 5 Card Cash [12]. The 5 Card Cash game is based on standard poker with a digital 52-card playing deck. A player purchases a system-generated ticket that has five randomly-selected cards. The player can win up to two times. The first win is an instant prize based on the composition of the cards on the player's ticket. The second win is when the lottery organizer randomly draws five cards from a deck that evening and the player is able to match two or more cards on the purchased ticket with the five randomly-drawn cards.

## 5.1    The Case

The 5 Card Cash game was suspended after it was suspected that lottery terminals may have been manipulated. Specifically, the game winnings were observed to be much larger than the game parameters should have allowed.

## 5.2    The Investigation

An investigation determined that some lottery ticket operators were manipulating their terminals to print more instant winner tickets and fewer losing tickets.

An investigator determined that an operator could slow down a lottery terminal by requesting a number of database reports or by entering several requests for lottery game tickets. While the reports or requests were being processed, the operator could enter sales for 5 Card Cash tickets. However, before a ticket was printed, the operator could see on the screen if the ticket was an instant winner. If the ticket was not a winner, the operator could cancel the sale of the ticket before it was printed.

## 5.3    The Examination

The examination focuses on testing the inferences made by the investigator. This is done by applying the principles and techniques of the case study method. The goal is to demonstrate how the inferences may have been determined and the certainty with which the inferences can be considered to be reliable.

Because the case itself does not provide much information about the design of the 5 Card Cash game, a generic design is used to illustrate the examination and the assumptions about the workings of the game system. The generic game system configuration presented in Figure 3 provides the context for the examination.

The system has six components, which perform functions such as generating lottery tickets, processing payments for tickets, printing tickets and generating reports. The output of one system component may also be an input to another component. This implies that certain system components must execute before another component can begin to exe-

| INPUT: Select(Lottery Game) | INPUT: Process(Details) | INPUT: Payment(Approved) |
|---|---|---|
| EXECUTE: Run(Option) | EXECUTE: Run(Payment) | EXECUTE: Generate(Ticket) |
| OUTPUT: Process(Details) | OUTPUT: Payment(Approved/ Declined) | OUTPUT: Ticket |

| INPUT: Select(Report) | INPUT: Ticket/Report | INPUT: Process(Cancellation) |
|---|---|---|
| EXECUTE: Generate(Report) | EXECUTE: Process(Ticket/Report) | EXECUTE: Process(Refund) |
| OUTPUT: Report | OUTPUT: Printout | OUTPUT: Start |

*Figure 3.* 5 Cash Card game system.

cute. For example, a ticket has to be generated before it can be displayed or printed. Also, reports have to be generated before they can be printed.

## 5.4    Hypotheses Formulation

From the initial investigation described above, the questions that the examiner may be asked can be framed as a decision problem and as a narrative problem. The decision problem addresses the examination in terms of the narrative and the narrative problem addresses the examination in terms of causality.

The two problems are stated as follows:

- **Decision Problem:** Are transactions deliberately canceled after the results are known?

- **Narrative Problem:** What enables the cancellation of transactions after the results are known?

The case study based on these two questions tests the hypothesis:

- **Hypothesis:** The terminal was manipulated in order to display the results in a manner that provided the operator with an undue advantage in determining favorable results and enabling the cancellation of unfavorable transactions.

The expected outcome of testing the hypothesis is to confirm its claim. In order to do this, the examination must demonstrate that unfavorable transactions were canceled after the results were known and that transactions considered to be favorable were allowed to continue. The alternative rival hypothesis is:

- **Rival Hypothesis:** The terminal was not manipulated in any way and the winnings are the result of legitimate transactions obtained within the scope of the game parameters.

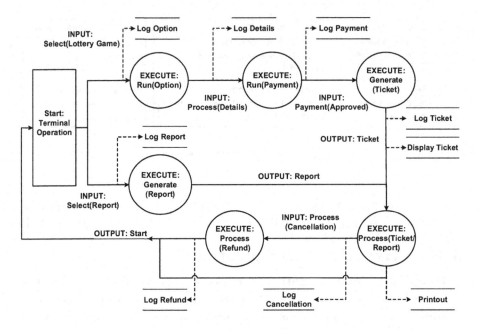

*Figure 4.* Cause and effect pattern (logic model).

## 5.5    Hypothesis Testing

Based on the game system configuration in Figure 3, a forensic examiner can express the system in terms of the cause and effect pattern or logic model shown in Figure 4. Figure 4 models the game system in terms of input, execution and output. An input to query the database using Select(Report) triggers the control logic to initiate the generation of the report; this initiates a passive effect to print the report.

Another pattern is observed in ticket generation. The selection of the lottery game triggers the program control logic to initiate the payment module, which issues the ticket and sends it to the printer without prompting the user. The ticket is also displayed as a passive effect.

In order to test the hypothesis that the terminal was manipulated, the examiner has to first specify the conditions that are necessary and sufficient to demonstrate the manipulation of the terminal. Specifying these conditions enables the examiner to know what to test. As stated above, necessary conditions are those without which an event cannot occur whereas sufficient conditions are those that guarantee the expected outcome.

The necessary conditions required to support the hypothesis that the terminal was manipulated are:

- There were sold tickets within a short time period before the transaction deadline.

- The terminal was busy or delayed during the time that the winning tickets were printed.

- Only unfavorable tickets during terminal busy/delay times were canceled.

These conditions are necessary in order for the operator to have an undue advantage in determining the results and cancelling unfavorable transactions.

The sufficient conditions are expected to provide a definite indicator of malicious activity. Specifically, it is sufficient to prove the hypothesis if it can be shown that:

- The activities specified under the necessary conditions occurred at numerous times.

- There is a consistent pattern with which these activities occurred.

In essence, the forensic examiner is required to demonstrate that, if there were late ticket sales and the terminal was busy, then the ticket sales made mostly involved winning tickets and the ticket sales canceled mostly involved unfavorable tickets. Also, the examiner may be able to show that this pattern occurred at numerous times in a consistent manner. Proving the hypothesis in this way eliminates the chance of having an alternative hypothesis that would take into consideration the necessary and sufficient conditions highlighted in the case. A hypothesis that cannot explain these conditions is excluded. Note that sufficient conditions may only be found if the hypotheses made are narrowed down to plausible explanations.

The specification of the necessary and sufficient conditions also helps establish a web of consistency. After observing the logs of system activities, the forensic examiner may be able to conduct a time-series analysis that displays the transactions along with their occurrence times.

Querying the log of generated tickets helps the examiner determine whether or not tickets were sold within a specified time period before the transaction deadline. The query provides the examiner with data that can be further analyzed to determine if tickets were processed when the terminal was busy or delayed. To do this, the results from querying the sold ticket log are compared with the results from the log of reports generated. This analysis is based on the knowledge that the terminal would be busy or delayed when the suspect tickets were generated and when the reports were being processed. The analysis provides the examiner with a smaller set of tickets that were generated when the terminal was busy or delayed. Using this set of tickets, the examiner would expect to discover that winning tickets were printed and unfavorable tickets were canceled. To determine whether only unfavorable tickets during terminal busy times were canceled, the set of tickets is compared with the log of canceled transactions. This could enable the examiner to show that a larger number of unfavorable tickets were canceled and the remaining tickets that were not canceled were primarily winning tickets.

The examiner successfully demonstrates the correctness of the hypothesis when the necessary conditions for the case have been proved. This indicates that the terminal could have been manipulated such that the results were known before the transactions were completed and unfavorable transactions were deliberately canceled.

In order to demonstrate sufficient proof of the hypothesis, the examiner may widen the scope of the analysis to other time frames for the same terminal, demonstrating that manipulations occurred multiple times and, thus, establishing a web of consistency. It may also be sufficient to demonstrate that the unfavorable tickets sold when the terminal was not busy were legitimate transactions conducted on behalf of a lottery user by the operator.

Using replication logic, the examiner can also expand the scope of the examination to consider multiple cases. By applying literal replication, the examiner could examine a number of suspected terminals using the same conditions and sufficiently demonstrate that manipulations occurred on the suspected terminals. This would further confirm and strengthen the hypothesis while enabling a web of consistency to be established.

By applying theoretical replication, the examiner can select another set of suspected terminals and examine them to invalidate the alternative hypothesis (i.e., falsify the hypothesis that the terminals were not manipulated). Another theoretical replication approach is to select a number of known "clean" terminals and show that the type of manipulation found on the suspected terminals could not be found on the clean terminals.

The identification, testing and validation of the necessary and sufficient conditions of a hypothesis and the application of analytic techniques and strategies in the case study method strengthen a forensic examination. In particular, demonstrating causal relationships and establishing a web of consistency ensure that the findings of the examination are consistent and reliable.

This case study has used a logic model to illustrate the application of an analytic technique in a forensic examination of a digital system. Other analytic techniques, namely pattern matching, explanation building, time-series analysis and cross-case synthesis, can also be applied to establish findings in digital forensic examinations.

## 6. Conclusions

This chapter has sought to demonstrate the practicality of the case study method in digital forensic examinations. The focus has been on applying the case study method to establish the findings of a forensic examination. The research clarifies the relationship between digital evidence – the effect – and its plausible causes, and how patterns can be identified and applied to demonstrate the findings. By applying Yin's case study method, an examiner can establish the relationships that support and validate the findings of a forensic examination.

Further research is required to demonstrate how the case study method can be applied to strengthen the findings of a forensic examination. The suitability and applicability of the four validity tests of Yin's method and the tactics applied to satisfy these tests need to be investigated for use in a digital forensic environment. Strengthening the findings of a forensic examination would ensure that a logical approach has been followed and that the findings follow from the underlying hypotheses.

## References

[1] M. Bunge, *Philosophy of Science: From Problem to Theory, Volume One*, Transaction Publishers, New Brunswick, New Jersey, 1998.

[2] B. Carrier, A Hypothesis-Based Approach to Digital Forensic Investigations, CERIAS Technical Report 2006-06, Center for Education and Research in Information Assurance and Security, Purdue University, West Lafayette, Indiana, 2006.

[3] E. Casey, *Digital Evidence and Computer Crime: Forensic Science, Computers and the Internet*, Academic Press, Waltham, Massachusetts, 2011.

[4] F. Cohen, *Digital Forensic Evidence Examination*, ASP Press, Livermore, California, 2010.

[5] S. Garfinkel, P. Farrell, V. Roussev and G. Dinolt, Bringing science to digital forensics with standardized forensic corpora, *Digital Investigation*, vol. 6(S), pp. S2–S11, 2009.

[6] P. Gladyshev and A. Patel, Formalizing event time bounding in digital investigations, *International Journal of Digital Evidence*, vol. 4(2), 2005.

[7] C. Grobler, C. Louwrens and S. von Solms, A multi-component view of digital forensics, *Proceedings of the IEEE International Conference on Availability, Reliability and Security*, pp. 647–652, 2010.

[8] L. Haber and R. Haber, Scientific validation of fingerprint evidence under Daubert, *Law, Probability and Risk*, vol. 7(2), pp. 87–109, 2008.

[9] K. Inman and N. Rudin, *Principles and Practice of Criminalistics: The Profession of Forensic Science*, CRC Press, Boca Raton, Florida, 2000.

[10] M. Kwan, K. Chow, F. Law and P. Lai, Reasoning about evidence using Bayesian networks, in *Advances in Digital Forensics IV*, I. Ray and S. Shenoi (Eds.), Springer, Heidelberg, Germany, pp. 275–289, 2008.

[11] Lottery Post, Six now face charges in CT lottery scheme (`www.lotterypost.com/news/301512`), March 23, 2016.

[12] Maryland Lottery, What is 5 card cash? Baltimore, Maryland (`www.mdlottery.com/games/5-card-cash`), 2017.

[13] National Institute of Justice and National Research Council, *Strengthening Forensic Science in the United States: A Path Forward*, National Academies Press, Washington, DC, 2009.

[14] M. Olivier, On complex crimes and digital forensics, in *Information Security in Diverse Computing Environments*, A. Kayem and C. Meinel (Eds.), IGI Global, Hershey, Pennsylvania, pp. 230–244, 2013.

[15] M. Olivier, Combining fundamentals, traditions, practice and science in a digital forensics course, presented at the *South African Computer Lecturers' Association Conference*, 2014.

[16] M. Olivier, Towards a digital forensic science, *Proceedings of the Information Security for South Africa Conference*, 2015.

[17] M. Olivier and S. Gruner, On the scientific maturity of digital forensics research, in *Advances in Digital Forensics IX*, G. Peterson and S. Shenoi (Eds.), Springer, Heidelberg, Germany, pp. 33–49, 2013.

[18] O. Oyelami and M. Olivier, Using Yin's approach to case studies as a paradigm for conducting examinations, in *Advances in Digital Forensics XI*, G. Peterson and S. Shenoi (Eds.), Springer, Heidelberg, Germany, pp. 45–59, 2015.

[19] J. Pearl, *Causality: Models, Reasoning and Inference*, Cambridge University Press, Cambridge, United Kingdom, 2009.

[20] M. Pollitt, Digital forensics as a surreal narrative, in *Advances in Digital Forensics V*, G. Peterson and S. Shenoi (Eds.), Springer, Heidelberg, Germany, pp. 3–15, 2009.

[21] M. Pollitt, History, historiography and the hermeneutics of the hard drive, in *Advances in Digital Forensics IX*, G. Peterson and S. Shenoi (Eds.), Springer, Heidelberg, Germany, pp. 3–17, 2013.

[22] S. Tewelde, M. Olivier and S. Gruner, Notions of hypothesis in digital forensics, in *Advances in Digital Forensics XI*, G. Peterson and S. Shenoi (Eds.), Springer, Heidelberg, Germany, pp. 29–43, 2015.

[23] S. Willassen, Hypothesis-based investigation of digital timestamps, in *Advances in Digital Forensics IV*, I. Ray and S. Shenoi (Eds.), Springer, Boston, Massachusetts, pp. 75–86, 2008.

[24] R. Yin, *Applications of Case Study Research*, Sage Publications, Thousand Oaks, California, 2012.

[25] R. Yin, *Case Study Research: Design and Methods*, Sage Publications, Thousand Oaks, California, 2013.

[26] T. Young, Forensic Science and the Scientific Method, Heartland Forensic Pathology, Kansas City, Missouri (`www.heartla ndforensic.com/writing/forensic-science-and-the-scienti fic-method`), 2007.

# Chapter 2

# A MODEL FOR DIGITAL EVIDENCE ADMISSIBILITY ASSESSMENT

Albert Antwi-Boasiako and Hein Venter

**Abstract**     Digital evidence is increasingly important in legal proceedings as a result of advances in the information and communications technology sector. Because of the transnational nature of computer crimes and computer-facilitated crimes, the digital forensic process and digital evidence handling must be standardized to ensure that the digital evidence produced is admissible in legal proceedings. The different positions of law on matters of evidence in different jurisdictions further complicates the transnational admissibility of digital evidence. A harmonized framework for assessing digital evidence admissibility is required to provide a scientific basis for digital evidence to be admissible and to ensure the cross-jurisdictional acceptance and usability of digital evidence. This chapter describes a harmonized framework that integrates the technical and legal requirements for digital evidence admissibility. The proposed framework, which provides a coherent techno-legal foundation for assessing digital evidence admissibility, is expected to contribute to ongoing developments in digital forensics standards.

**Keywords:**   Digital evidence, admissibility assessment framework

## 1. Introduction

Despite the significance of digital evidence in legal proceedings, digital forensics as a forensic science is still undergoing transformation. The rapidly advancing information and communications technology sector and the evolution of cyber crimes and legal responses underpin these developments. Digital evidence admissibility is a key issue that arises from the application of digital forensics in jurisprudence. However, a reproducible and standardized framework that provides a foundation for the admissibility of digital evidence in legal proceedings has not been addressed holistically in the literature on digital forensics harmonization

© IFIP International Federation for Information Processing 2017

Published by Springer International Publishing AG 2017. All Rights Reserved

G. Peterson and S. Shenoi (Eds.): Advances in Digital Forensics XIII, IFIP AICT 511, pp. 23–38, 2017.

DOI: 10.1007/978-3-319-67208-3_2

and standardization. This research addresses the gap by proposing a harmonized model that integrates technical and legal requirements to determine the admissibility of digital evidence in legal proceedings.

## 2.      Background

This section discusses digital forensics, digital evidence and previous research on digital forensics harmonization and standardization.

## 2.1      Digital Forensics and Digital Evidence

Digital forensics refers to the methodical recovery, storage, analysis and presentation of digital information [7]. Digital evidence is simply a product of a digital forensic process [11]. According to ISO/IEC 27037 [8], digital evidence is information or data stored or transmitted in binary form that may be relied upon as evidence. Digital evidence has become important because of the involvement of electronic devices and systems in criminal activities. A review of the literature and court documents suggests that digital evidence is generally admissible in many jurisdictions [14].

Digital forensics as a scientific discipline is rooted on classic forensic principles. It is underpinned by Locard's exchange principle, which states that contacts between two persons, items or objects will result in an exchange [4]. Thus, traces are left after interactions between persons, items or objects.

An example can establish the relationship between the exchange principle and digital forensics. In order for a laptop to be connected to a protected wireless network, the laptop must make its media access control (MAC) address available to the wireless network administrator (router) before receiving access. An exchange occurs between the two devices and traces are left after the connection is established (the router has logs of the wireless access and the laptop has artifacts pertaining to the access).

Computer users leave digital traces called digital footprints. Digital forensic examiners can identify computer crime suspects by collecting and analyzing these digital footprints.

The application of digital forensics in legal proceedings is significant. Digital forensics is applied in pure cyber crime cases and incidents as well as in cyber-facilitated incidents. This is because it is nearly impossible in today's information-technology-driven society to encounter a crime that does not have a digital dimension. Pure cyber crimes are those that can only be committed using computers, networks or other information technology devices or infrastructures; examples include hacking and denial-of-service (DoS) attacks. Cyber-facilitated crimes, on the other hand, are conventional crimes that are perpetrated using computers, networks or other information technology devices or infrastructures; examples include murder, human trafficking, narcotics smuggling and sales, and economic crimes such as financial fraud.

Digital evidence is highly volatile. Unlike other traditional types of evidence, digital evidence can be altered rapidly through computing-related activities [18]. A few mouse clicks on a file could alter its metadata, which is a key determinant of evidence admissibility. When a user clicks on a file, he may not necessarily intend to alter the file metadata. However, doing so potentially alters metadata such as the last accessed time, which may render the file inadmissible as evidence. In order to ensure that evidence is admissible, the court must be satisfied that the evidence conforms to established legal rules – the evidence must be scientifically relevant, authentic, reliable and must have been obtained legally [13].

The fragility of digital evidence also presents challenges [1]. The rapidly-changing nature of technology, the fragility of the media on which electronic data is stored and the intangible nature of electronic data all render digital evidence potentially vulnerable to claims of errors, accidental alteration, prejudicial interference and fabrication. These technical issues combined with legal missteps or difficulties could affect the admissibility of digital evidence. Even when digital evidence is admitted, these factors could impact the weight of the evidence in question. Several efforts have focused on harmonizing digital forensic processes and activities in order to address the technical and legal issues regarding the admissibility of digital evidence.

## 2.2    Harmonization and Standardization

According to Leigland and Krings [12], digital forensic processes and techniques are generally fragmented. Approaches for gathering digital evidence were initially developed in an *ad hoc* manner by investigators, primarily within law enforcement. Personal experience in digital investigations and expertise gained over time have led to the development of *ad hoc* digital investigation models and guidelines [12].

Several researchers and practitioners have attempted to develop harmonized digital forensic frameworks. The first attempt at the Digital Forensics Research Workshop (DFRWS) in 2001 produced a digital forensic process model that consists of seven phases [16]: (i) identification; (ii) preservation; (iii) collection; (iv) examination; (v) analysis; (vi) presentation; and (vii) design. Reith et al. [17] have proposed an abstract model of digital forensics. The Association of Chief Police Officers Good Practice Guide [2] and the U.S. Department of Justice Electronic Crime Scene Investigation Guide [21] are examples of efforts undertaken by law enforcement to harmonize digital forensics and provide common approaches for conducting digital forensic investigations. Valjarevic and Venter [23] have proposed a harmonized digital forensic model that attempts to resolve the fragmentation associated with digital forensic processes. The Scientific Working Group on Digital Evidence (SWGDE) [20] has published guidelines that cover specific incident investigations.

The standardization of digital forensics achieved major milestones when the International Organization for Standardization (ISO) published the ISO/IEC 27027 Standard – Guidelines for Identification, Collection, Acquisition and Preservation of Digital Evidence in 2012 [8] and the ISO/IEC 27043 Standard – Incident Investigation Principles and Processes in 2015 [10]. The two ISO/IEC standards provide guidelines for various incident investigations.

Despite the significant developments in digital forensics standardization, analysis suggests that current standards do not adequately address the issue of digital evidence admissibility. While it is essential to follow scientific investigative processes in conducting digital investigations, the admissibility of digital evidence is also impacted by other factors. Current standards are very applicable to digital forensic investigations, but they do not provide a basis for assessing the admissibility of digital evidence.

A review of the literature and court cases suggests that technical and legal requirements are considered when admitting digital evidence in legal proceedings [13]. However, the problem with digital evidence admissibility in the context of legal proceedings persists despite the formulation of standards for digital forensic processes. The question about which reproducible standardized criteria or benchmarks underpin digital evidence admissibility has not been answered by any of the existing digital forensic models. Therefore, it is imperative to develop a standardized model that harmonizes the technical and legal requirements in providing a foundation for digital evidence admissibility in legal proceedings.

## 3.    Requirements for Assessing Admissibility

This section discusses the need for harmonizing the technical and legal requirements in order to determine the admissibility of digital evidence. It also specifies the technical and legal requirements that underpin the admissibility of digital evidence in legal proceedings.

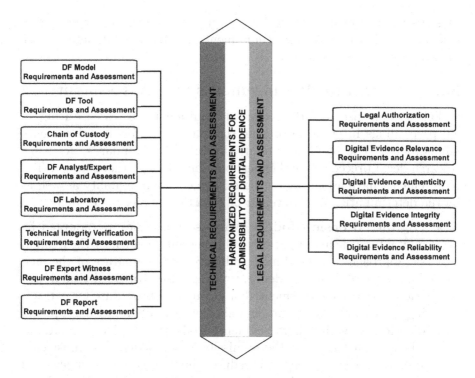

*Figure 1.* Technical and legal requirements for assessing admissibility.

## 3.1 Harmonization of Requirements

Analysis of the literature suggests that frameworks and standards pertaining to digital forensics do not address the question of digital evidence admissibility from a holistic perspective. In particular, the frameworks and standards specify technical processes and guidelines for incident investigators to follow when collecting digital evidence, but they fail to clarify the factors that underpin digital evidence admissibility.

Analysis of evidence admissibility in legal proceedings suggests the presence of technical and legal requirements that impact each other. In most jurisdictions, a legal authorization or search warrant (which is a legal requirement) is required before any digital device can be seized for a digital forensic examination (which is a technical requirement). Likewise, the manner in which digital evidence is retrieved during a digital forensic analysis (technical requirement) impacts the reliability of the evidence (legal requirement).

The harmonization of technical and legal requirements creates the foundation for determining the admissibility of digital evidence. Figure 1 presents the key technical and legal requirements that underpin digital evidence admissibility. These requirements are discussed in detail in the following sections.

## 3.2　　Technical Requirements and Assessment

This section discusses the technical requirements assessed during legal proceedings in order to provide the foundation for digital evidence admissibility. The requirements are derived from standards, academic research, legal precedents and expert opinion, among other sources. The requirements have a bearing on digital evidence admissibility as well as on the determination of the weight of a particular piece of evidence.

- **Digital Forensic Models:** Various approaches are adopted by digital forensic investigators to obtain digital evidence. Each forensic approach or procedure is influenced by the nature of the incident, type of digital evidence, typology of the target digital device and electronic environment. For example, a procedure for extracting digital evidence from a mobile device is different from a procedure for extracting digital evidence from a hard drive. As a result, when a court assesses the admissibility of evidence, it must consider the specific forensic procedures that were used to retrieve and process the evidence in question. Digital forensic models embody a number of guidelines to ensure that appropriate digital forensic procedures are followed when conducting investigations. Key guidelines for digital forensic processes and procedures have been proposed by the Association of Chief Police Officers in the United Kingdom [2], Scientific Working Group on Digital Evidence in the United States [20] and International Organization for Standardization via the ISO/IEC 27043 Standard [10].

- **Digital Forensic Tools:** Digital forensic practitioners have access to a number of open source and proprietary tools to assist in the collection, analysis and preservation of digital evidence. Although no explicit rules govern the use of digital forensic tools, there is generally a consensus in the scientific community that forensic tools should have been tested, validated and their error rates documented. The Daubert case in the United States [22] highlights the importance of digital forensic tool validation as a criterion for determining digital evidence admissibility. Organizations such as the National Institute of Standards and Technology (NIST), Scientific Working Group on Digital Evidence and International Organization for Standardization have developed frameworks and methods for testing digital forensic tools (see, e.g., ISO/IEC 27041 [9]).

- **Chain of Custody:** Chain of custody seeks to preserve the integrity of digital evidence. A document sponsored by the U.S. National Institute of Justice [15] defines chain of custody as a process used to maintain and document the sequential history of evidence. Chain of custody cuts across all the steps of an investigative process, but it is especially important during the digital evidence seizure stage. According to the Association of Chief Police Officers Good Practice Guide [2], an independent third party should be able to track the movement of evidence right from the crime scene all the way through the investigation chain to the courtroom. Giova [6] argues that digital evidence should be accepted as valid in court only if its chain of custody can be established.

- **Digital Forensic Analysts and Experts:** The qualifications of a digital forensic examiner are also an important requirement and assessment criterion related to digital evidence admissibility. Analysis suggests that digital forensics as a forensic science is a multidimensional discipline that encompasses computing (information technology), investigations and the law. A digital forensic examiner is expected to demonstrate his/her competence in digital forensics in order to handle digital evidence. Although no transnational competency standards have been created to validate the competence of digital forensic examiners, education and training, certifications and hands-on experience are generally considered to determine the suitability of an individual to handle digital evidence.

- **Digital Forensic Laboratories:** A well-organized digital forensic laboratory with standard operating procedures (SOPs) and quality assurance systems positively impacts investigative processes and, consequently, the quality of the produced evidence. The Association of Chief Police Officers Good Practice Guide [2] lists specific guidelines for setting up and operating digital forensics laboratories. For example, a failure to adopt relevant laboratory standard operating procedures could alter the original state of data stored on a mobile device. The use of a poor laboratory facility or inappropriate storage procedures could result in digital evidence being ruled inadmissible in legal proceedings [24].

- **Technical Integrity Verification:** Maintaining and verifying the integrity of digital evidence items are important technical considerations that could significantly impact their admissibility. Digital data is altered, modified or copied from one environment to another either through human actions or uncontrolled computing activities [18]. Forensic examiners adopt various methods for maintaining and demonstrating the integrity of digital evidence. The use of a write blocker, for example, is a standard digital forensic requirement to maintain the integrity of evidence. Digital signatures, encryption and hash algorithms are also employed to maintain, validate and demonstrate the integrity of digital evidence.

- **Digital Forensic Expert Witnesses:** Individuals with relevant expertise, knowledge and skills are often called upon to serve as expert witnesses in legal proceedings [19]. According the U.S. Federal Rules of Evidence, an expert witness must be qualified on the basis of knowledge, expertise, experience, education and/or training. The scientific, technical and other specialized knowledge possessed by an expert witness enables the individual to testify to the facts in question [19].

- **Digital Forensic Reports:** The report produced by a digital forensic investigation is an important technical consideration that underpins digital evidence admissibility. Garrie and Morrissy [5] maintain that a digital forensic report must have conclusions that are reproducible by independent third parties. They also argue that conclusions that are not reproducible should be given little credence in legal proceedings. In Republic vs. Alexander Tweneboah (Ghana Suit No. TB 15/13/15 of 2016), the high court judge in the financial court division ruled against a report submitted by an expert witness from the e-Crime Bureau because the judge deemed that the report did not fully represent the digital evidence contained on an accompanying CD.

## 3.3    Legal Requirements and Assessment

Most jurisdictions have legal requirements that provide the grounds for admissibility of digital evidence in legal proceedings. This section discusses the legal issues pertaining to the admissibility of digital evidence as listed in Figure 1.

- **Legal Authorization:** Assessing digital evidence often requires legal authorization. Human rights, data protection and privacy impacts on accused parties and victims must be respected. Although there may be exceptions, the law generally provides safeguards for protecting the rights of individuals. Obtaining a legal authorization grants judicial legitimacy to the evidence in question; indeed, this may be the most important step in obtaining and handling digital evidence. Search warrants are normally required to seize electronic devices and digital evidence. Failure to obtain a legal authorization may undermine the best evidence rule and jeopardize the case [13]. Admitting evidence that is not supported by legal authorizations could result in prosecutors and law enforcement (i.e., the state) trampling on civil liberties [9].

- **Digital Evidence Relevance:** Relevance is an important determinant of digital evidence admissibility. According to Mason [14], in order for evidence to be admissible, it must be "sufficiently relevant" to the facts at issue. Evidence cannot be admissible if it is not deemed to be relevant [12]. For a piece of evidence to be deemed relevant in legal proceedings, it must tend to prove or disprove a fact in the proceedings [3]. Evidence that has probative value must prove the fact in question to be more (or less) probable than it would be without the evidence.

- **Digital Evidence Authenticity:** Authenticity is another important criterion that impacts the reliability of evidence. According to Mason [14], for digital evidence to be admitted in a court of law, there must be adduced evidence that the evidence in question is indeed what it is purported to be. For example, for a digital record to be admissible, the court would have to be convinced that the record was indeed generated by the individual who is purported to have authored the record. The American Express Travel Related Services Company Inc. vs. Vee Vinhnee case [14] highlights the importance of the authenticity requirement. In this case, the judge felt that American Express failed to authenticate certain digital records and proceeded to rule against American Express on the basis of its failure to authenticate the records. American Express subsequently appealed, but the appeals court affirmed the lower court decision.

- **Digital Evidence Integrity:** Integrity refers to the "wholeness and soundness" of digital evidence [14]. Integrity also implies that the evidence is complete and unaltered. An assessment of evidence integrity is a primary requirement for digital evidence admissibility and serves as the basis for determining the weight of evidence. Mason [14] contends that digital evidence integrity is not an absolute condition but a state of relationships. In assessing the integrity of digital evidence, courts, therefore, consider several factors and relationships – primarily the technical requirements discussed in the previous section. Courts require the integrity of evidence to be established and guaranteed during investigations and the evidence to be preserved from modifications during its entire lifecycle [13]. In the Republic of South Africa, the originality of digital evidence depends on its integrity as outlined in Section 14(2) of the Electronic Communications and Transactions Act of 2002.

- **Digital Evidence Reliability:** In order for evidence to be admissible in court, the proferrer of the evidence must establish that no aspect of the evidence is suspect. Leroux [13] states that, for evidence to be deemed reliable, "there must be nothing that casts doubt about how the evidence was collected and subsequently handled." The Daubert case [22] provides the basis for assessing the reliability of scientific evidence in the United States. In particular, this celebrated case specifies five criteria for evaluating the reliability (and by extension, the admissibility) of digital evidence: (i) whether the technique has been tested; (ii) whether the technique has undergone peer review; (iii) whether there is a known error rate associated with the technique; (iv) whether standards controlling its operations exist and were maintained; and (v) whether the technique is generally accepted by the scientific community.

The integration of the technical and legal requirements discussed above provides the foundation of a harmonized framework for assessing digital evidence admissibility. It must be emphasized that cross examination in legal proceedings is an important element that impacts the assessment of the technical and legal requirements. The next section explores the relationships between the requirements and the considerations involved in determining digital evidence admissibility.

## 4.     Model for Assessing Evidence Admissibility

This section discusses the proposed harmonized model for digital evidence admissibility assessment and its application in legal proceedings. A harmonized conceptual model was developed in order to integrate the requirements discussed above. The conceptual model shown in Figure 2 provides a framework for establishing the dependencies and relationships between the various requirements and assessment considerations.

The conceptual model encapsulates three levels of harmonization, called phases, which are integrated in the proposed harmonized model for digital evidence admissibility assessment. The three phases are integrated but differ from each other in terms of their functional relevance to digital evidence admissibility assessment. Figure 3 presents the proposed harmonized model for digital evidence admissibility assessment.

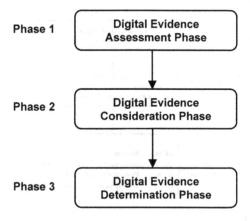

*Figure 2.* Digital evidence admissibility assessment model schema.

## 4.1 Phase 1: Evidence Assessment Phase

The digital evidence assessment phase establishes the legal foundation of the digital evidence in question. For example, when digital evidence residing on a hard drive belonging to a suspect is presented in court, the first consideration of the court is to determine the legal basis for the seizure of the hard drive. Essentially, the legal authority of the prosecution to seize the device has to be firmly established. In most jurisdictions, a court order may satisfy this requirement. Organizational policies and protocols may also provide the basis for the legal authority. Therefore, Phase 1 addresses the preliminary questions related to the legal admissibility of digital evidence. Generally, digital evidence is deemed inadmissible if it fails to meet the requirements imposed in this important phase. Indeed, Phase 1 also provides the grounds for further consideration of the digital evidence in question.

## 4.2 Phase 2: Evidence Consideration Phase

This phase focuses on the technical standards and requirements that underpin digital evidence admissibility. Technical considerations associated with the handling and processing of digital evidence are considered after the legal basis of the evidence has been established. This phase is subdivided into three categories:

- **Pre-Requisite Requirements:** These requirements must be considered before any core technical activities are conducted. The requirements include digital forensic model, tool, analyst/expert and laboratory requirements and assessments.

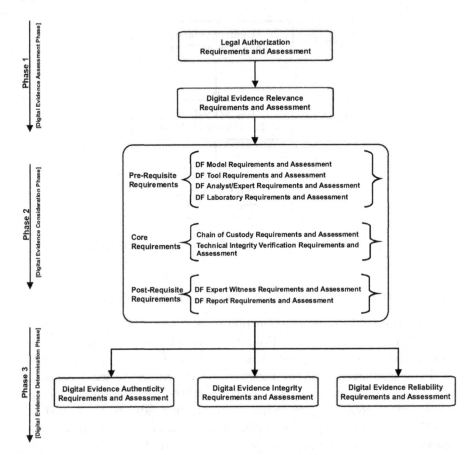

*Figure 3.* Harmonized model for digital evidence admissibility assessment.

- **Core Requirements:** These principal technical requirements significantly impact the determination of the admissibility of digital evidence. The requirements comprise chain of custody and technical integrity verification requirements and assessments.

- **Post-Requisite Requirements:** These requirements further elaborate or explain the requirements in the two previous categories. The requirements comprise digital forensic expert witness and report requirements and assessments.

Phase 2 focuses on the technical requirements and considerations of digital evidence. The phase is very important because judicial conclusions (Phase 3) are based primarily on the assessment outcomes of the technical requirements.

## 4.3     Phase 3: Evidence Determination Phase

This phase underpins court decisions in determining the admissibility and weight of digital evidence. The determinations of the Phase 3 requirements are based on the assessment outcomes of the Phase 2 requirements (technical requirements). The determination of the weight of a piece of digital evidence is based on the results of the various technical considerations; each technical criterion has a specific impact (impact factor) on the evidence. For example, although the lack of a digital forensic laboratory may impact a case involving digital evidence, the failure to document and track the chain of custody of a piece of digital evidence could have a wider impact on the evidence than the lack of a laboratory facility.

## 5.     Application in Legal Proceedings

The harmonized model provides a holistic techno-legal foundation for assessing digital evidence admissibility in legal proceedings. The model integrates the key technical requirements associated with digital forensics and the legal principles that underpin evidence admissibility across different jurisdictions. As a result, the harmonized model helps address the issue of digital evidence admissibility from a trans-jurisdictional perspective with particular emphasis on the cross-border handling of digital evidence. By incorporating best practices for digital evidence assessment and exchange across different jurisdictions, the harmonized model also contributes to digital forensics standardization efforts.

In summary, the proposed harmonized model for digital evidence admissibility assessment is designed to provide a techno-legal foundation for: (i) determining if digital evidence is admissible; and (ii) determining the weight of digital evidence that has already been admitted subject to further research.

## 6.     Conclusions

Developments in computer science and information technology are expected to significantly impact the technical and legal requirements that provide the foundation for the admissibility of digital evidence. The proposed harmonized model for digital evidence admissibility assessment has been created to ensure that future technological developments in the fields are integrated into the digital forensic process. As such, the proposed model contributes to ongoing efforts in digital forensics standardization being undertaken by academia, industry and law enforcement.

The problem of admissibility of digital evidence is the central theme
of this research. The novelty lies in the introduction of a reproducible,
trans-jurisdictional and standardized model that underpins the admissibility of digital evidence in legal proceedings. Key technical and legal
requirements are identified and integrated within the framework for assessing digital evidence admissibility.

Different technical requirements have different impacts on the determination of evidentiary weight. Future research will investigate the
impact level of each requirement in the harmonized model on the determination of the weight of a piece of evidence. In addition, future
research will evaluate practical applications of the harmonized model in
legal proceedings, with the goal of creating an expert system that would
provide advice, guidance and assessments of the admissibility and weight
of digital evidence.

# References

[1] J. Ami-Narh and P. Williams, Digital forensics and the legal system:
A dilemma of our time, *Proceedings of the Sixth Australian Digital
Forensics Conference*, 2008.

[2] Association of Chief Police Officers, Good Practice Guide for
Computer-Based Evidence, London, United Kingdom, 2008.

[3] S. Brobbey, *Essentials of the Ghana Law of Evidence*, Datro Publications, Accra, Ghana, 2014.

[4] E. Casey, *Digital Evidence and Computer Crime: Forensic Science, Computers and the Internet*, Academic Press, Waltham, Massachusetts, 2011.

[5] D. Garrie and J. Morrissy, Digital forensic evidence in the courtroom: Understanding content and quality, *Northwestern Journal of
Technology and Intellectual Property*, vol. 12(2), article no. 5, 2014.

[6] G. Giova, Improving chain of custody in forensic investigations of
electronic digital systems, *International Journal of Computer Science and Network Security*, vol. 11(1), 2011.

[7] M. Grobler, Digital forensic standards: International progress,
*Proceedings of the South African Information Security Multi-Conference*, pp. 261–271, 2010.

[8] International Organization of Standardization, Information Technology – Security Techniques – Guidelines for Identification, Collection, Acquisition and Preservation of Digital Evidence, ISO/IEC
27037:2012 Standard, Geneva, Switzerland, 2012.

[9] International Organization of Standardization, Information Technology – Security Techniques – Guidance on Assuring Suitability and Adequacy of Incident Investigative Methods, ISO/IEC 27041:2015 Standard, Geneva, Switzerland, 2015.

[10] International Organization of Standardization, Information Technology – Security Techniques – Incident Investigation Principles and Processes, ISO/IEC 27043:2015 Standard, Geneva, Switzerland, 2015.

[11] G. Kessler, Judges' awareness, understanding and application of digital evidence, *Journal of Digital Forensics, Security and Law*, vol. 6(1), pp. 55–72, 2011.

[12] R. Leigland and A. Krings, A formalization of digital forensics, *International Journal of Digital Evidence*, vol. 3(2), 2004.

[13] O. Leroux, Legal admissibility of electronic evidence, *International Review of Law, Computers and Technology*, vol. 18(2), pp. 193–222, 2004.

[14] S. Mason, *Electronic Evidence*, Butterworths Law, London, United Kingdom, 2012.

[15] National Forensic Science Technology Center, Crime Scene Investigation: A Guide for Law Enforcement, Largo, Florida, 2013.

[16] G. Palmer, A Road Map for Digital Forensic Research, DFRWS Technical Report, DTR-T001-01 Final, Air Force Research Laboratory, Rome, New York, 2001.

[17] M. Reith, C. Carr and G. Gunsch, An examination of digital forensic models, *International Journal of Digital Evidence*, vol. 1(3), 2002.

[18] E. Roffeh, *Practical Digital Evidence: Law and Technology, Part I*, CreateSpace Independent Publishing Platform, Seattle, Washington, 2015.

[19] S. Schroeder, How to be a digital forensic expert witness, *Proceedings of the First International Conference on Systematic Approaches to Digital Forensic Engineering*, pp. 69–85, 2005.

[20] Scientific Working Group on Digital Evidence, SWGDE Best Practices for Computer Forensics, Version 3.1 (www.swgde.org/documents/Current%20Documents/SWGDE%20Best%20Practices%20for%20Computer%20Forensics), 2014.

[21] Technical Working Group for Electronic Crime Scene Investigation, Electronic Crime Scene Investigation: A Guide for First Responders, National Institute of Justice, Washington, DC, 2001.

[22] U.S. Supreme Court, Daubert v. Merrell Dow Pharmaceuticals Inc., *United States Reports*, vol. 509, pp. 579–601, 1983.

[23] A. Valjarevic and H. Venter, Harmonized digital forensic process model, *Proceedings of the Information Security for South Africa Conference*, 2012.

[24] C. Vecchio-Flaim, Developing a Computer Forensics Team, InfoSec Reading Room, SANS Institute, Bethesda, Maryland, 2001.

II

# MOBILE AND EMBEDDED DEVICE FORENSICS

Chapter 3

# EVALUATING THE AUTHENTICITY OF SMARTPHONE EVIDENCE

Heloise Pieterse, Martin Olivier and Renier van Heerden

**Abstract**    The widespread use and rich functionality of smartphones have made them valuable sources of digital evidence. Malicious individuals are becoming aware of the importance of digital evidence found on smartphones and may be interested in deploying anti-forensic techniques to alter evidence and thwart investigations. It is, therefore, important to establish the authenticity of smartphone evidence.

This chapter focuses on digital evidence found on smartphones that has been created by smartphone applications and the techniques that can be used to establish the authenticity of the evidence. In order to establish the authenticity of the evidence, a better understanding of the normal or expected behavior of smartphone applications is required. This chapter introduces a new reference architecture for smartphone applications that models the components and the expected behavior of applications. Seven theories of normality are derived from the reference architecture that enable digital forensic professionals to evaluate the authenticity of smartphone evidence. An experiment conducted to examine the validity of the theories of normality indicates that the theories can assist forensic professionals in identifying authentic smartphone evidence.

**Keywords:** Smartphone forensics, evidence, authenticity, reference architecture

## 1.    Introduction

The 21$^{st}$ century has witnessed the emergence and continuous evolution of smartphones. Smartphones are compact devices that combine traditional mobile phone features with personal computer functionality [22]. The popularity of smartphones is the result of ever increasing functionality provided by the hardware, operating systems such as Google Android and Apple iOS, and their associated applications [28].

© IFIP International Federation for Information Processing 2017                                    41

Published by Springer International Publishing AG 2017. All Rights Reserved

G. Peterson and S. Shenoi (Eds.): Advances in Digital Forensics XIII, IFIP AICT 511, pp. 41–61, 2017.

DOI: 10.1007/978-3-319-67208-3_3

The ubiquitous use of smartphones in daily activities has rendered these devices rich sources of digital evidence. This digital evidence is important when smartphones are linked to criminal, civil, accident and corporate investigations.

Digital evidence stored on smartphones, referred to as smartphone evidence, includes information of probative value that is generated by an application or transferred to the smartphone by the user. Malicious individuals are becoming increasingly aware of the importance of smartphone evidence and may attempt to manipulate, fabricate or alter the evidence [15]. In particular, they would attempt to apply anti-forensic techniques and tools to compromise the evidence [11]. Anti-forensics can be described as "attempts to compromise the availability or usefulness of evidence to the forensic process" [16]. It is, therefore important for digital forensic professionals to mitigate anti-forensic actions and to establish the authenticity of smartphone evidence. Authenticity refers to the preservation of evidence from the time it was first generated and the ability to prove that the integrity of the evidence has been maintained over the entire period of time [5, 6, 24]. Authentic smartphone evidence is, thus, evidence that originates as a result of the normal behavior of a smartphone application or user.

Smartphone evidence primarily resides in three components: (i) subscriber identity module (SIM) card; (ii) internal storage; and (iii) portable storage such as a micro SD card [1, 7]. While all these components contain valuable evidence, this work focuses on application-related smartphone evidence that is stored directly on a smartphone. Establishing the authenticity of smartphone evidence requires a better understanding of the applications that create the evidence. Developing a better understanding of smartphone applications can be achieved by designing a reference architecture that captures the common architectural elements and their expected behavior [8].

This chapter introduces a new reference architecture for smartphone applications that models the components as well as the normal or expected behavior of smartphone applications. The reference architecture is designed to enable digital forensic professionals to easily comprehend smartphone applications and to understand how the associated evidence originates. The architecture is used to derive theories of normality for smartphone applications. The theories of normality capture the normal or expected behavior of smartphone applications and assist digital forensic professionals in identifying authentic smartphone evidence and helping eliminate unreliable evidence from being considered in arriving at the final conclusions.

## 2.    Related Research

Evidence on a smartphone can provide a digital forensic professional with valuable insights about the interactions that took place involving the smartphone. Smartphone evidence is, however, vulnerable to change and can be altered, manipulated or fabricated either maliciously or by accident without leaving obvious signs [5, 15]. A digital forensic professional must, therefore, establish the authenticity of smartphone evidence before arriving at the final conclusions.

Many software applications have safeguards, such as audit logs and integrity checks, to ensure that the data is valid and has not been tampered with [30]. Such safeguards could assist forensic professionals in establishing the authenticity of smartphone evidence. However, smartphone applications generally do not have audit logs or similar safeguards. Meanwhile, commercial tools, such as the Cellebrite Universal Forensic Device (UFED) and FTK Mobile Phone Examiner, provide limited support in establishing authenticity [31]. Therefore, new techniques and tools are required to determine the authenticity of smartphone evidence.

Pieterse et al. [26] have introduced an authenticity framework for Android timestamps that enables digital forensic professionals to establish the authenticity of timestamps found on Android smartphones. The framework determines the authenticity of timestamps found in SQLite databases using two methods. The first method explores the Android filesystem (EXT4) for artifacts that indicate potential manipulations of the SQLite databases. The second method identifies inconsistencies in the SQLite databases. The presence of specific filesystem changes and inconsistencies in the associated SQLite databases are indicators that the authenticity of the stored timestamps may have been compromised.

Verma et al. [31] have proposed a technique for identifying malicious tampering of dates and timestamps in Android smartphones. The technique gathers kernel-generated timestamps of events and stores them in a secure location outside the Android smartphone. During a digital forensic investigation, the preserved timestamps can be used to establish the authenticity of the dates and times extracted from the smartphone under examination.

Govindaraj et al. [13] have designed iSecureRing, a system for securing iOS applications and preserving dates and timestamps. The system incorporates two modules. One module wraps an iOS application in an additional layer of protection while the other module preserves authentic dates and timestamps of events relating to the application.

All the solutions described above can assist digital forensic professionals in evaluations of smartphone evidence, especially with regard to authenticity. However, the solutions are either platform-specific or require software to be installed on a smartphone prior to an investigation. Clearly, there is a need for additional solutions that can enable digital forensic professionals to determine the authenticity of smartphone evidence.

A promising solution is to consider the structure and behavior of smartphone applications that create the evidence in question. This can be achieved by modeling smartphone applications using a reference architecture that captures the common architectural elements of applications as well as their behavior [8]. Reference architectures have been specified for several domains, including web browsers [14] and web servers [17]. In the case of smartphone applications, a reference architecture only exists for Android applications [27]. At this time, no generic reference architecture exists for smartphone applications across different platforms.

## 3.     Reference Architecture

A large quantity of smartphone evidence is the result of executing applications. This evidence enables a digital forensic professional to make informed conclusions about application usage. Should the tampering of smartphone evidence not be detected, the digital forensic professional could come up with inaccurate or false conclusions. Therefore, it is important to establish the authenticity of smartphone evidence before attempting to make any conclusions. Identifying authentic smartphone evidence requires the digital forensic professional to have a good understanding of the normal or expected behavior of smartphone applications. Using a reference architecture to model smartphone applications enables the forensic professional to comprehend the structure and behavior of applications and understand how the associated evidence originated.

Designing a reference architecture for smartphone applications requires the evaluation of architectural designs of applications created for various smartphone operating systems. From the architectural designs, common architectural components are identified to create the reference architecture. Finally, the interactions within and between the components are modeled to complete the design of the reference architecture.

## 3.1     Architectural Designs of Applications

The most common mobile platforms are Google's Android (83% market share) and Apple's iOS (15% market share) [18, 28]. Their popularity is directly related to their functionality, advanced capabilities and numerous third-party applications. Applications designed for these platforms adhere to specific architectural designs to ensure visual attractiveness and enhanced performance. Examination of the documentation of Android and iOS smartphone applications provides insights into their architectural designs. The combined 98% market share of Android and iOS smartphones has motivated the emphasis on Android and iOS applications in this research.

**Android Applications.** The visual design and user interface of Android applications are determined by specific themes, styles and structured layouts. A style is a collection of properties that specifies the look and feel of a single view; the properties typically include height, width, padding and color of the view. A theme is a style that is applied to the entire application, enabling all the views to have a similar presentation. Layouts define the visual structure and determine how the views are organized.

Developers use the Extensible Markup Language (XML) to define the theme, styles and layouts for the user interface of an Android application [12]. The user interface facilitates interactions between a user and an application. The interactions are captured by an activity, which contains a window holding the user interface. Activities interact with the user as well as with background processes such as broadcast receivers and services. Broadcast receivers respond to system-wide announcements while services perform longer running operations. Activities, broadcast receivers and services realize the logic of an Android application.

Android applications may require access to persistent data. This access is provided by functions and procedures, captured in storage-specific application programming interfaces (APIs). Android applications have several data storage options: shared preferences, internal storage, external storage and SQLite databases [3]. One or more of the options may be used by an Android application to store data.

Pieterse et al. [27] have proposed a reference architecture for Android applications. The reference architecture has two core components: (i) application activity; and (ii) SQLite database. The application activity component captures the user interface design and logic of the application while the SQLite database component describes the data retention policy [27]. The current reference architecture only models Android applications that use SQLite databases to retain data. Therefore, the architecture is not a complete solution and smartphone applications on other platforms must be investigated to design a reference architecture for smartphone applications in general.

**iOS Applications.** Developers of iOS applications tend to follow the model-view-controller (MVC) architectural design pattern [21]. The pat-

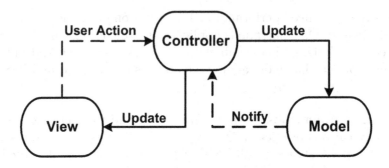

Figure 1.  Model-view-controller architecture [19].

tern assigns objects in an iOS application to one of three roles: (i) model; (ii) view; or (iii) controller. As illustrated in Figure 1 [19], the pattern also defines the communications between the objects.

The model object encapsulates the domain data specific to an iOS application [19] and interacts with the physical storage. A view object, which is visible to a user, renders the graphical user interface [19]. View objects are populated with standard user interface elements provided by the UIKit; they often include labels, buttons, tables and text fields [21]. View objects display data from an application model to a user and enable the user to interact with persistent data.

Four common approaches for data persistence are available for iOS applications: (i) user defaults; (ii) property lists; (iii) SQLite databases; and (iv) core data (relational object-oriented model) [20]. The controller object acts as a mediator between the view and model objects [19]. It receives actions from the user and acts accordingly [21]. The controller is also responsible for altering the model object and updating the view object with the changes. The business logic of an iOS application is, thus, realized by the controller object.

Although iOS applications have a different architectural design than Android applications, it is possible to identify certain similar characteristics. These similar characteristics enable the specification of a reference architecture for modeling Android and iOS smartphone applications.

## 3.2    Reference Architecture Components

Close examination of the architectural designs of Android and iOS applications reveals four similar architectural elements: (i) user interface; (ii) application logic; (iii) data management; and (iv) data storage. Table 1 describes the architectural elements.

The first component is the user interface, which captures the graphical design and presents an interface for user-application interactions. The

*Table 1.*  Architectural similarities of Android and iOS applications.

|  | **Android** | **iOS** |
|---|---|---|
| Visual Components | Themes, styles and layouts created using XML | View objects containing visual elements created using UIKit |
| Core Functions and Logic | Activities, broadcast receivers and services | Controller objects |
| Data Management | Management of stored data using content providers | Management of stored data using model objects |
| Data Storage | Shared preferences and SQLite databases | User defaults and SQLite databases |

interactions allow for the effective operation of the application by permitting the user to perform a limited selection of actions, including the submission of data. This implies that there are common actions, which lead to expected results. The user interface conveys the implemented operations and the received results in a simplistic manner to the user.

The second component is the application logic, which captures the core functions and workflow of the application. The application logic implements the functions responsible for validating, processing and executing the actions and data received from the user interface component. During processing, the data included along with an action can be consumed by the process. Certain actions also cause the data or portions of the data to be kept in their original form and produced as part of the result. After the data is processed, the application logic executes the received action and produces results that are passed to the user interface. Some applications may require all or parts of the data received during an action to be maintained in persistent storage.

The data management component receives data from the application logic component and transforms the data into a suitable format for storage or presentation in the user interface.

The final data storage component stores persistent data and makes the stored data available to applications.

Figure 2 presents the four components of the reference architecture for smartphone applications. The figure shows the architectural ordering of the components and the basic interactions between the components. The current design only provides a high-level overview of the components. In order to obtain a better understanding of the normal or expected behavior of smartphone applications, the reference architecture must capture detailed information about the interactions within and between the architectural components.

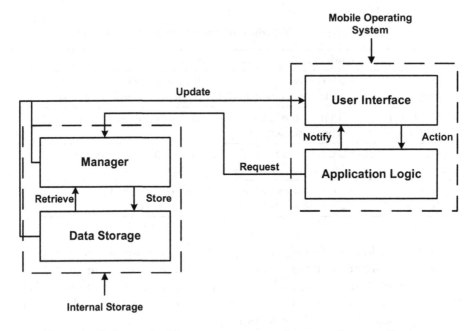

*Figure 2.*   Reference architecture components for smartphone applications.

## 3.3    Modeling Application Behavior

Modeling smartphones at a fine level of granularity requires a detailed exploration of the behavior of smartphone applications. The internal behavior of smartphone applications is the result of interactions that occur within and between the architectural components. Modeling these interactions provides additional insights into the normal or expected behavior of smartphone applications.

Figure 3 presents a state diagram that models the internal behavior of smartphone applications. The state diagram abstracts the behavior of smartphone applications in terms of four stages:

- **User Interface Stage:** The user interface stage has three states: (i) Idle; (ii) Ready; and (iii) Update. The successful installation of a smartphone application places it the Idle state. An inactive application remains in the Idle state waiting for a user to launch the application or for an external event to occur. An application opened by a user or external event causes it to transition from the Idle state to the Ready state.

    An application in the Ready state can accept an action from a user, the same application (internal action) or another application (external action). An application transitions from the Ready state

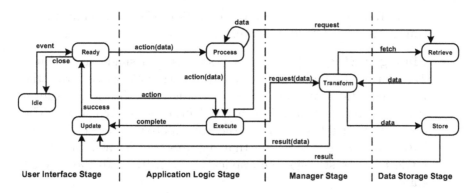

*Figure 3.*   Internal behavior of smartphone applications.

to the Process state upon receiving an action that includes data. An action involving no data causes the application to transition directly to the Execute state.

After an action completes, an application transitions to the Update state. In the Update state, the user interface is updated based on the completed action; this can involve updating the data or elements displayed by the interface. After this is completed, the application returns to the Ready state. Note that an application transitions to the Idle state only when it is closed by a user.

- **Application Logic Stage:** The application logic stage has two states: (i) Process; and (ii) Execute. An application transitions to the Process state upon receiving an action that includes data. The Process state is responsible for separating the action from the data and processing the data accordingly. The processing may involve data validation or the application of security measures such as encryption and encoding. Data processing may involve multiple iterations and the application transitions to the Execute state only after the processing has completed.

An application in the Execute state executes a received action. If the action involves no data, the application transitions to the Update state after completing the action. An action involving data can cause several outcomes. First, the action may completely consume the data and cause a transition to the Update state. If the data or portion of the data have to be retained in storage, the application transitions to the Transform state. Whether or not an action involves data, it can require data that is maintained in data storage. In order to retrieve the data, the application moves to the Retrieve state. After the data is received, the application transitions to the Update state.

- **Manager Stage:** The manager stage has a single state called Transform. An application moves to the Transform state from the Execute or Retrieve states after receiving data. In the Transform state, the received data is converted into the desired form. The application then transitions to the Store state in order to store the data. To complete an action that requires transformed data to be retrieved from storage, the application transitions to the Update state.

- **Data Storage Stage:** The data storage state has two states: (i) Retrieve; and (ii) Store. An application moves to the Store state after it accepts transformed data from the Transform state; it then proceeds to store the data in a database or file. After the data is stored, the application transitions to the Update state. The Retrieve state fetches data from storage and the application transitions to the Transform state to transform the data into an acceptable form.

## 3.4     Exploring an Android Application

The proposed reference architecture provides an abstraction of smartphone applications, enabling a digital forensic professional to easily comprehend the applications and their associated evidence. From this abstraction, the following general characteristics regarding smartphone applications can be identified:

- Only a smartphone application can access and/or update the stored data.

- Data stored by a smartphone application is only accessible via an executed action.

- Data displayed by the user interface directly corresponds to the stored data.

- Changes to data stored by a smartphone application can only occur after an action is received.

- An action can only be provided by a human user, the current smartphone application (internal action) or some other smartphone application (internal action).

- A smartphone application only accepts a fixed set of actions.

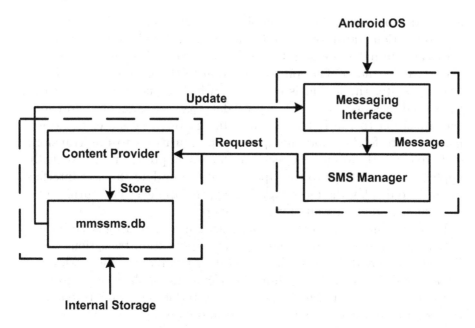

*Figure 4.* Modeling Android's default messaging application.

- An action in the fixed set leads to an expected result.

To illustrate the value and generality of the reference architecture, Android's default messaging application is modeled according to the reference architecture. Android smartphones are equipped with basic messaging functionality. A user can employ the default messaging application that is pre-installed on a smartphone to send and receive text or multimedia messages [9].

Figure 4 shows how the reference architecture is used to identify and model the core components of the application. The messaging interface enables users to view, delete, send and receive text or multimedia messages. The SMS manager, which contains the workflow logic of the messaging application, is implemented by SmsManger, an Android class that manages the messaging operations [2]. The SmsManger class uses public methods to implement the requested actions. The management functions transform data into a suitable format for storage, which includes the creation of timestamps and the extraction of additional information such as the service center number. After it is transformed, the data is retained in the `mmssms.db` SQLite database.

The behavior of the messaging application is illustrated by sending a new text message. The interactions involved in sending a text message involve three phases. In the first phase, human user opens the messaging application on the Android smartphone. Upon receiving the open event, the application transitions from the Idle state to the Ready state and receives an internal action to retrieve all the stored messages. The received action causes the application to transition to the Execute state. In the Execute state, the action is evaluated, which requests the retrieval of the stored messages from the SQLite database (`mmssms.db`) and causes the transition to the Retrieve state. In the Retrieve state, the stored messages are fetched and the application transitions to the Transform state to correctly format the messages for visual presentation. Next, the application transitions to the Update state to update the user interface in order to display the messages. Finally, the application returns to the Ready state where it waits for a new action.

In the second phase, the user provides a new action by selecting the option to create a new text message. The application transitions to the Execute state and, because the action does not request the retrieval or storage of data, the action completes. Next, the application transitions to the Update state and updates the user interface accordingly, enabling the user to enter one or more recipients and write the new text message. Finally, the application returns to the Ready state.

During the third and final phase, the user enters the recipient(s) and the text message. Pressing the send button generates an action that includes the data entered by the user, causing the application to move to the Process state. In the Process state, the data is validated (i.e., length of the phone number and text message) before the application transitions to the Execute state. In the Execute state, the text message is sent, but the message must be recorded in the `mmssms.db` database. Therefore, the application proceeds to the Transform state where the data is formatted correctly, after which the application transitions to the Store state. The application then transitions to the Update state to update the user interface and show that the text message was sent. Finally, the application returns to the Ready state.

Modeling Android's default messaging application according to the reference architecture enables a digital forensic professional to identify valuable information about the application. Specifically, the architecture serves as a valuable template for a forensic professional to gain a good understanding of the normal or expected behavior of the messaging application. Although modeling the messaging application can offer insights about the origin of evidence related to the smartphone application, as discussed in the next section, additional criteria are required to efficiently identify authentic smartphone evidence.

# 4. Theories of Normality

Despite its utility, the information provided by modeling a smartphone application is insufficient to establish the authenticity of the related evidence. Seven theories of normality are specified to assist digital forensic professionals in evaluating the authenticity of smartphone evidence. The theories capture the normal or expected behavior of smartphone applications and can assist forensic professionals in identifying authentic smartphone evidence. The following seven theories of normality stem from the research conducted when designing the reference architecture:

- **Data Correspondence:** Many smartphone applications include actions that retrieve or store data in persistent storage such as a database. This data is made accessible to a user via the user interface of the application. Unauthorized changes made to stored data may not be immediately reflected in the user interface because of cached data. Authentic smartphone evidence requires the stored data to correspond to the data presented by the user interface. Should the application allow for bi-directional communications (i.e., text messaging or telephone calls), the stored data must also correspond to the data stored on the other smartphone involved in the communications (if the other smartphone is available for examination).

- **Data Storage Consistency:** Smartphone applications have several options for storing persistent data, one of the most popular is an SQLite database [4, 10]. Authentic smartphone evidence should have consistent database records. A consistent record in a SQLite database is one that is listed correctly when ordered according to the auto-incremented primary key and a field containing a date or timestamp.

- **File System Consistency:** Files containing stored data have specific permissions and owners that allow/restrict modifications to the data. When a file is created for the first time, the responsible application is given ownership of the file and is assigned the necessary read/write permissions. Authentic smartphone evidence requires file permissions and ownership to remain unaltered.

- **Smartphone Reboot:** Tampering with smartphone evidence may require a system reboot for the changes to be reflected on the smartphone and on the user interface of the smartphone application [27]. A system reboot is generally performed after a file containing stored data has been modified. A timestamp associated with a system reboot that follows soon after the modification of the file is a possible indicator of evidence tampering.

- **Presence of Anti-Forensic Tools:** Anti-forensic tools for smartphones can be used to destroy, hide, manipulate or prevent the creation of evidence [29]. Smartphone applications, such as File Shredder (Android) or iShredder (iOS), can be used to destroy data; data can be hidden using StegDroid or MobiStego (both Android) applications. Eliminating the presence of anti-forensic applications on a smartphone limits the possibility of evidence tampering.

- **Smartphone Rooting/Jailbreaking:** Data stored by a smartphone application is inaccessible to users. Access to the application and the data can be obtained by rooting (Android) or jailbreaking (iOS) the smartphone [23, 25]. Although rooting or jailbreaking is not a direct indication of data tampering, a rooted or jailbroken smartphone lacks the additional protection measures against data tampering that are required to ensure evidence authenticity.

- **Application Usage:** The internal behavior of a smartphone application, illustrated in the state diagram, shows that only actions can create or alter stored data. Users (humans, the smartphone application itself or another smartphone application) are the only entities capable of providing actions; therefore, their presence must be confirmed. Verifying that a user created or altered the data increases its authenticity.

The seven theories of normality indicate whether or not the evidence produced by a smartphone application is the result of normal or expected behavior of the application. A digital forensic professional can, therefore, use the theories of normality to evaluate the authenticity of smartphone evidence.

An experiment was conducted to confirm the validity of the seven theories of normality. The experiment involved the tampering of text messages produced by Android's default messaging application. The manipulation of the text messages involved the following steps

- **Step 1:** Root the test Android smartphone (Samsung Galaxy S5 Mini running Android version 4.4.4).

- **Step 2:** Copy the `mmssms.db` and `mmssms.db-wal` SQLite database files that contain all the text messages to the `/sdcard/` location on the Android smartphone and then to a computer.

```
<pkg name="eu.chainfire.supersu">
  <comp name="eu.chainfire.supersu.PromptActivity" lrt="1469541224910"/>
</pkg>
```

*Figure 5.* Confirmation of SuperSu application use in `usage-history.xml`.

- **Step 3:** Use SQLite Expert Personal to alter the text messages.

- **Step 4:** Remove the `mmssms.db` and `mmssms.db-wal` SQLite database files from the Android smartphone using the `rm` command.

- **Step 5:** Copy the altered `mmssms.db` SQLite database file to the Android smartphone and move the file to the `/data/data/com.android.provider.telephony/databases/` location.

- **Step 6:** Change the permissions of the `mmssms.db` SQlite database file using the command `chmod 666 mmssms.db`.

- **Step 7:** Reboot the Android smartphone.

- **Step 8:** Unroot the Android smartphone.

In the experiment, the seven theories of normality were used to evaluate the text messages and determine whether or not the messages originated as a result of the normal behavior of the messaging application. First, the installed applications on the Samsung Galaxy S5 Mini were viewed. No anti-forensic applications were installed on the smartphone. Traditional root applications, such as SuperSU and Superuser, were also not present on the smartphone. However, their absence is not a definite indicator that the smartphone was not rooted; this is because a root application could have been uninstalled or root could have been removed. Examination of the `/data/system/usage/usage-history.xml` file, which contains log entries showing when the user last used an application, revealed that the SuperSu application was previously installed on the smartphone.

Figure 5 presents a snippet of the `usage-history.xml` file. Conversion of the timestamp revealed that the SuperSu application was last used on `26/07/2016 15:53:44 GMT+2:00`. The log entry offers a positive indication that the smartphone was rooted.

The `usage-history.xml` file in Figure 6 also shows that the default messaging application (identified by the `com.android.mms` package name) was last used on `23/07/2016 14:09:44 GMT+2:00` (Figure 6).

Figure 7 shows the timestamps of the SQLite database files associated with the default messaging application. The timestamps contradict the log entry in the `usage-history.xml` file. In fact, the timestamps of the

```
<pkg name="com.android.mms">
    <comp name="com.android.mms.ui.ConversationComposer" lrt="1469275784131"/>
    <comp name="com.android.mms.settings.NotificationSettings" lrt="1426085288917"/>
    <comp name="com.android.mms.settings.CheckDefaultSmsAppsActivity" lrt="1411617622059"/>
    <comp name="com.android.mms.settings.EntrancePrefActivity" lrt="1440400537806"/>
    <comp name="com.android.mms.settings.MultimediamessagesSettings" lrt="1440400533905"/>
    <comp name="com.android.mms.ui.ClassZeroActivity" lrt="1444779525868"/>
    <comp name="com.android.mms.ui.ForwardMessageActivity" lrt="1466240005345"/>
    <comp name="com.android.mms.ui.ReservationMessageManager" lrt="1390041980198"/>
    <comp name="com.android.mms.prioritysender.AddGlanceListActivity" lrt="1451841909782"/>
    <comp name="com.android.mms.cover.MissedMsgActivity" lrt="1429775515108"/>
```

*Figure 6.*    Confirmation of SMS application use in `usage-history.xml`.

```
root@kminilte:/data/data/com.android.providers.telephony/databases # ls -l
-rw-rw----  radio       radio       1273856 2016-06-09 13:03 mmssms.db
-rw-rw----  radio       radio         32768 2014-01-18 12:35 mmssms.db-shm
-rw-rw----  radio       radio       4152992 2014-01-15 09:22 mmssms.db-wal
-rw-rw----  radio       radio         32768 2014-09-24 10:00 nwk_info.db
-rw-rw----  radio       radio         25136 2014-01-01 02:01 nwk_info.db-journal
-rw-rw----  radio       radio        188416 2014-01-18 12:35 telephony.db
-rw-------  radio       radio             0 2014-01-01 02:24 telephony.db-journal
```

*Figure 7.*    Original timestamps in the `mmssms.db` SQLite database.

SQLite database files (`mmssms.db` and `mmssms.db-wal`) indicate that the application was last used on **26/07/2016 16:01:00 GMT+2:00**.

```
root@kminilte:/data/data/com.android.providers.telephony/databases # ls -l
-rw-rw-rw-  root        root        1302528 2016-07-26 15:57 mmssms.db
-rw-rw-rw-  radio       radio         32768 2016-07-26 16:01 mmssms.db-shm
-rw-rw-rw-  radio       radio          4152 2016-07-26 16:01 mmssms.db-wal
-rw-rw----  radio       radio         32768 2014-09-24 10:00 nwk_info.db
-rw-rw----  radio       radio         25136 2014-01-01 02:01 nwk_info.db-journal
-rw-rw----  radio       radio        188416 2016-07-26 16:01 telephony.db
-rw-------  radio       radio             0 2014-01-01 02:24 telephony.db-journal
```

*Figure 8.*    Changed timestamps in the `mmssms.db` SQLite database.

Closer inspection of the SQLite database files in Figure 8 indicate changes to the file permissions and ownership. To confirm the consistency of the SQLite database records, the database records were viewed and the records were found to be listed correctly. It was also discovered that the records stored in the SQLite database corresponded to the text messages displayed on the user interface.

Finally, the log files associated with a system reboot were examined. Figure 9 indicates that a system reboot occurred shortly after the SQLite database was modified.

The specific findings – inconsistent usage of the default messaging application, filesystem inconsistencies, subsequent rebooting and the rooting of the smartphone – lead to the conclusion that the text messages

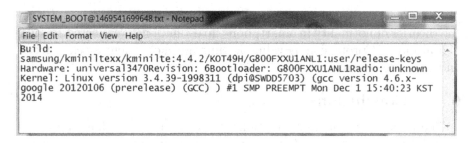

*Figure 9.* Confirmation of reboot on 26/07/2016 16:01:39 GMT+2:00.

stored on the Android smartphone may have been tampered with and that the authenticity of the text messages cannot be established.

## 5. Discussion

The proposed reference architecture for smartphone applications allows for the abstraction of a diverse collection of Android and iOS applications. To support the diversity, the reference architecture captures the essential components of applications and identifies the behaviors of the architectural components. The simplistic design clearly and concisely describes the role of each component, enabling the easy comprehension of modeled smartphone applications. The design is also flexible, providing digital forensic professionals with the ability to model smartphone applications at different levels of complexity. Using the reference architecture, forensic professionals can swiftly obtain a better understanding of the normal or expected behavior of smartphone applications as well as the smartphone evidence related to the applications. The reference architecture is limited to Android and iOS applications, but it is readily extended to model applications that run on other operating systems. However, although the reference architecture offers insights into the internal behavior of applications, it is not sufficient to establish the authenticity of the related smartphone evidence.

The seven theories of normality derived from the reference architecture capture the normal or expected behavior of smartphone applications. Digital forensic professionals can use the theories of normality to evaluate smartphone evidence. Based on an evaluation, a forensic professional can decide whether to consider or disregard the smartphone evidence. The experiment conducted as part of this research demonstrates that the theories of normality provide a forensic professional with the support needed to determine whether or not evidence originated as a result of the normal behavior of a smartphone application. While the theories of normality cannot directly pinpoint the tampering of smartphone evidence, they can assist in eliminating unreliable evidence. Using the theories of normality in smartphone investigations is expected to save digital forensic professionals valuable time and help them reach correct and accurate conclusions.

## 6.     Conclusions

The popularity and rich functionality of smartphones have required digital forensic professionals to examine large quantities of smartphone evidence. However, the integrity of smartphone evidence can be compromised by anti-forensic tools, malware and malicious users. It is, therefore, necessary to establish whether or not smartphone evidence is the result of the normal or expected behavior of smartphone applications. The reference architecture described in this chapter models the components of smartphone applications and their expected behavior. The reference architecture helps derive seven theories of normality that assist digital forensic professionals in evaluating the authenticity of smartphone evidence. An experiment involving the manipulation of evidence produced by Android's default messaging application validates the use of the normality theories. Indeed, the experiment demonstrates that the normality theories provide significant investigatory assistance to digital forensic professionals while enabling them to identify unreliable evidence so that it can be eliminated when arriving at the final conclusions.

Future research will engage the theories of normality to create a smartphone evidence classification model that will enhance the ability to establish the authenticity of evidence. The classification model will also be evaluated against authentic and manipulated smartphone evidence.

## References

[1] M. Al-Hadadi and A. AlShidhani, Smartphone forensics analysis: A case study, *International Journal of Computer and Electrical Engineering*, vol. 5(6), pp. 576–580, 2013.

[2] Android Developers, SmsManager (`developer.android.com/reference/android/telephony/SmsManager.html`), 2015.

[3] Android Developers, Storage Options (`developer.android.com/guide/topics/data/data-storage.html`), 2016.

[4] M. Bader and I. Baggili, iPhone 3GS forensics: Logical analysis using Apple iTunes Backup Utility, *Small Scale Digital Device Forensics Journal*, vol. 4(1), 2010.

[5] E. Casey, *Digital Evidence and Computer Crime: Forensic Science, Computers and the Internet*, Academic Press, Waltham, Massachusetts, 2011.

[6] F. Cohen, *Digital Forensic Evidence Examination*, Fred Cohen & Associates, Livermore, California, 2009.

[7] K. Curran, A. Robinson, S. Peacocke and S. Cassidy, Mobile phone forensic analysis, in *Crime Prevention Technologies and Applications for Advancing Criminal Investigations*, C. Li and A. Ho (Eds.), IGI Global, Hershey, Pennsylvania, pp. 250–262, 2012.

[8] W. Eixelsberger, M. Ogris, H. Gall and B. Bellay, Software architecture recovery of a program family, *Proceedings of the Twentieth International Conference on Software Engineering*, pp. 508–511, 1998.

[9] W. Enck, M. Ongtang and P. McDaniel, On lightweight mobile phone application certification, *Proceedings of the Sixteenth ACM Conference on Computer and Communications Security*, pp. 235–245, 2009.

[10] F. Freiling, M. Spreitzenbarth and S. Schmitt, Forensic analysis of smartphones: The Android Data Extractor Lite (ADEL), *Proceedings of the ADFSL Conference on Digital Forensics, Security and Law*, pp. 151–160, 2011.

[11] S. Garfinkel, Anti-forensics: Techniques, detection and countermeasures, *Proceedings of the Second International Conference on i-Warfare and Security*, pp. 77–84, 2007.

[12] M. Goadrich and M. Rogers, Smart smartphone development: iOS versus Android, *Proceedings of the Forty-Second ACM Technical Symposium on Computer Science Education*, pp. 607–612, 2011.

[13] J. Govindaraj, R. Verma, R. Mata and G. Gupta, iSecureRing: Forensic-ready secure iOS apps for jailbroken iPhones, poster paper presented at the *IEEE Symposium on Security and Privacy*, 2014.

[14] A. Grosskurth and M. Godfrey, A reference architecture for web browsers, *Proceedings of the Twenty-First IEEE International Conference on Software Maintenance*, pp. 661–664, 2005.

[15] M. Hannon, An increasingly important requirement: Authentication of digital evidence, *Journal of the Missouri Bar*, vol. 70(6), pp. 314–323, 2014.

[16] R. Harris, Arriving at an anti-forensics consensus: Examining how to define and control the anti-forensics problem, *Digital Investigation*, vol. 3(S), pp. S44–S49, 2006.

[17] A. Hassan and R. Holt, A reference architecture for web servers, *Proceedings of the Seventh Working Conference on Reverse Engineering*, pp. 150–159, 2000.

[18] International Data Corporation Research, Smartphone Growth Expected to Drop to Single Digits in 2016, Led by China's Transition from Developing to Mature Market, According to IDC, Press Release, Framingham, Massachusetts, March 3, 2016.

[19] T. Iulia-Maria and H. Ciocarlie, Best practices in iPhone programming: Model-view-controller architecture – Carousel component development, *Proceedings of the International Conference on Computer as a Tool*, 2011.

[20] B. Jacobs, iOS from Scratch with Swift: Data Persistence and Sandboxing on iOS, *Envato Tuts+* (`code.tutsplus.com/tutorials/ios-from-scratch-with-swift-data-persistence-and-sandboxing-on-ios--cms-25505`), December 25, 2015.

[21] M. Joorabchi and A. Mesbah, Reverse engineering iOS mobile applications, *Proceedings of the Nineteenth Working Conference on Reverse Engineering*, pp. 177–186, 2012.

[22] A. Kubi, S. Saleem and O. Popov, Evaluation of some tools for extracting e-evidence from mobile devices, *Proceedings of the Fifth International Conference on the Application of Information and Communication Technologies*, 2011.

[23] J. Lessard and G. Kessler, Android forensics: Simplifying cell phone examinations, *Small Scale Digital Device Forensics Journal*, vol. 4(1), 2010.

[24] M. Losavio, Non-technical manipulation of digital data, in *Advances in Digital Forensics*, M. Pollitt and S. Shenoi (Eds.), Springer, Boston, Massachusetts, pp. 51–63, 2005.

[25] C. Miller, Mobile attacks and defense, *IEEE Security and Privacy*, vol. 9(4), pp. 68–70, 2011.

[26] H. Pieterse, M. Olivier and R. van Heerden, Playing hide-and-seek: Detecting the manipulation of Android timestamps, *Proceedings of the Information Security for South Africa Conference*, 2015.

[27] H. Pieterse, M. Olivier and R. van Heerden, Reference architecture for Android applications to support the detection of manipulated evidence, *SAIEE Africa Research Journal*, vol. 107(2), pp. 92–103, 2016.

[28] A. Prasad, Android to rule smartphone market with 85% share in 2020 says IDC report, *International Business Times*, March 5, 2016.

[29] I. Sporea, B. Aziz and Z. McIntyre, On the availability of anti-forensic tools for smartphones, *International Journal of Security*, vol. 6(4), pp. 58–64, 2012.

[30] L. Thomson, Mobile devices: New challenges for admissibility of electronic evidence, *Scitech Lawyer*, vol. 9(3), 2013.

[31] R. Verma, J. Govindaraj and G. Gupta, Preserving dates and time-stamps for incident handling in Android smartphones, in *Advances in Digital Forensics X*, G. Peterson and S. Shenoi (Eds.), Springer, Heidelberg, Germany, pp. 209–225, 2014.

# Chapter 4

# FORENSIC EVALUATION OF AN AMAZON FIRE TV STICK

Logan Morrison, Huw Read, Konstantinos Xynos and Iain Sutherland

**Abstract**    This chapter presents the results of a forensic acquisition and analysis of an Amazon Fire TV Stick, a popular streaming media device. Although the primary functions of the Fire TV Stick are streaming videos and playing non-intensive video games, it is a reasonably powerful device that runs an Android operating system. This chapter explores the additional capabilities being developed for Fire TV Sticks in the hacker/enthusiast community and considers the implications that alterations to the devices could have with regard to digital forensics. An empirical assessment is conducted to identify the potential for misuse of Fire TV Sticks and to provide guidance to forensic investigators who analyze these devices.

**Keywords:** Embedded systems, Fire TV Stick, forensic evaluation

## 1.    Introduction

One aspect of digital convergence is the ability of users to replace wired entertainment systems such as cable television with wireless media streaming services [3]. Streaming service providers have responded to this demand by introducing devices like the Fire TV Stick. Such a device brings streaming services to a user's television set by merely attaching a USB device to the set without any other connections. Over time, these devices have become very popular – current estimates indicate that more than 50% of U.S. homes have a television set connected to the Internet via one of these devices. It is also estimated that global shipments will increase from 240 million devices in 2016 to 382 million devices by 2021 [7]. The increased use of these devices has caused streaming media forensics to become its own specialty area.

© IFIP International Federation for Information Processing 2017

Published by Springer International Publishing AG 2017. All Rights Reserved

G. Peterson and S. Shenoi (Eds.): Advances in Digital Forensics XIII, IFIP AICT 511, pp. 63–79, 2017.

DOI: 10.1007/978-3-319-67208-3_4

During the first quarter of 2015, it was reported that there were 4.5 million Fire TV devices in use [8] and the number of these devices has surely grown since then. This figure incorporates Fire TV Sticks into its calculation. Meanwhile, there is little information about the data stored on a Fire TV Stick and how to acquire an image of the data in a forensically-sound manner. This chapter discusses the information stored on a Fire TV Stick that may be of interest to forensic investigators. Also, it presents guidance on conducting a forensic evaluation of a Fire TV Stick.

## 2.     Related Work

Streaming media devices present unique challenges when it comes to accessing data, since many of them may require hardware modifications in order to access data. Some research related to the forensic acquisition and analysis of data from similar streaming media devices has been attempted, but little, if any, research has focused on the Amazon Fire TV Stick. It is possible to understand the challenges that may be experienced with regard to potential acquisition methods by reviewing work on similar media streaming devices and other small-scale devices.

## 2.1     Chromecast

Researchers have analyzed the files contained in a crash report generated by a Google Chromecast device [9]. However, this involves crashing the device, which causes major changes to the device; it is, therefore, less than ideal in a digital forensic investigation. The primary challenges are that the universal asynchronous receiver/transmitter (UART) connection provides minimal data and that the flash chip is encrypted with a unique (per device) key. These challenges make data acquisition and analysis very difficult. Nevertheless, the analysis of the crash report, which is in the form of a ZIP file, provides information about the layout of the NAND chip, useful timestamps and data pertaining to streamed videos.

## 2.2     Measy A2W Miracast

An analysis of the Measy A2W Miracast device [9] is more interesting because of the larger number of acquisition possibilities and the amount of useful data that can be recovered. Hardware experiments have accessed the UART interface by physically connecting to several pins on the main circuit board. This enables Hexdump to be used to extract a memory dump. However, employing the UART interface can change the device memory and, therefore, may not be forensically sound.

Experiments with the `curl` binary in the device firmware revealed that files can be posted to a Wi-Fi enabled server, but this is inconsistent and unreliable. An experiment that imaged the NAND flash chip revealed that the chip could be imaged effectively and in a forensically-sound manner using a toolkit with a write blocker [9]. Experiments using a Netcat listener to acquire files over Wi-Fi were also conducted.

Researchers were also able to recover MAC addresses, links, image files, URLs, firmware data, timestamps regarding device usage, WPA2 passwords and SSIDs using toolkits and techniques such as file carving [9]. This work is of interest because it discusses: (i) multiple methods for acquiring data from a streaming media device; (ii) a forensically-sound data acquisition technique, (iii) challenges that can arise when working with the devices; and (iv) potential methods for overcoming the challenges. However, some of the methods present risks that may keep them from being used in digital forensic investigations, including the possibility of permanently disabling (i.e., "bricking") the devices [2].

## 2.3 Amazon Kindle Fire HD

Research by Iqbal et al. [6] is of particular interest due to the similarities between the Kindle Fire HD and Fire TV Stick. Both devices run Amazon's Fire operating system and have an EXT4 file system [4]. Therefore, the experimental results for the Kindle Fire HD could be useful for the Fire TV Stick as well.

An experiment conducted by Iqbal et al. used a modified USB cable and a QEMU automated root exploit to gain root access. Next, the Android debug bridge (ADB) was used to image the userdata partition. The analysis of the userdata partition revealed that app data, user data, photographs, browsing data, audio data, cloudsync status and other useful data could be recovered.

The research on the Kindle Fire suggests an initial approach should focus on the userdata partition of a Fire TV Stick. It also demonstrates the challenges in achieving – and the importance of having – root access to the device in order to access the partition. However, this method requires the USB debugging function to be enabled on the device, which poses problems when this feature is disabled. Note that enabling USB debugging may result in the modification of the device and, thus, affect the forensic soundness of the recovered information.

## 3. Proposed Forensic Methodology

Forensic soundness is an extremely important characteristic of an evidence extraction methodology. This is accomplished by limiting, if not eliminating, the changes made to the evidentiary device before and/or during data extraction. Thus, all the experiments conducted on the Fire TV Stick in this research have paid special attention to this requirement.

A literature survey and an exploration of the Fire TV Stick functionality were performed to identify potential methods and areas of interest on the device. The research on Amazon Kindle Fire HD forensics by Iqbal et al. [6] was extremely useful from this perspective. The Fire TV Stick research involved reviewing its functionality as well as powering the device and going through the various menus to ascertain the kinds of artifacts that may reside on the device. The focus was to identify commonly-used functionalities, applications providing the functionalities and locations where artifacts related to user actions reside on the device. It was identified empirically that the userdata partition would be the most likely location to find artifacts of interest. Specifically, the following features of interest to a typical user and the applications associated with these features were identified:

- Video streaming through Netflix, YouTube and free Amazon content.

- Music streaming through Spotify and Pandora.

- Gaming through Amazon's App Store.

- Uploading/viewing photographs through Amazon's Cloud Drive.

- App downloading through Amazon's App Store.

- Sideloading of Android apps through the Android debug bridge.

## 3.1    Experimental Methodology

Table 1 summarizes the experimental methodology. The methodology was developed by exploring the device functionality, device state (on/off) and various physical, logical and manual acquisition options. The goal was to determine if it was possible to retrieve data generated by the various features and applications. This involved simulating typical user behavior using the available features and applications in order to introduce data and discover if it could be retrieved for subsequent analysis. Towards the end of the experiment, a new software update became available for the Fire TV Stick (version 5.0.5.1). This update caused problems with some of the acquisition methods. Due to time constraints, the update and its effects could not be explored fully.

*Table 1.* Amazon Fire TV Stick experimental methodology.

| Method | Description |
| --- | --- |
| Evaluate Fire TV Stick Condition | Examine a new out-of-the-box device with/without USB debugging enabled, with/without root enabled, before/after user interactions. |
| Select Method | Select physical method (ADB raw device imaging with root), logical method (file copying with custom Python script and ADB) or manual method (visual inspection of menus, etc.). |
| Activate Video Capture | Record the time, create a record of actions. |
| Power on the Device | Record time, note boot sequence of device, default menus, etc. |
| Empirically Assess Features | Systematically traverse through the identified features and applications, interact with them, record content consumed/created, observations and times for future retrieval. |
| Power off the Device | Record the time, turn off the Fire TV Stick and video capture device. |
| Attempt Data Recovery | Create an image of the Fire TV Stick using a physical, logical or manual method. Record the success or failure of the method and any pertinent image-specific data. |
| Investigate Images | Use forensic tools (FTK Imager v.3.4.0.1, AccessData Labs v.5.1) to retrieve data. |

## 3.2    Sample Data

The Fire TV Stick is designed to be registered to a specific Amazon account in order to access Amazon content. An Amazon account was created for the device under the name "Fire Stick." A gaming profile was also created locally on the device under a pseudonym. An author's accounts for Netflix, Pandora and Spotify were used to test the video and music streaming features.

To assess the video streaming features, Netflix and YouTube applications were installed and accessed. The Netflix application was then used to stream the first ten minutes of several sample movies and television shows. The YouTube application was used to stream several sample videos. Finally, Amazon's free streaming video content was used to stream sample videos.

The assessment of the music streaming feature involved the installation of the Spotify and Pandora apps. Spotify was used to stream several sample music tracks. The Pandora app was used to stream music from a radio station.

The gaming feature was assessed by first setting up a local gaming profile on the Fire TV Stick. This profile was created and named automatically without direct action by the user. It appeared after the first game was downloaded and launched on the system. Amazon's App Store was then used to download two sample games, *Flappy Birds Family* and *Crossy Road*. The apps were then launched individually and two rounds of each game were played.

In order to assess the photograph uploading and viewing feature via Amazon's Cloud Drive, a free trial for the Cloud Drive was obtained using the Fire Stick Amazon account and an email address. Photos were then uploaded using the Fire Stick account, Cloud Drive website and a desktop personal computer. After the photographs were uploaded, they were viewed via the Fire TV Stick's photo tab. The photo tab was then used to view the Test and Favorites albums and to add the photographs to the albums.

Amazon's App Store and the app downloading feature were assessed by downloading additional programs. NBC and HBO Go apps were downloaded from the App Store to assess this feature. The idea was to see the kind of information that could be recovered about apps that were downloaded but never used.

The sideloading of Android apps from sources other than Amazon's App Store was assessed using the Android debug bridge and ES File Explorer. ES File Explorer was used to download Kodi, formerly known as the Xbox Media Center, directly from its download page. This was done by creating a Favorites tab in Kodi to navigate to a web page and using the remote to navigate the website. Kodi was then launched to ensure that it worked properly. The `install` command of the Android debug bridge can be used from a workstation to obtain downloaded Android APK files and install them on the Fire TV Stick. This method was used to install the Firefox and Google Chrome web browser apps. The apps were then launched to ensure that they worked properly. The web browsers were used to navigate and log into a Facebook account and the remote was used to navigate to the page.

## 4.     Forensic Assessment

Various tests were devised and conducted to assess the ability of a digital forensic investigator to acquire an image and identify artifacts of user actions and device information on a Fire TV Stick. Test data was introduced at different times during the testing process. Timestamps were found to be consistent in all the tests; specifically, when files could be retrieved during the assessments, the timestamps were reflective of the simulated interactions with the system. This was confirmed using FTK Imager to triage the extracted information and compare the file timestamps against the recorded times.

## 4.1 ADB Extraction Test

The `pull` command of the Android debug bridge was used to create an image of the userdata partition without root permissions. The test began by powering on the Fire TV Stick, setting it up, enabling USB debugging and powering off the Fire TV Stick. The device was then disconnected from the TV and connected to a Windows workstation. An Android debug bridge server was then started on the workstation and a connection was established with the Fire TV Stick. The `mount` command was then used to identify the location of the userdata partition. After it was identified, the `pull` command was used to attempt to image the partition, but this failed due to the lack of root permissions. The `dd` command was also attempted, but it failed for the same reason. Thus, the Android debug bridge extraction test failed to extract an image from the device and, therefore, could not help identify any useful information on the device.

## 4.2 UFED Touch Test

The UFED Touch v.1.9.0.130 from Cellebrite was used to attempt physical and logical filesystem extractions from the Fire TV Stick. Research by Horowitz [5] has revealed that a physical extraction from the Amazon Kindle Fire HDX could be performed using Cellebrite's UFED Touch Ultimate. Because the two devices use similar operating systems, it was expected that this method could work for the Fire TV Stick.

The experiment involved connecting the Fire TV Stick to the UFED Touch and working through its menus to attempt physical and logical extractions. However, the version of the UFED Touch available at the time of this writing was unable to recognize or read the Fire TV Stick.

## 4.3 Python Script Test

This experiment attempted to use a custom Python script to extract a logical image of the Fire TV Stick using the Android debug bridge functionality without root permissions. Komodo edit 9, Python 3.5 and the `pyadb` module were used to create the script. The script incorporated native Android debug bridge commands to extract/pull all the files that it could extract, create hashes before and after file transfer (MD5 is

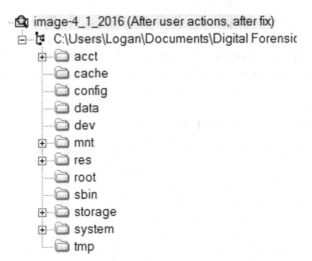

*Figure 1.*  File structure of the test data image produced by the Python script.

available on the Fire TV Stick without any additional modification), compare the hashes, recreate the directory structure and then store all the original timestamps for the files that were extracted. The script was used to create logical images of the Fire TV Stick before and after the test data was added.

FTK Imager v.3.4.0.1 was used to examine the images obtained using the Python script. Figure 1 shows the file structure of the image created after the test data was added. An analysis of the image revealed that some artifacts of user actions were present and could be recovered. The artifacts included remnants of the sideloading process with Kodi, list of installed apps, files and APKs associated with installed apps, app thumbnails and APK files for sideloaded apps. Other system artifacts included the language setting of the device and APK/ODEX files corresponding to background apps.

Certain points regarding the image need to be highlighted. First, many useful data items and artifacts of user actions came from having the ES File Explorer app installed on the device. If this app had not been previously installed on the device, most of what was found in the image would not be present. Second, the data directory, which contains much of the useful user data, could not be extracted due to problems with permissions (i.e., root privileges are required).

## 4.4    Rooting Test

This experiment was designed to address the problem of not having root permissions to the Fire TV Stick, which hinders access to certain areas of the device. The experiment involved the use of KingRoot v.4.8.5. FireOS on the first-generation Fire TV and Fire TV Stick can be rooted using the KingRoot automatic rooting app [1] up to and including FireOS v.5.0.5. Thus, a copy of the KingRoot APK was downloaded to a workstation and the Android debug bridge was used to install it on the Fire TV Stick. However, the KingRoot GUI is designed to work with a mouse, not the Fire TV Stick remote. Therefore, a Bluetooth mouse had to be connected to the Fire TV Stick to run KingRoot. The Fire TV Stick was successfully rooted and the SuperSU APK was sideloaded using an Android debug bridge install. An Android debug bridge connection was established from the workstation to the Fire TV Stick and the su command was executed, successfully gaining root permissions on the device.

After gaining root permissions, the Python script was modified to use root permissions in an attempt to extract files. Initial tests with the modified script revealed that timestamps were not extracted correctly. After changing the operating system on the acquisition workstation from Windows to Linux (Ubuntu), the MAC times were copied correctly.

## 4.5    ADB Extraction Test

Enabling root permissions on the device reduced the challenges encountered when using the previous Android debug bridge extraction method. Therefore, the test was repeated with root permissions to see if an image could be produced that included the userdata partition.

The procedure involved starting an Android debug bridge server with root permissions to the Ubuntu workstation. A connection was then established to the Fire TV Stick and the Android debug bridge mount command was used to locate the userdata partition. The su command was executed to gain root permissions. Next, the chmod command was used to provide temporary (until reboot) world-read permissions on the userdata block. The Android debug bridge pull command was used to successfully extract an image of the Fire TV Stick's userdata partition. Two images were created using this method: (i) test image created initially while working through the empirical process; and (ii) test image after the initial sample data was added.

After adding test data, attempts were made to create another image, but an automatic software update changed the operating system from v.5.0.5 to v.5.0.5.1, rendering the version of KingRoot unable to root

Table 2. Artifacts in the Amazon Fire TV Stick.

| Artifacts | Description |
|---|---|
| Timestamp | Last access time reflective of user interaction. |
| Browser History | The browser.db file contains evidence of navigating to websites using Mozilla Firefox. |
| Pictures | [root]/data/com.amazon.bueller.photos/files/ cmsimages contains pictures from the Amazon Cloud Drive. Images extracted directly from the Cloud Drive have the same hash values as the originals, but images found at this location in the Fire TV Stick do not. It appears that images in the Fire TV Stick are formatted for better viewing in the system menu. Two files, each identical in name except for *-full.jpg and *-thumb.jpg suffixes may be found. Figure 3 shows the original image (left), fPM452RvROeOv-iKfAaOSQ-full.jpg (center) and fPM452RvROeOv-iKfAaOSQ-thumb.jpg (right). |
| Bluetooth Devices | [root]/data/com.amazon.device.controllermanager/ databases/devices contains the names and MAC addresses of devices connected via Bluetooth (Razer Orochi mouse and Amazon Fire TV remote). |
| Amazon Logs | [root]/data/com.amazon.device.logmanager/files contains several log files, including Log.amazon\main. |

the (at the time of writing) up-to-date Fire TV Stick. The acquisition experiment was halted at this point.

It should be noted that a digital forensic investigator would not put such a device online while working on an active case. The update occurred only because connectivity was required in order to generate the test data needed to assess the Fire TV Stick. However, it was still possible to continue the analysis of the image taken with the initial test data. AccessData Labs v.5.1 was used to analyze the images created using the Android debug bridge pull command. Figure 2 shows the file structure of the test image created after the test data was added.

Analysis of the image revealed that a large amount of useful information could be recovered (Table 2). In addition to the artifacts commonly encountered in Android devices, it was also possible to recover several Amazon-specific artifacts.

While the images produced using the Android debug bridge extraction method proved to be extremely useful, a few points regarding the method should be highlighted. First, the method requires permissions to the partition to be changed in order to use the Android debug bridge

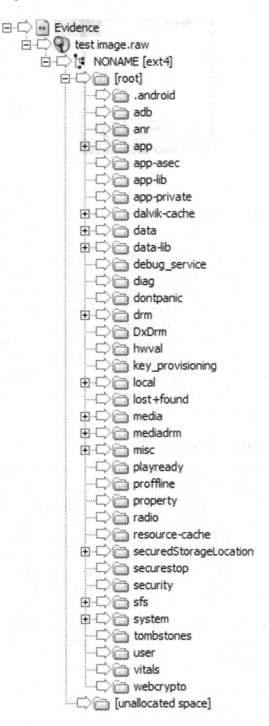

*Figure 2.*   File structure of the userdata image obtained via ADB extraction.

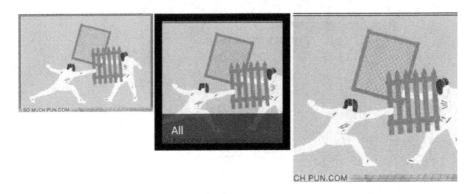

*Figure 3.*   Visual comparison of images obtained from the Fire TV Stick.

pull command for extraction. Thus, a change has to be made to the system, which is certainly not ideal with regard to the forensic soundness of the method. Upon closer inspection, the version of KingRoot used was found to have not made significant changes to the userdata partition; however, this would have to be considered for every future root/exploit method. Forensic soundness is still preserved during extraction because the userdata partition is only granted world-read, not world-write, permissions (the permissions are reset after the device is rebooted). Thus, the Android debug bridge cannot modify the data during a pull operation.

## 4.6    Manual Acquisition Test

In order to handle a device that cannot be rooted, additional experiments were performed to elicit artifacts using traditional manual means – specifically, video recordings, photographs and note-taking to capture and analyze the menus visible to a regular user. The test began by powering on the Fire TV Stick and recording the time. The user accessible menus/pages were then examined starting with the Home tab. Each tab/menu was fully documented before proceeding to the next tab. Figure 4 shows a photograph that documents the Home tab of the Fire TV Stick.

An analysis of the videos and photographs revealed that a large amount of useful information could be recovered. Artifacts of user actions that were recovered include:

- Recently accessed apps/content.

- Games downloaded by the user.

- User's gaming profile.

*Figure 4.* Fire TV Stick Home tab with recent activity feed highlighted.

- List of apps downloaded by the user (sideloaded apps are distinguished by the message "This app was not downloaded from Amazon").
- Amazon Prime music/account content.
- User's Amazon Cloud Drive images/albums.
- Metadata for Cloud Drive images (e.g., name, taken and uploaded timestamps, dimensions).
- Email address associated with the registered user's Amazon account.
- Bluetooth devices synced with the Fire TV Stick.
- Full list of installed apps with metadata (e.g., version, size, storage).
- Name of the registered Amazon account.

Furthermore, the following useful system information was recovered:

- Device name.
- Amazon remote, game controller and other Bluetooth device information (e.g., name, version, serial number).
- Device storage capacity.
- Operating system/software version.
- Device serial number.
- Device date and time.
- SSID of the connected Wi-Fi network.
- Device IP address.
- Wi-Fi adapter MAC address.

- Number of connected controllers/Bluetooth devices.

- System update timestamps.

- Available Wi-Fi networks.

- ZIP code of the location.

- Country and timezone.

- Language settings.

However, this acquisition method is problematic because it requires the device to be analyzed live, which results in changes to the system.

## 5.      Recommended Forensic Analysis Method

Figure 5 outlines the digital forensic methodology recommended for acquiring an image from an Amazon Fire TV Stick.

Step 1 creates the environment for imaging a rooted Fire TV Stick. The Android debug bridge is used to obtain shell access to the device. SuperSU provides root access to the device, enabling all the files to be captured.

Step 2 is the standard best practice for a live investigation. All interactions with the system must be recorded and notes should be taken along with the times in case the device time has been altered.

Step 3 turns the device on. Step 4 sets up the environment variables in the Fire TV Stick to allow the installation of the SuperSU root APK. Step 5 injects the files into the system, establishes root access with the assistance of a Bluetooth mouse (Fire TV Stick does not have a USB port for external peripherals) and confirms that root access is established.

Step 6 uses the Android debug bridge server on the Ubuntu workstation to connect to the Fire TV Stick's shell; the built-in `mount` command is used to identify which partition/block device stores data. Step 7 navigates to the `/dev/block` directory to locate the correct device. Step 8 executes the `su` command on the device to obtain root privileges; following this, the permissions of the userdata partition can be updated to 755, enabling global read access (but importantly, not global write).

Step 9 exits the Fire TV Stick shell and, given the temporary changes made to the userdata area, maximizes data acquisition via the Android debug bridge `pull` command. Step 10 concludes the data acquisition, powers off the Fire TV Stick and video capture device, and records the times of both actions.

## 6.      Conclusions

An Amazon Fire TV Stick contains a plethora of information, some of it related to user activity and other information related to the system

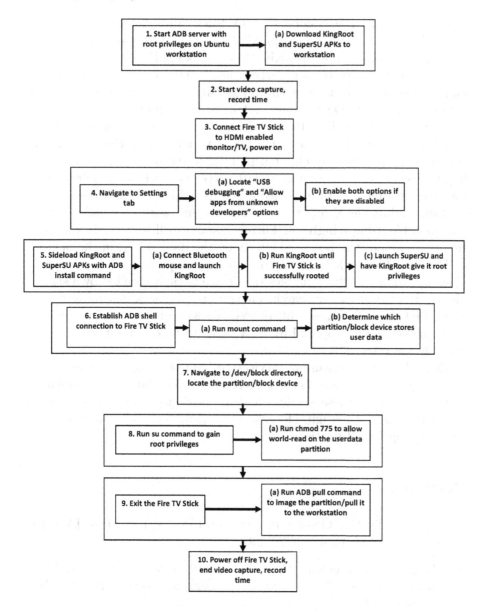

*Figure 5.* Forensic analysis method for the Amazon Fire TV Stick.

itself. The proposed method for imaging Fire TV Sticks enables digital forensic investigators to perform analyses of these popular streaming media devices. Efforts are taken to minimize, if not eliminate, data alteration. Thus, the method can be considered to be "semi" forensically sound.

Whether or not a particular Fire TV Stick can be imaged successfully using the proposed method depends on the operating system/software version. It is possible to use KingRoot to root a Fire TV Stick device that runs a Fire OS version earlier than v.5.0.5.1; rooting the device makes it possible to acquire an image using the proposed method. A device running Fire OS version v.5.0.5.1 or later cannot be rooted using the current version of KingRoot and, thus, an image of the device cannot be extracted via the proposed method. An automatic Fire OS update increases the potential of eliminating root access to a device, making it imperative to ensure that the update server is blocked by a firewall or the forensic analysis of the device is conducted in a Faraday cage.

Downgrading the Fire TV Stick software/firmware may make the device rootable using KingRoot. Future research will investigate this possibility as well as the potential effects on the data stored in the device.

The Fire TV Stick has a remote app, a companion application provided by Amazon, which enables the device to be controlled by a smartphone. It provides voice search, navigation, playback control and keyboard text entry features. Future research will analyze the interactions between the remote app and Fire TV Stick to determine if any forensic artifacts are retrievable.

Meanwhile, new streaming services and applications are emerging as streaming media devices become increasingly popular. Future research will also examine these services and applications, which may provide artifacts of interest to digital forensic investigators as well as new avenues for analyzing Fire TV Sticks.

# References

[1] AFTVnews, Fire OS 5 on the Amazon Fire TV 1 and Fire TV Stick can be rooted, February 20, 2016.

[2] T. Cushing, Amazon Fire TV firmware update bricks rooted devices, prevents rollback to previous firmware versions, *Techdirt*, December 5, 2014.

[3] B. Evangelista, Cord cutting accelerated in 2015, on track to continue next year, *San Francisco Chronicle*, December 31, 2015.

[4] K. Fairbanks, An analysis of Ext4 for digital forensics, *Digital Investigation*, vol. 9(S), pp. S118–S130, 2012.

[5] J. Horowitz, Kindle Fire HDX Forensics (`kindlefirehdxforen sics.blogspot.com`), April 15, 2014.

[6] A. Iqbal, H. Al Obaidli, A. Marrington and I. Baggili, Amazon Kindle Fire HD forensics, *Proceedings of the International Conference on Digital Forensics and Cyber Crime*, pp. 39–50, 2014.

[7] J. Smith, Here's why consumers are increasingly turning to streaming media devices to view content, *Business Insider*, June 16, 2016.

[8] N. Terry, Amazon Fire TV takes 30% of the streaming market, *Android Headlines*, June 5, 2015.

[9] P. van Bolhuis and C. Van Bockhaven, Forensic Analysis of Chromecast and Miracast Devices, Cybercrime and Forensics Project, Master's Program in System and Network Engineering, University of Amsterdam, Amsterdam, The Netherlands, 2014.

# Chapter 5

# DETECTING ANOMALOUS PROGRAMMABLE LOGIC CONTROLLER EVENTS USING MACHINE LEARNING

Ken Yau and Kam-Pui Chow

**Abstract**    Industrial control system failures can be hazardous to human lives and the environment. Programmable logic controllers are major components of industrial control systems that are used across the critical infrastructure. Attack and accident investigations involving programmable logic controllers rely on forensic techniques to establish the root causes and to develop mitigation strategies. However, programmable logic controller forensics is a challenging task, primarily because of the lack of system logging. This chapter proposes a novel methodology that logs the values of relevant memory addresses used by a programmable logic controller program along with their timestamps. Machine learning techniques are applied to the logged data to identify anomalous or abnormal programmable logic controller operations. An application of the methodology to a simulated traffic light control system demonstrates its effectiveness in performing forensic investigations of programmable logic controllers.

**Keywords:** Programming logic controllers, forensics, machine learning

## 1. Introduction

Industrial control systems, which are widely used in the critical infrastructure, contribute to safety and convenience in every aspect of modern society. These systems have served reliably for decades, but a changing technological environment is exposing them to risks that they were not designed to handle [4]. In particular, their reliance on networking technologies, including remote access and control over the Internet, significantly increase the likelihood of attacks.

© IFIP International Federation for Information Processing 2017
Published by Springer International Publishing AG 2017. All Rights Reserved
G. Peterson and S. Shenoi (Eds.): Advances in Digital Forensics XIII, IFIP AICT 511, pp. 81–94, 2017.
DOI: 10.1007/978-3-319-67208-3_5

A common approach when investigating attacks and anomalies involving an industrial control system is to concentrate on the central server of the digital control system or supervisory control and data acquisition (SCADA) system [4]. These servers typically use commodity operating systems, enabling the use of standard digital forensic tools. However, field devices in an industrial control system such as programmable logic controllers (PLCs) and remote terminal units (RTUs) typically rely on proprietary hardware and embedded operating systems, and, therefore, require specialized digital forensic tools and techniques. Unfortunately, these tools and techniques are very limited in their functionality or simply do not exist.

Programmable logic controllers, which interact with and manage sensors and actuators, are important components of industrial control systems. As a result, they are attractive targets for attackers. A notable example is the Stuxnet malware that targeted Siemens programming logic controllers that operated Iran's uranium hexafluoride centrifuges [3]. The malware reprogrammed programmable logic controller code to cause malfunctions and damage while providing fabricated data to the operators in order to mask the attacks.

Unlike traditional digital forensics, no standard guidelines, procedures and tools are available for performing programmable logic controller forensics. A key challenge is the lack of system logging for forensic investigations. This chapter proposes a forensic methodology that captures the values of relevant memory addresses used by a programmable logic controller program in a log file. Machine learning techniques are applied to the logged data to identify anomalous or abnormal programmable logic controller operations. The methodology is applied to the popular Siemens Simatic S7-1212C programmable logic controller. Experiments with a simulated traffic light control system demonstrate the effectiveness and utility of the methodology in forensic investigations of incidents involving programmable logic controllers.

## 2.     Programmable Logic Controllers

A programmable logic controller is a special microprocessor-based device that uses programmable memory to store instructions and implement functions such as logic, sequencing, timing, counting and arithmetic in order to monitor and control equipment and processes [2]. Figure 1 shows a schematic diagram of a programmable logic controller.

The programming of controllers is an important task when designing and implementing control applications. Each programmable logic controller has to be loaded with a program that controls the status of

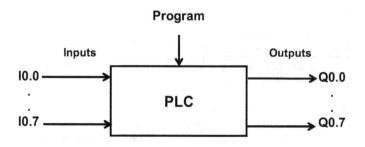

*Figure 1.* Programmable logic controller.

outputs based on the status of inputs. A programmable logic controller identifies each input or output according to its memory address. In the case of Siemens programmable logic controllers, the addresses of inputs and outputs are expressed in terms of their byte and bit numbers. For example, I0.1 is an input at bit 1 in byte 0 and Q0.7 is an output at bit 7 in byte 0.

A programmable logic controller exhibits anomalous operations in the following situations: (i) hardware failure; (ii) incompatible firmware version; (iii) control program bugs created by an authorized programmer or attacker; (iv) stop and start attacks [1]; and (v) memory read and write attacks [1].

The first step in detecting these anomalous operations is to capture the values of the inputs and outputs used by the control program in a log file. Machine learning techniques are subsequently applied to the logged data in order to detect anomalous operations.

## 3.    Forensic Challenges

Digital forensic guidelines, procedures and tools have been developed for traditional information technology infrastructures and environments. A digital forensic process includes identification, collection, analysis and reporting. However, performing digital forensic techniques on programmable logic controllers is subject to several challenges [11]:

- **Lack of Documentation:** Low-level documentation of proprietary hardware, firmware and applications is usually not available for programmable logic controllers.

- **Lack of Domain-Specific Knowledge and Experience:** Digital forensics of programmable logic controllers is hindered by the lack of expertise and experience on the part of investigators.

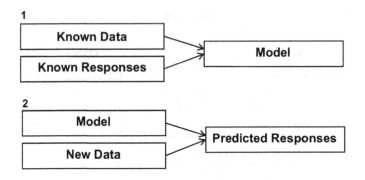

*Figure 2.* Supervised learning.

- **Lack of Logging Mechanisms:** Programmable logic controllers typically do not log data for forensic purposes.

- **Lack of Forensic Tools:** Limited, if any, forensic tools are available for conducting investigations of incidents involving programmable logic controllers.

- **Availability/Always On:** The availability of programmable logic controllers in an industrial control environment is a priority. It is extremely difficult to shut down a control system and physical process in order to conduct a forensic investigation.

## 4.    Machine Learning

Machine learning is a data analysis method that automates model building. By leveraging algorithms that iteratively learn from data, machine learning enables computer systems to find hidden insights without being explicitly programmed [12]. Machine learning techniques have been applied in a number of areas, including pattern and image recognition, email spam filtering and network intrusion detection.

Supervised learning is the most common machine learning approach and several algorithms such as decision trees, support vector machines and artificial neural networks have been developed to implement supervised learning. In general, a supervised learning algorithm takes a known set of input data and known responses to the data, and creates a model that effectively predicts the responses to new input data [7].

Figure 2 shows a schematic diagram of the supervised learning approach. The experiments conducted in this research leveraged decision tree (DT) and support vector machine (SVM) learning algorithms to analyze log file data in order to detect anomalous programmable logic controller operations.

## 5. Related Work

The Stuxnet attack [3] significantly increased research efforts related to industrial control system security, including intrusion detection and anomaly detection. However, very little research has specifically focused on applying machine learning techniques to detect intrusions and anomalous operations. An example is the work of Morris et al. [9], which trained a classifier on log data captured from a laboratory-scale gas pipeline and used it to detect 35 cyber attacks.

Another example is the research of Mantere et al. [6], which leveraged network traffic features to detect anomalies in specific industrial control systems. Mantere and colleagues used machine learning to decrease the amount of manual customization required to deploy network security monitors and intrusion detection systems in industrial control systems.

The research presented in this chapter differs from related work in that it concentrates on monitoring and capturing data directly from programmable logic controllers to support forensic investigations of intrusions and anomalous operations.

## 6. Experimental Setup and Methodology

This section describes the experimental setup and the methodology for identifying anomalous programmable logic controller operations.

### 6.1 Experimental Setup

The experiments used a Siemens S7-1212C programmable logic controller loaded with the TLIGHT traffic light control program. TLIGHT is a sample program provided with the Siemens SIMATIC S7-300 Programmable Controller Quick Start User Guide [16]. As shown in Figure 3, the TLIGHT program controls vehicles and pedestrian traffic at an intersection.

In order to simulate the hardware configuration of a traffic light control system, the programmable logic controller inputs I0.0 and I0.1 were connected to switches and the outputs Q0.0, Q0.1, Q0.5, Q0.6 and Q0.7 were connected to traffic lights. Figure 4 shows the input/output connections of the Siemens S7 1212C programmable logic controller. The Ethernet port of the programmable logic controller was used to establish a network connection for communicating with a peripheral device such as a laptop for programming the system.

*Figure 3.* TLIGHT control system.

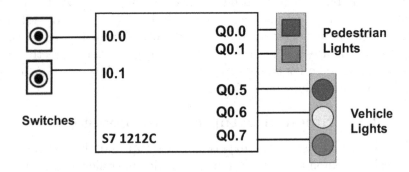

*Figure 4.* Siemens S7 1212C showing the input/output connections.

A program using the libnodave open source library [5] was used to log the values of relevant memory addresses used by the TLIGHT program. In particular, the program monitored the programmable logic controller memory addresses over the network and recorded the values along with their timestamps. To simplify the supervised learning process, all the non-binary values of memory addresses (e.g., timers) were converted to binary values.

## 6.2    Classifying Anomalous Operations

A machine learning technique typically splits the available data into two parts: (i) training set for learning the properties of the data; and (ii) testing set for evaluating the learned properties of the data. The accuracy of response prediction was evaluated using the testing set [14].

Table 1. TLIGHT control program instructions.

| Instruction | Address | Description |
|---|---|---|
| Outputs | Q 0.0 | Red for pedestrians |
| | Q 0.1 | Green for pedestrians |
| | Q 0.5 | Red for vehicles |
| | Q 0.6 | Yellow for vehicles |
| | Q 0.7 | Green for vehicles |
| Inputs | I 0.0 | Switch on the right-hand side of the street |
| | I 0.1 | Switch on the left-hand side of the street |
| Memory Bit | M 0.0 | Memory bit for switching the signal after a green request from a pedestrian |
| Timers (On-Delay) | T 2 | Red for pedestrians |
| | T 3 | Green for pedestrians |
| | T 4 | Red for vehicles |
| | T 5 | Yellow for vehicles |
| | T 6 | Green for vehicles |

In order to implement supervised leaning, it was first necessary to understand the TLIGHT program logic. The TLIGHT program comprises instructions that involve inputs, outputs, memory bits and timers. Table 1 provides details about the TLIGHT instructions. Figure 5 shows the input and output signal states during the TLIGHT sample program sequence [16].

The supervised learning approach involved the following steps:

- **Step 1: Training Set Creation:** A training example corresponds to a pair of input objects (values of relevant addresses) and known responses (normal/anomalous operations of the traffic lights). Normal and anomalous operations of TLIGHT were determined according to the values at the relevant addresses (timers and outputs). The seven normal operations of TLIGHT presented in Figure 5 are based on the values of the timers and outputs at various time intervals. Table 2 shows the input objects and known responses for the seven normal operations of TLIGHT. These were transformed to the input data matrix format for use in supervised learning.

The training set was generated by running the traffic light control system and logging system to capture the values of relevant addresses (inputs, outputs and timers) used by TLIGHT. Anomalous operations were created by altering some values in address locations using Snap7, an open-source, 32/64 bit, multi-platform

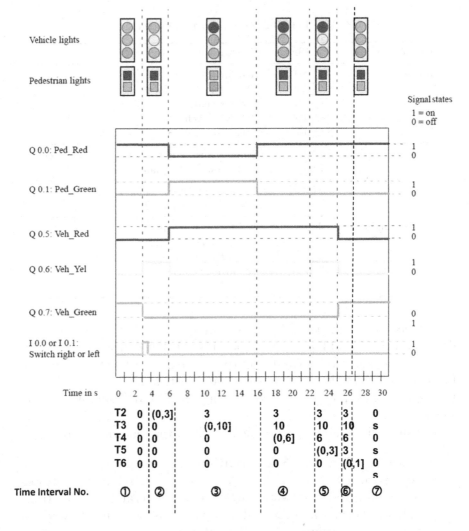

*Figure 5.* Input and output signal states during the TLIGHT program sequence.

Ethernet communications suite for interfacing with Siemens S7 programmable logic controllers [10]. Thus, the generated log file contained normal and anomalous traffic light operations.

- **Step 2: Supervised Learning Algorithm Selection:** Decision tree (DT) and support vector machine (SVM) supervised learning algorithms were employed in the experiments. A decision tree algorithm was selected to classify anomalous operations of TLIGHT for several reasons [8]. First, the target function has discrete output

Table 2.   Seven normal TLIGHT operations.

| Time Interval | Input Objects | | | | | | | | | | Known Response |
| --- | --- | --- | --- | --- | --- | --- | --- | --- | --- | --- | --- |
| | Yes=1; No=0 | | | | | On=1; Off=0 | | | | | Yes=1; No=0 |
| | T2=3? | T3=10? | T4=6? | T5=3? | T6=1? | Q0.0 | Q0.1 | Q0.5 | Q0.6 | Q0.7 | Normal? |
| 1 | 0 | 0 | 0 | 0 | 0 | 1 | 0 | 0 | 0 | 1 | 1 |
| 2 | 0 | 0 | 0 | 0 | 0 | 1 | 0 | 0 | 1 | 0 | 1 |
| 3 | 1 | 0 | 0 | 0 | 0 | 0 | 1 | 1 | 0 | 0 | 1 |
| 4 | 1 | 1 | 0 | 0 | 0 | 1 | 0 | 1 | 0 | 0 | 1 |
| 5 | 1 | 1 | 1 | 0 | 0 | 1 | 0 | 1 | 1 | 0 | 1 |
| 6 | 1 | 1 | 1 | 1 | 0 | 1 | 0 | 0 | 0 | 1 | 1 |
| 7 | 0 | 0 | 0 | 0 | 1 | 1 | 0 | 0 | 0 | 1 | 1 |

values (TLIGHT operations). Additionally, a decision tree algorithm is fairly robust at handling training data errors, including mislabeled attribute values. Indeed, somewhat noisy data (e.g., due to errors in assigning response values) do not pose much of a problem for a decision tree algorithm. A decision tree algorithm can also handle data with missing attribute values (e.g., missing values at memory addresses during data capture).

In addition to a decision tree algorithm, a support vector machine supervised learning algorithm was used. This was done to determine if any obvious differences in accuracy and performance occur when a different machine learning algorithm is used. Furthermore, the support vector machine algorithm performs well even with small training datasets

- **Step 3: Supervised Learning Algorithm Application:** The captured data was assigned response values corresponding to normal or anomalous operations and was subsequently transformed to a matrix format for input to the supervised learning algorithms (Table 2). Decision tree and support vector machine classifiers provided by scikit-learn [15] were used for model training. Table 3 lists the settings of the classifiers used in the experiments. The classifiers were implemented using default values of the input parameters. No $k$-fold cross validation was applied to the training samples. Finally, the accuracy of response prediction was evaluated based on the testing data.

Table 3.   DT and SVM classifier settings in scikit-learn.

|  | DT | SVM |
|---|---|---|
| Class | tree.DecisionTreeClassifier | svm.SVC |
| Training Samples | Transaction records in data log files with assigned known responses | |
| • Input Objects | Memory addresses used in TLIGHT | |
| • Known Responses | Operational status of TLIGHT (normal/anomalous) | |
| Parameter Settings | Default settings | |

Table 4.   Classification accuracy.

|  | Dataset 1 | | Dataset 2 | |
|---|---|---|---|---|
| Training Records | 560 | | 1,600 | |
| Testing Records | 2,240 | | 6,400 | |
| Learning Algorithm | DT | SVM | DT | SVM |
| Accuracy | 99.91% | 99.91% | 99.94% | 99.60% |

## 7.     Experimental Results and Discussion

In order to evaluate the accuracy of the learned models, two datasets were prepared for the decision tree and support vector machine learning algorithms. The first set (Dataset 1) contained 2,800 records, 560 for training and 2,240 for testing. The second set (Dataset 2) contained 8,000 records, 1,600 for training and 6,400 for testing. Table 4 shows the classification accuracy. The accuracy rates with Dataset 1 for the decision tree and support vector machine learning algorithms were 99.91% while the accuracy rates with Dataset 2 for the decision tree and support vector machine learning algorithms were 99.94% and 99.60%, respectively.

In the experiments, transaction records in the log file corresponding to anomalous operations were identified by machine learning. Because the values at the relevant addresses used by TLIGHT were recorded along with timestamps in the log file, it was possible to trace which values had been altered and when they were altered, and subsequently identify the anomalous TLIGHT operations. However, a log file alone may be insufficient in a forensic investigation because it does not contain information about what (e.g., IP address) induced an anomalous operation and how it was induced. For this reason, a forensic investigator should use a network packet analyzer such as Wireshark to capture

**Corresponds to Table 2 Training Data**

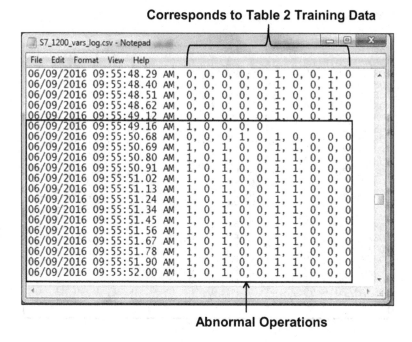

*Figure 6.* Log file with anomalous operations.

packets while employing the logging system to record the relevant addresses used by TLIGHT. Wireshark supports the PROFINET industrial data communications standard in order to record and analyze Ethernet message frames. It can be used to dissect the ISO-on-TCP packets in Siemens S7 programmable logic controller communications after adding the Wireshark S7 dissector plugin. Note that S7 is a function-oriented or command-oriented protocol in that each transmission contains a command or a reply.

After collecting and analyzing the log file and network packet data, a forensic investigator can discover where the compromise originated, how it was carried out and, possibly, who was responsible for the incident. For example, the machine learning algorithms (decision tree and support vector machine) identified that anomalous operations started on 09 June 2016 at 09:55.49.16 AM (Figure 6) and on 29 August 2016 at 09:27:38.96 PM (Figure 7). This step saves a forensic investigator considerable time in identifying anomalous transactions. Based on the timestamps in the log file, an investigator can focus on checking the actions performed on the system (e.g., firmware or user control program updates by authorized operators and alterations performed by unauthorized entities).

```
S7_1200_vars_log.csv - Notepad                                      ⸻ ▢ ✕

File   Edit   Format   View   Help
08/29/2016 09:27:38.96 PM, 0, 0, 0, 0, 1, 1, 0, 0, 0, 1
08/29/2016 09:27:39.07 PM, 0, 0, 0, 0, 1, 1, 0, 0, 0, 1
08/29/2016 09:27:39.18 PM, 0, 0, 0, 0, 1, 1, 0, 0, 0, 1
08/29/2016 09:27:39.29 PM, 0, 0, 0, 0, 1, 1, 0, 0, 0, 1
08/29/2016 09:27:39.40 PM, 0, 0, 0, 0, 1, 1, 0, 0, 0, 1
08/29/2016 09:27:39.51 PM, 0, 0, 0, 0, 1, 1, 0, 0, 0, 1
08/29/2016 09:27:39.62 PM, 0, 0, 0, 0, 1, 1, 0, 0, 0, 1
08/29/2016 09:27:39.73 PM, 0, 0, 0, 0, 1, 1, 0, 0, 0, 1
08/29/2016 09:27:39.84 PM, 0, 0, 0, 0, 1, 1, 0, 0, 0, 1
08/29/2016 09:27:39.95 PM, 0, 0, 0, 0, 1, 1, 0, 0, 0, 1
08/29/2016 09:27:40.06 PM, 0, 0, 0, 0, 1, 1, 0, 0, 0, 1
08/29/2016 09:27:40.16 PM, 0, 0, 0, 0, 1, 1, 0, 0, 0, 1
08/29/2016 09:27:40.27 PM, 0, 0, 0, 0, 1, 1, 0, 0, 0, 1
08/29/2016 09:27:40.38 PM, 0, 0, 0, 0, 1, 1, 0, 0, 0, 1
08/29/2016 09:27:40.49 PM, 0, 0, 0, 0, 0, 1, 0, 0, 1, 0
08/29/2016 09:27:40.60 PM, 0, 0, 0, 0, 0, 1, 0, 0, 1, 0
08/29/2016 09:27:40.71 PM, 0, 0, 0, 0, 0, 1, 0, 0, 1, 0
08/29/2016 09:27:40.82 PM, 0, 0, 0, 0, 0, 1, 0, 0, 1, 0
08/29/2016 09:27:40.93 PM, 0, 0, 0, 0, 0, 1, 0, 0, 1, 0
08/29/2016 09:27:41.04 PM, 0, 0, 0, 0, 0, 1, 0, 0, 1, 0
08/29/2016 09:27:41.15 PM, 0, 0, 0, 0, 0, 1, 0, 0, 1, 0
08/29/2016 09:27:41.26 PM, 0, 0, 0, 0, 0, 1, 0, 0, 1, 0
08/29/2016 09:27:41.37 PM, 0, 0, 0, 0, 0, 1, 0, 0, 1, 0
08/29/2016 09:27:41.47 PM, 0, 0, 0, 0, 0, 1, 0, 0, 1, 0
```

*Figure 7.*   Anomalous operations.

In the experiment, the anomalous operations that started on 09 June 2016 at 09:55.49.16 AM were the result of a programmable logic controller self-test and the anomalous operations that started on 29 August 2016 at 09:27:38.96 PM were due to a simulated attack (Snap7) [10]. These examples demonstrate that machine learning can help a forensic investigator filter unnecessary log data and narrow the scope of the forensic investigation.

The methodology presented in this chapter can be extended to other brands of programmable logic controllers and other control programs. However, it is not possible to create a single logging system for all programmable logic controller applications because different applications require different control programs. Therefore, each programmable logic controller application should have its own logging system. In order to create a logging system, it is necessary to understand the design of the control program and identify the programmable logic controller memory addresses that must be monitored and analyzed.

In order to simplify machine learning, the experiments did not consider the time sequences of normal programmable logic controller operations. Therefore, the accuracy of the results may vary. Note also that supervised learning is by no means the only way to identify anomalous programmable logic controller operations. In fact, the work described in this chapter serves as an initial approach to determine whether or not supervised learning is feasible for programmable logic controller forensics. Indeed, the experimental results demonstrate that supervised learning can help predict anomalous operations with uncertain inputs and responses, even in the case of complicated user control programs.

## 8. Conclusions

A log containing the values at the relevant memory addresses used by a programmable logic controller program along with their timestamps can be very valuable in a forensic investigation of an industrial control system incident. In particular, machine learning techniques can applied to the logged data to identify anomalous programmable logic controller operations. The application of the methodology to a simulated traffic light control system demonstrates its effectiveness in a forensic investigation involving a programmable logic controller. Since different programmable logic controller applications require different control programs, each application should have its own logging system. In order to create the logging system, it is necessary to understand the design of the control program and identify the programmable logic controller memory addresses that must be monitored and analyzed. However, a log file alone may be insufficient in a forensic investigation because it may not contain information about what induced an anomalous operation and how it was induced. Therefore, it is recommended to augment the log file with data from a network packet analyzer such as Wireshark.

This research is an initial step in developing forensic capabilities for programmable logic controllers. Future research will attempt to apply and refine machine learning techniques to various industrial control system applications to support forensic investigations of intrusions and anomalous behavior in these vital systems that permeate the critical infrastructure.

## References

[1] D. Beresford, Exploiting Siemens Simatic S7 PLCs, presented at *Black Hat USA*, 2011.

[2] W. Bolton, *Programmable Logic Controllers*, Newnes, Burlington, Massachusetts, 2009.

[3] N. Falliere, L. O'Murchu and E. Chien, W32.Stuxnet Dossier, Symantec, Mountain View, California, 2011.

[4] L. Folkerth, Forensic Analysis of Industrial Control Systems, In-foSec Reading Room, SANS Institute, Bethesda, Maryland, 2015.

[5] T. Hergenhahn, `libnodave` (`sourceforge.net/projects/libnodave`), 2014.

[6] M. Mantere, M. Sailio and S. Noponen, Network traffic features for anomaly detection in a specific industrial control system network, *Future Internet*, vol. 5(4), pp. 460–473, 2013.

[7] MathWorks, Supervised Learning Workflow and Algorithms, Natick, Massachusetts (`www.mathworks.com/help/stats/supervised-learning-machine-learning-workflow-and-algorithms.html?requestedDomain=www.mathworks.com`), 2017.

[8] T. Mitchell, *Machine Learning*, WCB/McGraw-Hill, Boston, Massachusetts, 1997.

[9] T. Morris, Z. Thornton and I. Turnipseed, Industrial control system simulation and data logging for intrusion detection system research, *Proceedings of the Seventh Annual Southeastern Cyber Security Summit*, 2015.

[10] D. Nardella, Step 7 Open Source Ethernet Communication Suite, Bari, Italy (`snap7.sourceforge.net`), 2016.

[11] H. Patzlaff, D 7.1 Preliminary Report on Forensic Analysis for Industrial Systems, CRISALIS Consortium, Symantec, Sophia Antipolis, France, 2013.

[12] SAS Institute, Machine Learning: What it is and Why it Matters, Milan, Italy (`www.sas.com/it_it/insights/analytics/machine-learning.html`), 2016.

[13] S. Sayad, *An Introduction to Data Mining*, University of Toronto, Toronto, Canada, 2011.

[14] scikit-learn Project, An Introduction to Machine Learning with scikit-learn (`scikit-learn.org/stable/tutorial/basic/tutorial.html`), 2016.

[15] scikit-learn Project, Supervised Learning (`scikit-learn.org/stable/supervised_learning.html#`), 2016.

[16] Siemens, SIMATIC S7-300 Programmable Controller Quick Start, Primer, Preface, C79000-G7076-C500-01, Nuremberg, Germany, 1996.

# III

# NETWORK AND
# CLOUD FORENSICS

# Chapter 6

# A FORENSIC METHODOLOGY FOR SOFTWARE-DEFINED NETWORK SWITCHES

Tommy Chin and Kaiqi Xiong

**Abstract**    This chapter presents a forensic methodology for computing systems in a software-defined networking environment that consists of an application plane, control plane and data plane. The methodology involves a forensic examination of the software-defined networking infrastructure from the perspective of a switch. Memory images of a live switch and southbound communications are leveraged to enable forensic investigators to identify and locate potential evidence for triage in real time. The methodology is evaluated using a real-world testbed exposed to network attacks. The experimental results demonstrate the effectiveness of the methodology for forensic investigations of software-defined networking infrastructures.

**Keywords:** Software-defined networks, incident response, forensics, switches

## 1.    Introduction

Software-defined networking (SDN) is a popular enterprise technology that employs a number of security mechanisms [4, 5, 8]. However, attackers often erase log files and historical data in targeted systems to mask their malicious activities. This requires the application of forensic techniques to investigate the compromised systems. Several researchers have studied the forensic aspects of software-defined networking, including data centers [2], traceback techniques [6] and the management layer [10]. However, little, if any, research has focused on triage techniques for software-defined networking infrastructures, specifically for switching devices.

Several attacks have been developed that target software-defined networks [7, 9, 11]. Defensive mechanisms for combating these attacks

© IFIP International Federation for Information Processing 2017
Published by Springer International Publishing AG 2017. All Rights Reserved
G. Peterson and S. Shenoi (Eds.): Advances in Digital Forensics XIII, IFIP AICT 511, pp. 97–110, 2017.
DOI: 10.1007/978-3-319-67208-3_6

heavily depend on sophisticated detection techniques based on signatures and heuristic patterns [5, 23]. Switching software such as Open vSwitch (OVS) [16] is widely deployed to forward traffic in software-defined network infrastructures (Open vSwitch traditionally executes in an operating system of choice). However, in the case of a data breach or other compromise, it may be necessary to conduct forensic analyses of all the devices in a software-defined network infrastructure.

This chapter presents a forensic methodology for analyzing switching devices in software-defined networking environments. The methodology leverages memory images of a live switch with traffic capture from southbound communications, where a southbound interface enables a network component to communicate with a lower-level component. Note that southbound communications refers to the exchange of software-defined networking messages between a switch and controller. On the other hand, northbound communications refers to traffic between an application-oriented system interface and controller that involves procedural calls. Northbound communications ties applications with controllers, but this traffic is out of scope because the focus is on switching devices. The forensic methodology was evaluated using the Global Environment for Network Innovation (GENI), a heterogeneous testbed that provides extensive capabilities for software-defined networking research [3]. Specifically, a series of network attacks was used to thoroughly examine areas of interest in a forensic investigation.

## 2.     Background

Network forensic approaches are applied to network devices that transport data of relevance to investigations [2, 10]. However, traditional approaches provide limited results due to the proprietary, vendor-specific nature of networking devices. Statistical information about networking devices can be derived from Simple Network Management Protocol (SNMP) traffic and logging services such as syslog. Other sources of information include configuration files and settings that are backed up remotely or locally depending on administrative needs. However, analyzing such information using available forensic techniques (e.g., [2, 6, 10]) often provides limited network event and system notification data.

Software-defined network switching devices, which come in hardware and software variants, contain potentially valuable forensic information. Software-based switching devices commonly reside in Linux-based computing systems [5, 19] and can therefore be investigated using traditional host-based forensic methods. Although valuable information may be obtained about the software-defined networking infrastructure, limited information is obtained if only local files are considered. System memory also contains useful information about running services and programs and can be forensically analyzed using the Volatility Framework [18]. However, there is limited research related to these aspects in software-defined networks.

A switching device in a software-defined network forwards traffic from one location to other destinations. This traffic originates from a variety of users, some of whom may be malicious. The switching device, which has no way of divining user intent, simply forwards the traffic to its destination. After a security incident, a forensic analyst can use network device statistics to discern the point-of-entry and other information about a malicious actor. However, a switching device is also a valuable source of evidence and, as such, should be considered during a forensic investigation.

The proposed methodology addresses the two main challenges involved in forensic analyses of networking devices. The first challenge deals with the timeline of events following a compromise, which is critical to an investigation. In a traditional network, memory contents may be erased due to normal operations, leading to the loss of valuable event information. Fortunately, software-based switches traditionally reside in virtualized systems that provide real-time snapshots of memory. The experimental evaluation conducted in this research examined the amount of time that an incident response team requires to collect event information from memory before the normal operations of a virtual machine (VM) clear the memory contents.

The second challenge deals with local storage in a software-defined networking device. A software-defined switching device traditionally has minimal secondary memory (hard drive) space and maximizes RAM and processing power to obtain adequate network transmission performance. Open vSwitch, a common distributed virtual multilayer switch used in software-defined networks, has numerous logging mechanisms that enable a variety of event information to be stored locally. If the virtual machine has limited storage space during the operation of the switch, older historical data is overwritten with new events in a continuous cycle. Remote storage of system logs can be implemented; however, due to the design of a software-defined network, this storage would have to reside in the control plane. A design limitation of software-defined networks prevents access from the data plane to the control plane; this requires a potentially costly solution to be implemented to obtain information. The experimental evaluation conducted in this research examines some problems related to the local storage of software-defined switches.

## 3.    Related Work

A software-defined network is interesting from the security perspective because its controller provides an overall view of the managed network [15] and because the network is programmable [16, 17]. Security research related to software-defined networks has primarily concentrated on the detection and mitigation of link flooding [12], denial-of-service, man-in-middle and other attacks [8, 19]. However, most studies have employed Mininet [14] to conduct simulations for performance and security evaluations; however, these experiments are often not very realistic.

While traditional network forensics is a mature area, limited research has focused on forensic analysis techniques for software-defined networks. The work of Bates et al. [2] stands out in that it employs software-defined networking as a tool for digital forensics. However, the approach requires a middlebox system to collect traffic information in a software-defined network and save it to local storage.

This approach has two limitations. First, while a middlebox enables a full network traffic capture for analysis of a variety of events, the capture does not include the southbound communications from a controller, which provide critical information about events leading up to the incident and post incident. The second limitation is that adequate memory is essential to the functioning of a software-defined switch, but the preservation of memory contents is vital to forensic analysis because the memory contains crucial information about switch operation. The use of a middlebox is reasonable, but the memory contents may not be accessed without root privileges, which poses a major security risk.

Thus, the approach of Bates et al. [2] may not provide a forensic investigator with adequate information about a security incident. On the other hand, the proposed forensic methodology enables an investigator to examine and catalog incident information.

## 4.    Proposed Forensic Methodology

A software-defined networking environment is impacted by security risks to switching devices, controllers and network peripherals. As more devices and peripherals are incorporated in a network, the number of vulnerabilities increase and, therefore, additional risks are introduced. This work assumes that a threat actor launches an attack from outside the network topology (wide-area network). It also assumes that the threat actor has compromised an internal computing system and has wiped all the content of the local hard drive. Finally, it is assumed the threat actor cannot access the switching device operating system (Open vSwitch) and controller (Floodlight) [17].

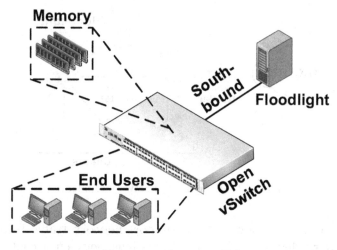

*Figure 1.* Threat model.

Figure 1 presents the threat model. The critical areas of investigation are the memory and the southbound communications of a software-defined switch captured by local logging mechanisms as determined by the software configuration. The figure shows a general switch configuration in which multiple computing devices are attached to the switch via physical or virtual configurations.

It is assumed that a threat actor resides in the group of end users. End users are targeted by the threat actor, but the software-defined network design ensures that Open vSwitch and Floodlight are untouched. Additionally, the activities of the threat actor leave forensic artifacts in memory and southbound communications traffic.

By leveraging the two main components of a switch, memory and network traffic, along with the service log files, a forensic investigator can identify and analyze artifacts related to a network compromise:

- **Memory Artifacts:** A network switch has memory components in a variety of specifications and sizes. The memory components provide rapid-access storage locations for network switching. From the perspective of forensic analysis, remnants of software variables and other artifacts stored in memory can provide useful information about the operations of the switch. Forensic tools such as Volatility, edb and Strings may be used for memory analysis. The experimental evaluation analyzed the amount of time various artifacts remain in the memory of an Open vSwitch.

- **Southbound Traffic:** During the operation of a software-defined network switch, a software-defined network controller provides in-

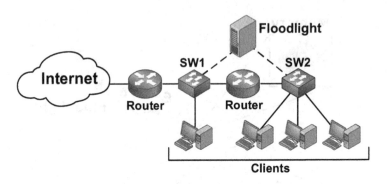

*Figure 2.* Experimental network topology.

structions and flow data to support network traffic to and from network devices. The communications between a controller and switch is known as southbound traffic, which mainly comprises OpenFlow messages [15]. The communications can contain a variety of artifacts that are valuable to a forensic investigation. The experimental evaluation used the `tcpdump` tool to capture and analyze southbound communications.

- **Service Log Files:** An Open vSwitch generates several log files that exclude operating system events. The log files reside in various locations of local storage and can be collected and analyzed for events of interest in a forensic investigation. The experimental evaluation considered some critical files for analysis and identified the information that can be utilized for forensic purposes. The events of interest include flow insertions, performance alerts and fault errors, among others.

## 5.     Experimental Evaluation

This section describes the application of the proposed forensic analysis methodology on a software-defined network that uses an Open vSwitch. The experiments identify the valuable information that can be recovered and help provide a timeline for the incident under investigation.

## 5.1    Experimental Setup

The experimental evaluation of the proposed forensic methodology used GENI [3], which virtualized all the network nodes. Figure 2 presents the topology of the experimental network. Two switch placements were configured: SW1 positioned between two routers and SW2 positioned behind a router. SW1 and SW2 were positioned to emulate a demilita-

*Table 1.* Attack timeline.

| Time | Actions |
|------|---------|
| 00:00 | Start (Authenticate) |
| 00:15 | Plant Meterpreter Shell |
| 00:20 | Exfiltrate Data |
| 08:53 | Wipe Target Drive |
| 08:54 | End (Exit Network) |

rized zone (DMZ) and an internal network, respectively. All the nodes in the GENI topology had the same hardware specifications: 2.10 GHz Intel Xeon CPU E5-2450 with 1 GB RAM and 16 GB hard drive running Ubuntu 14.04. All the network links were set to 100 mbps and the routers were Linux nodes with routing functionality. No latency, loss or link degradation occurred in the experimental configuration.

## 5.2 Attack Scenario

A threat actor could be an insider or an external entity. The attack scenario considered in the evaluation assumed that the attacker resides in the Internet cloud. It was also assumed that the actor could conduct reconnaissance to obtain network topology information.

Clients in the GENI topology were configured to have compromised SSH accounts. The threat actor targeted a client in the demilitarized zone and internal network. A remote shell was set up on the targeted machine. The Metasploit Framework [13] was then used to plant a Meterpreter shell in the targeted machine and various configuration files were subsequently exfiltrated to the Internet cloud.

Table 1 presents the timeline of the events involved in the attack on the software-defined network infrastructure. The threat actor gained access to the client using a compromised administrative access account, planted the shell, exfiltrated data, wiped the target drive and exited the network. Note that the time required to exfiltrate the data and wipe the target hard drive depends on the system resources and the quantity of data involved. However, in this scenario, after exfiltrating the data, the threat actor simply initiated the process to wipe the drive and exited the network.

## 5.3 Memory Analysis

Open vSwitch executes on a computing platform whose memory potentially contains valuable artifacts. Figure 3 presents the three-step

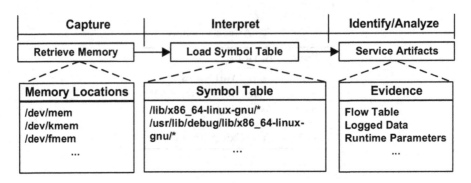

*Figure 3.* Memory analysis.

approach for conducting a memory analysis of an Open vSwitch. The three-step approach includes: (i) capture; (ii) interpretation; and (iii) identification and analysis.

Memory artifacts can be obtained via root-level access from several locations as shown in Figure 3. The following artifacts were discovered during the experiments:

- **Flow Table:** The flow table is used by the Open vSwitch to forward traffic to the correct destinations. The flow table is stored in memory and can be utilized to identify the origin of an attack and the path traversed within the network by the threat actor. The information collected included MAC addresses, switch port interfaces through which traffic traversed and port descriptors such as link states, speed and the number of packets sent. This information can be used by a forensic investigator to reconstruct the software-defined network topology up to one neighboring device.

- **Logged Data:** Open vSwitch has several logging mechanisms that can be leveraged in a forensic investigation. Although the log entries are written to local storage, the memory analysis of Open vSwitch revealed that logged events were stored for well over 20 minutes. Network activity and memory capacity determine when the events are erased and replaced. Note that network activity refers to the number of network connections between hosts. A large data transfer between two clients generates just one event whereas microtransactions between clients generate many events.

- **Runtime Parameters:** An administrator has to configure Open vSwitch to tailor it to the network requirements. The parameters and configurations stored in memory are of value in a forensic

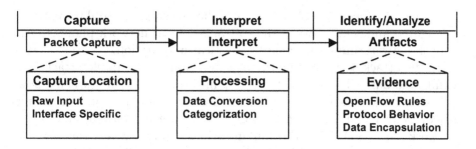

*Figure 4.* Southbound communications analysis.

investigation. These provide information about the logging mechanisms, controller and Open vSwitch plugins.

## 5.4 Southbound Traffic Analysis

Southbound communications are vital to the operation of a software-defined network because the controller utilizes this channel to send a variety of commands to a switch. In a forensic investigation, southbound traffic may be captured and analyzed to discover traces of the threat actor depending on how much time has elapsed.

Figure 4 shows the three-step approach for analyzing southbound communications. Southbound communications traffic can be captured using a variety of networking tools. Analysis of the captured communications during the experimental evaluation revealed OpenFlow traffic, but this quickly disappeared after the software-defined network flow timed out. Note that a software-defined network flow is inserted into a switch for data communications between a source and destination. The flow information has a timeout period in order to maintain the size of the flow table. If communications traffic stops after a period of time set by the administrator, then the flow disappears and the controller is informed. The timing of these communications depends heavily on the configuration of the Open vSwitch and the attached controller. The experiments used a default setting of five seconds and several runs were performed to analyze this issue. Note that a software-defined network uses several protocols to implement the desired network functionality, and this traffic can be analyzed in a forensic investigation.

A software-defined network controller has numerous other mechanisms to implement the network topology. The mechanisms can be identified by the behavioral aspects and data encapsulation techniques used to maintain and operate the network topology. For example, OpenFlow has two protocol-specific flags, OF Type 13 and OF Type 10, that enable data plane traffic to be transmitted and received by the controller, respectively. Specially-crafted packets that leverage these flags may be configured and sent between the software-defined network planes to establish network links and collect statistical information.

In the attack scenario, the threat actor launched a simple attack and exfiltrated data. The associated communications are visible when a flow is inserted into a switching device, when a flow is updated and when link discovery protocols are used to maintain statistical information about a network path. Southbound communications can also reveal the transfer of exfiltrated data via delay analysis techniques that identify link latency. An investigator can use this information to carefully verify the location of the threat actor and the path traversed to the targeted machine.

## 5.5    Service-Level Event Logging

Although memory and southbound communications analyses can provide detailed information about a software switch, local logging mechanisms can also be employed by default on Open vSwitch to capture relevant events pertaining to software-based networking services. Open vSwitch provides three key log files:

- **ovs-ctl.log:** This log file contains information about the start and stop times of Open vSwitch. The artifacts can be used to verify the time sequence of network events and to show that Open vSwitch was running during an incident and that it was not killed or restarted during analysis.

- **ovsdb-server.log:** This log file provides event information related to a running database that maintains the Open vSwitch flow table. While this log file provides minimal details about network characteristics, the logged information is useful for investigating denial-of-service attacks that use spoofed IP addresses.

- **ovs-vswitchd.log:** This log file provides the most valuable artifacts related to traffic flows and controller communications. Analysis of the log file in the attack scenario revealed the threat actor's initial communications and network exit times. While limited details are provided about southbound communications, information in the log file provides a useful high-level overview of the channel. Indeed, using the logged information in conjunction with a southbound traffic capture can help verify the integrity of the southbound link.

## 5.6    Discussion

The attack scenario considered in the experimental evaluation involved a threat actor who entered the configured GENI network, compromised a targeted client, exfiltrated data and erased all the information related to the attack. However, the software switch could not be tampered with by the threat actor due to access control limitations imposed by the software-defined network configuration.

Three components of interest in forensic investigations of software-defined networks are memory, southbound traffic and service-level log files. Memory analysis revealed several artifacts that can be used to identify a threat actor's point-of-entry into the network along with a timeline. This information can be used along with residual information in southbound communications to verify the timing of key events, depending, of course, on how long after the compromise the incident response is conducted. While southbound communications might provide limited information due to a delay in incident response, service-level local log files can provide adequate information to correlate events and their times. An event timeline is an important aspect of a forensic investigation and can be very helpful in identifying the threat actor.

The following configurations are recommended to enhance forensic investigations of software-defined networks:

- **Memory Snapshots:** Analysis of the memory of a switching device is vital to a forensic investigation. The software switch considered in this study was merely a virtual machine running Open vSwitch on a hypervisor. Due to the nature of virtualization, several hypervisor platforms provide memory snapshot functionality. Periodic memory snapshots should be taken to record a history. However, since a memory image can be very large depending on the amount of memory allocated to a virtual machine, it is advisable to focus the snapshots on important areas of memory. Additionally, compression or historical data rotation could be used to ensure that data is not lost.

- **Centralized Logging Service:** In a software-defined network, limited amount of hard drive space may be allocated to a software switch due to hardware constraints or space conservation. Therefore, it is recommended to use a centralized logging service to collect information stored in service-level log files related to a switch in order to offload the hard drive space and facilitate data querying and analysis. The centralized logging service should be located in the data plane, but this can present a risk to the software-defined network infrastructure because this device would have access to the data and control planes. Consequently, the centralized logging service should be positioned in the control plane or application to ensure the secure collection of relevant information without interactions with data plane users.

## 6.    Conclusions

Software-defined network controllers are widely used to manage network traffic, allocate computing resources [1, 20–22], control network policies and detect and mitigate security attacks. However, limited research has focused on forensic analysis techniques for software-defined network controllers and devices. This chapter has attempted to address the gap by proposing an approach for forensically analyzing a software-defined network infrastructure from the perspective of a switch. The chapter also identifies the important artifacts that can be found in the memory image of a software switch and in southbound communications traffic. While several researchers have used Mininet to provide simulation results pertaining to their approaches, this research has employed real-time attacks on a real-world software-defined network to demonstrate the efficacy of the proposed approach.

Future research will focus on re-targeting the proposed approach to forensically analyze software-defined network controllers. Efforts will also concentrate on extending the approach to conducting forensic analyses of large-scale networks and applications.

## Acknowledgement

This research was partially supported by the National Science Foundation under Grant Nos. CNS 1620871, CNS 1633978 and CNS 1636622; by the BBN/GPO Project 1936 under Grant No. CNS 1346688; and by a seed grant from the Florida Center for Cybersecurity (FC$^2$).

## References

[1] A. Akella and K. Xiong, Quality of service (QoS) guaranteed network resource allocation via software-defined networking (SDN), *Proceedings of the Twelfth International Conference on Dependable, Autonomic and Secure Computing*, pp. 7–13, 2014.

[2] A. Bates, K. Butler, A. Haeberlen, M. Sherr and W. Zhou, Let SDN be your eyes: Secure forensics in data center networks, *Proceedings of the Network and Distributed System Security Workshop on Security of Emerging Network Technologies*, 2014.

[3] M. Berman, J. Chase, L. Landweber, A. Nakao, M. Ott, D. Raychaudhuri, R. Ricci and I. Seskar, GENI: A federated testbed for innovative network experiments, *Journal of Computer Networks*, vol. 61, pp. 5–24, 2014.

[4] T. Chin, X. Mountrouidou, X. Li and K. Xiong, An SDN-supported collaborative approach for DDoS flooding detection and containment, *Proceedings of the IEEE Military Communications Conference*, pp. 659–664, 2015.

[5] T. Chin, X. Mountrouidou, X. Li and K. Xiong, Selective packet inspection to detect DoS flooding using software-defined networking, *Proceedings of the Thirty-Fifth IEEE International Conference on Distributed Computing Systems Workshops*, pp. 95–99, 2015.

[6] J. Francois and O. Festor, Anomaly traceback using software-defined networking, *Proceedings of the IEEE International Workshop on Information Forensics and Security*, pp. 203–208, 2014.

[7] S. Hong, L. Xu, H. Wang and G. Gu, Poisoning network visibility in software-defined networks: New attacks and countermeasures, *Proceedings of the Twenty-Second Annual Network and Distributed System Security Symposium*, 2015.

[8] H. Hu, W. Han, G. Ahn and Z. Zhao, FlowGuard: Building robust firewalls for software-defined networks, *Proceedings of the Third Workshop on Hot Topics in Software Defined Networking*, pp. 97–102, 2014.

[9] M. Kang, S. Lee and V. Gligor, The crossfire attack, *Proceedings of the IEEE Symposium on Security and Privacy*, pp. 127–141, 2013.

[10] S. Khan, A. Gani, A. Wahab, A. Abdelaziz and M. Bagiwa, FML: A novel forensic management layer for software-defined networks, *Proceedings of the Sixth IEEE International Conference on Cloud System and Big Data Engineering (Confluence)*, pp. 619–623, 2016.

[11] D. Kreutz, F. Ramos and P. Verissimo, Towards secure and dependable software-defined networks, *Proceedings of the Second ACM SIGCOMM Workshop on Hot Topics in Software-Defined Networking*, pp. 55–60, 2013.

[12] C. Liaskos, V. Kotronis and X. Dimitropoulos, A novel framework for modeling and mitigating distributed link flooding attacks, *Proceedings of the Thirty-Fifth IEEE International Conference on Computer Communications*, 2016.

[13] D. Maynor, K. Mookhey, J. Cervini, F. Roslan and K. Beaver, *Metasploit Toolkit for Penetration Testing, Exploit Development and Vulnerability Research*, Syngress, Burlington, Massachusetts, 2007.

[14] Mininet, Mininet (`mininet.org`), 2017.

[15] Open Networking Foundation, OpenFlow Switch Specification, Version 1.5.1 (Protocol Version `0x06`), ONF TS-025, Menlo Park, California, 2015.

[16] B. Pfaff, J. Pettit, T. Koponen, E. Jackson, A. Zhou, J. Rajahalme, J. Gross, A. Wang, J. Stringer, P. Shelar, K. Amidon and M. Casado, The design and implementation of Open vSwitch, *Proceedings of the Twelfth USENIX Symposium on Networked Systems Design and Implementation*, pp. 117–130, 2015.

[17] Project Floodlight, Floodlight (`www.projectfloodlight.org/flo odlight`), 2017.

[18] Volatility Foundation, Volatility Framework (`www.volatilityfoun dation.org`), 2017.

[19] H. Wang, L. Xu and G. Gu, FloodGuard: A DoS attack prevention extension in software-defined networks, *Proceedings of the Forty-Fifth IEEE/IFIP International Conference on Dependable Systems and Networks*, pp. 239–250, 2015.

[20] K. Xiong, Web services performance modeling and analysis, *Proceedings of the International Symposium on High Capacity Optical Networks and Enabling Technologies*, 2006.

[21] K. Xiong, Multiple priority customer service guarantees in cluster computing, *Proceedings of the IEEE International Symposium on Parallel and Distributed Processing*, 2009.

[22] K. Xiong, *Resource Optimization and Security for Cloud Services*, John Wiley and Sons, Hoboken, New Jersey, 2014.

[23] A. Zaalouk, R. Khondoker, R. Marx and K. Bayarou, OrchSec: An orchestrator-based architecture for enhancing network security using network monitoring and SDN control functions, *Proceedings of the Twenty-Sixth Network Operations and Management Symposium*, 2014.

# Chapter 7

# IDENTIFYING EVIDENCE FOR CLOUD FORENSIC ANALYSIS

Changwei Liu, Anoop Singhal and Duminda Wijesekera

**Abstract**       Cloud computing provides benefits such as increased flexibility, scalability and cost savings to enterprises. However, it introduces several challenges to digital forensic investigations. Current forensic analysis frameworks and tools are largely intended for off-line investigations and it is assumed that the logs are under investigator control. In cloud computing, however, evidence can be distributed across several machines, most of which would be outside the control of the investigator. Other challenges include the dependence of forensically-valuable data on the cloud deployment model, large volumes of data, proprietary data formats, multiple isolated virtual machine instances running on a single physical machine and inadequate tools for conducting cloud forensic investigations.

This research demonstrates that evidence from multiple sources can be used to reconstruct cloud attack scenarios. The sources include: (i) intrusion detection system and application software logs; (ii) cloud service API calls; and (iii) system calls from virtual machines. A forensic analysis framework for cloud computing environments is presented that considers logged data related to activities in the application layer as well as lower layers. A Prolog-based forensic analysis tool is used to automate the correlation of evidence from clients and the cloud service provider in order to reconstruct attack scenarios in a forensic investigation.

**Keywords:** Cloud forensics, attack scenarios, OpenStack

## 1.     Introduction

Digital forensics involves the identification, collection, examination and analysis of data while preserving its integrity and maintaining strict chain of custody during post-incident investigations [9]. Network forensics is a component of digital forensics that primarily focuses on the analysis of network traffic and other data from intrusion detection systems

© IFIP International Federation for Information Processing 2017

Published by Springer International Publishing AG 2017. All Rights Reserved

G. Peterson and S. Shenoi (Eds.): Advances in Digital Forensics XIII, IFIP AICT 511, pp. 111–130, 2017.

DOI: 10.1007/978-3-319-67208-3_7

and logs [14]. Cloud forensics is an emerging branch of network forensics, which involves post-incident analysis of systems with distributed
processing, multi-tenancy, virtualization and mobility of computations.
Ruan et al. [16] identify several challenges associated with cloud forensics. These include the dependence of forensically-valuable data on the
cloud deployment model and methods, large volumes of data, proprietary data formats, large numbers of diverse, simultaneously-executing
virtual machine instances, lack of monitoring and alerts by hypervisors
that run virtual machines, and limited techniques and tools designed
specifically for cloud forensic investigations.

The National Institute of Standards and Technology (NIST) [7] has
published a cloud computing standards roadmap that emphasizes cloud
governance, security and risk assessment. A key recommendation in
the roadmap and by members of the digital forensics research community [14, 16] is the implementation of forensics-enabled clouds. However,
most approaches focus on evidence gathering from infrastructure-as-a-
service cloud model deployments. No formal approach currently exists
for reconstructing attack scenarios based on evidence collected in virtualized cloud environments. This research demonstrates that evidence
from multiple sources can be used to reconstruct cloud attack scenarios.
The sources include: (i) intrusion detection system and application software logs; (ii) cloud service API calls; and (iii) system calls from virtual
machines. A Prolog-based forensic analysis tool is used to automate the
correlation of evidence from the three sources in order to reconstruct
attack scenarios in cloud forensic investigations.

## 2.    Background and Related Work

Cloud computing has three principal service deployments: (i) software-
as-a-service (SaaS); (ii) platform-as-a-service (PaaS); and (iii) infrastructure-as-a-service (IaaS) [12]. A software-as-a-service model enables consumers to use service provider applications running on a cloud infrastructure. A platform-as-a-service model allows consumers to deploy
their own applications or acquired applications using programming languages, libraries, services and tools supported by the service provider.
An infrastructure-as-a-service model provides consumers with the ability to provision processing, storage, networks and other fundamental
computing resources, including operating systems and applications.

Cloud forensics is a subset of network forensics that uses techniques
tailored to cloud computing environments [16]. For example, data acquisition is different in the software-as-a-service and infrastructure-as-
a-service models because an investigator has to depend entirely on the

cloud service provider in the case of a software-as-a-service model whereas an investigator can acquire virtual machine images from a customer in an infrastructure-as-a-service model.

Several techniques have been proposed to collect evidence from cloud environments, including remote data acquisition, management plane acquisition, live forensics and snapshot analysis [15]. Dykstra and Sherman [3] have retrieved volatile and non-volatile data from the Amazon EC2 cloud active user instance platform using traditional forensic tools such as EnCase and FTK. However, these tools do not validate the integrity of the collected data. Dykstra and Sherman [4] subsequently developed the FROST toolkit, which can be integrated within OpenStack to collect logs from the operating system that runs the virtual machines; this technique assumes that the cloud provider is trustworthy. Zawoad et al. [19] have designed a complete, trustworthy and forensics-enabled cloud.

Hay and Nance [5] have conducted live digital forensic analyses on clouds with virtual introspection, a process that enables the hypervisor or any other virtual machine to observe the state of a chosen virtual machine. They also developed a suite of virtual introspection tools for Xen (VIX tools). At this time, live forensic tools have not been incorporated as a commercial service by cloud providers.

Snapshot technology enables cloud customers to freeze virtual machines in specific states [2]. A frozen snapshot image may be restored by loading it to a target virtual machine, following which information about the running state of the virtual machine can be obtained. Several hypervisors, including Xen, VMWare, ESX and Hyper-V, support snapshot features.

In order to reduce the time and effort involved in forensic investigations, researchers have proposed the use of rules to automate evidence correlation and attack reconstruction [10, 18]. Liu et al. [10] have integrated a Prolog rule-based tool with a vulnerability database and an anti-forensic database to ascertain the admissibility of evidence and explain missing evidence due to the use of anti-forensic tools. However, these rule-based forensic analysis frameworks have been developed for networks, not for cloud environments.

## 3. Attack Reconstruction

Liu et al. [10, 11] have described an application of the MulVAL logic-based network security analyzer [13] that uses rules representing generic attack techniques to ascertain the causality between different items of evidence collected from a compromised network to reconstruct the attack steps. The rules, which are based on expert knowledge, are used as hypotheses by an investigator to link chains of evidence that are written in the form of Prolog predicates in order to create attack steps. Attack scenarios are reconstructed in the form of acyclic graphs as defined below [11].

**Definition 1 (Logical Evidence Graph (LEG)):** A logical evidence graph $LEG = (N_f, N_r, N_c, E, L, G)$ is a six-tuple where $N_f$, $N_r$ and $N_c$ are three disjoint sets of nodes in the graph (called fact, rule and consequence fact nodes, respectively), $E \subseteq ((N_f \cup N_c) \times N_r) \cup (N_r \times N_c)$ is the evidence, $L$ is a mapping from nodes to labels and $G \subseteq N_c$ is a set of observed attack events.

Every rule node has one or more fact nodes or consequence fact nodes from prior attack steps as its parents and a consequence fact node as its only child. Node labels consist of instantiations of rules or sets of predicates specified as follows:

1. A node in $N_f$ is an instantiation of predicates that codify system states, including access privileges, network topology and known vulnerabilities associated with host computers. The following predicates are used:

   - hasAccount(_principal, _host, _account), canAccessFile(_host, _user, _access, _path) and other predicates model access privileges.

   - attackerLocated(_host) and hacl(_src, _dst, _prot, _port) model network topology, including the attacker's location and network reachability information.

   - vulExists(_host, _vulID, _program) and vulProperty(_vulID, _range, _consequence) model node vulnerabilities.

2. A node in $N_r$ describes a single rule of the form $p \leftarrow p_1 \wedge p_2 \cdots \wedge p_n$. The rule head $p$ is an instantiation of a predicate from $N_c$, which is the child node of $N_r$ in the logical evidence graph. The rule body comprises $p_i$ ($i = 1..n$), which are predicate instantiations of $N_f$ from the current attack step and $N_c$ from one or more prior attack steps that comprise the parent nodes of $N_r$.

3. A node in $N_c$ represents the predicate that codifies the post-attack state as the consequence of an attack step. The two predicates execCode(_host, _user) and netAccess(_machine, _protocol, _port) are used to model the attacker's capability after an attack step. Valid instantiations of these predicates after an attack update valid instantiations of the three predicates listed in item 1 above.

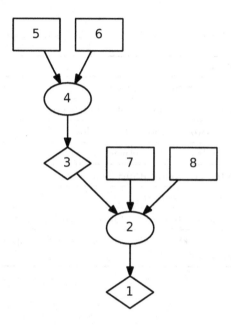

*Figure 1.* Example logical evidence graph.

Figure 1 shows an example logical evidence graph; Table 1 describes the nodes in Figure 1. In Figure 1, fact, rule and consequence fact nodes are represented as boxes, ellipses and diamonds, respectively. Consequence fact nodes (Nodes 1 and 3) codify the attack status obtained from event logs and other forensic tools that record the postconditions of attack steps. Fact nodes (Nodes 5, 6, 7 and 8) include network topology (Nodes 5 and 6), computer configuration (Node 7) and software vulnerabilities obtained by analyzing evidence captured by forensic tools (Node 8). Rule nodes (Nodes 2 and 4) represent rules that change the attack status using attack steps. These rules, which are based on expert knowledge, are used to link chains of evidence as consequences of attack steps. Linking a chain of evidence using a rule creates an investigator's hypothesis of an attack step given the evidence.

## 4. Reconstructing Attack Scenarios

This section demonstrates how three experimental attacks launched on a private cloud are reconstructed using evidence from the cloud.

### 4.1 Experimental Setup

OpenStack was used to create a private cloud. OpenStack is a collection of Python-based software projects that manage access to pooled

Table 1. Descriptions of the nodes in Figure 1.

| Node | Notation |
|------|----------|
| 1 | execCode(workStation1, user) |
| 2 | THROUGH 3 (remote exploit of a server program) |
| 3 | netAccess(workStation1, tcp, 4040) |
| 4 | THROUGH 8 (direct network access) |
| 5 | hacl(internet, workStation1, tcp, 4040) |
| 6 | attackerLocated(internet) |
| 7 | networkServiceInfo(workStation1, httpd, tcp, 4040, user) |
| 8 | vulExists(workStation1, 'CVE-2009-1918', httpd, remoteExploit, privEscalation) |

storage and computing and network resources that reside in one or more machines corresponding to a cloud. The collection has six core projects: (i) Neutron (networking); (ii) Nova (computing); (iii) Glance (image management); (iv) Swift (object storage); (v) Cinder (block storage); and (vi) Keystone (authentication and authorization). OpenStack can be used to deploy software-as-a-service, platform-as-a-service and infrastructure-as-a-service cloud models; however, it is mostly deployed as an infrastructure-as-a-service cloud.

DevStack is a series of extensible scripts that can invoke an OpenStack environment quickly. DevStack was used to deploy a private infrastructure-as-a-service cloud with a version of Juno on an Ubuntu computer that was accessed from IP address 172.16.168.100. An authenticated user can manage OpenStack services by entering the IP address 172.16.168.100 on a browser to access the cloud control dashboard Horizon as shown in Figure 2.

Two virtual machine instances were deployed in the private cloud, a web server named WebServer with IP address 172.16.168.226 and a file server named FileServer with IP address 172.16.168.229. The instances were managed by an authenticated user named admin. WebServer was an Apache server with a MySQL database that enabled SQL queries to be issued via web applications. Also, SSH was set up on FileServer to enable authenticated users to access it remotely. The Kali ethical hacking Linux distribution tool was set up in the same network at IP address 172.16.168.173 in order to launch attacks.

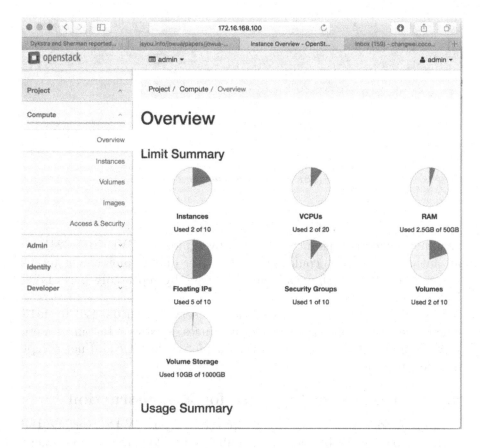

*Figure 2.* OpenStack web user interface (Horizon).

## 4.2 Experimental Attacks

A SQL injection attack, distributed denial-of-service (DDoS) attack and denial-of-service (DoS) attack were launched at the two virtual machines in the infrastructure-as-a-service cloud. The SQL injection attack exploited an unsanitized user input (CWE89 vulnerability) to the web server. The DDoS attack involved a TCP connection flood that used nping in Kali to prevent legitimate requests from reaching the file server. The SQL injection and DDoS attacks could target any network (including a cloud) that has the associated vulnerabilities. However, only privileged users in the infrastructure-as-a-service cloud can resize and delete a virtual machine by launching the DoS attack that exploits vulnerability CVE-2015-3241 in OpenStack Nova versions 2015.1 through 2015.1.1 and 2014.2.3 and earlier. The process of resizing and deleting an instance in this way is called instance migration. The migration process does not

| | Instance Name | Image Name | IP Address | Size | Key Pair | Status | Availability Zone |
|---|---|---|---|---|---|---|---|
| ☐ | FileServer | - | 10.0.0.13 Floating IPs: 172.16.168.229 | ds1G | default | Confirm or Revert Resize/Migrate | nova |
| ☐ | WebServer | - | 10.0.0.5 Floating IPs: 172.16.168.226 | m1.small | default | Active | nova |

*Figure 3.* Resizing the file server.

terminate when an instance is deleted by exploiting CVE-2015-3241, so an authenticated user could bypass the user quota enforcement mechanism to deplete all the available disk space by repeatedly performing instance migration.

Figure 3 shows the resizing of the file server from `ds512M` to `ds1G` where the availability zone of the instances is Nova. Instances were resized and deleted until Nova was so depleted that it could not accept any new instances.

## 4.3 Collecting Evidence for Reconstruction

In order to obtain evidence for forensic analysis, WebServer and the SQL database in WebServer were configured to log accesses and query history. Also, Snort was installed on the virtual machines in WebServer and FileServer while Wireshark was deployed in the Ubuntu host machine to monitor network traffic. Snort was configured to capture the SQL injection attack, which generated alerts based on the pre-set rules while Wireshark was configured to capture packets associated with the DDoS and DoS attacks.

Figure 4 lists example Snort alerts and MySQL query logs for the SQL injection attack. Note that the attack was launched using `or '1'='1'` to bypass the SQL query syntax check.

Figure 5 shows a snapshot of the packets captured by Wireshark. Kali Linux at IP address `172.16.168.173` sent numerous SYN packets to FileServer at IP address `172.16.168.229` and FileServer sent numerous SYN-ACK packets back to Kali Linux.

A Prolog-based forensic tool [10, 11] was used to automate the process of correlating items of evidence to reconstruct the SQL injection and DDoS attacks. This was accomplished by coding the evidence and the cloud configuration as Prolog predicates to create the input file shown

```
[**] SQL Injection Attempt --1=1 [**]
08/16-14:37:27.818279 172.16.168.173:1715 -> 172.16.168.226:80
TCP TTL:128 TOS:0x0 ID:380 IpLen:20 DgmLen:48 DF
******S* Seq: 0xDEDBEABF  Ack: 0x0  Win: 0xFFFF  TcpLen: 28
TCP Options (4) => MSS: 1460 NOP NOP SackOK


160813 14:37:29 40 Connect
...
40 QuerySET GLOBAL general_log = 'ON' 40 Queryselect * from profiles where
name='Alice' AND password='alice' or '1'='1'
Gen_log 2: 130813 14:39:56
...
```

*Figure 4.* Example Snort alerts and MySQL query logs.

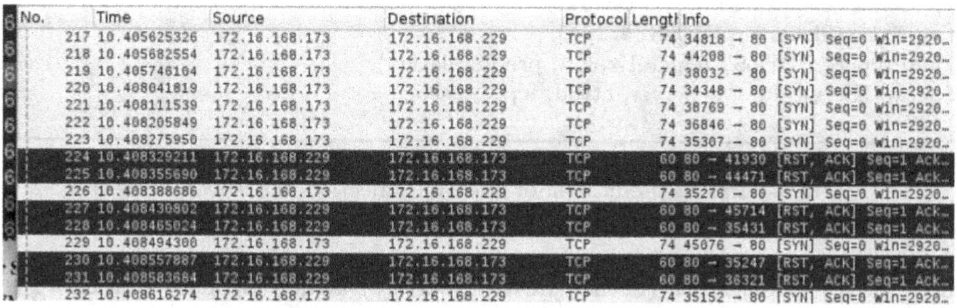

| No. | Time | Source | Destination | Protocol | Length | Info |
|---|---|---|---|---|---|---|
| 217 | 10.405625326 | 172.16.168.173 | 172.16.168.229 | TCP | 74 | 34818 → 80 [SYN] Seq=0 Win=2920… |
| 218 | 10.405682554 | 172.16.168.173 | 172.16.168.229 | TCP | 74 | 44208 → 80 [SYN] Seq=0 Win=2920… |
| 219 | 10.405746104 | 172.16.168.173 | 172.16.168.229 | TCP | 74 | 38032 → 80 [SYN] Seq=0 Win=2920… |
| 220 | 10.408041819 | 172.16.168.173 | 172.16.168.229 | TCP | 74 | 34348 → 80 [SYN] Seq=0 Win=2920… |
| 221 | 10.408111539 | 172.16.168.173 | 172.16.168.229 | TCP | 74 | 38769 → 80 [SYN] Seq=0 Win=2920… |
| 222 | 10.408205849 | 172.16.168.173 | 172.16.168.229 | TCP | 74 | 36846 → 80 [SYN] Seq=0 Win=2920… |
| 223 | 10.408275950 | 172.16.168.173 | 172.16.168.229 | TCP | 74 | 35307 → 80 [SYN] Seq=0 Win=2920… |
| 224 | 10.408329211 | 172.16.168.229 | 172.16.168.173 | TCP | 60 | 80 → 41930 [RST, ACK] Seq=1 Ack… |
| 225 | 10.408355690 | 172.16.168.229 | 172.16.168.173 | TCP | 60 | 80 → 44471 [RST, ACK] Seq=1 Ack… |
| 226 | 10.408388686 | 172.16.168.173 | 172.16.168.229 | TCP | 74 | 35276 → 80 [SYN] Seq=0 Win=2920… |
| 227 | 10.408430802 | 172.16.168.229 | 172.16.168.173 | TCP | 60 | 80 → 45714 [RST, ACK] Seq=1 Ack… |
| 228 | 10.408465024 | 172.16.168.229 | 172.16.168.173 | TCP | 60 | 80 → 35431 [RST, ACK] Seq=1 Ack… |
| 229 | 10.408494300 | 172.16.168.173 | 172.16.168.229 | TCP | 74 | 45076 → 80 [SYN] Seq=0 Win=2920… |
| 230 | 10.408557887 | 172.16.168.229 | 172.16.168.173 | TCP | 60 | 80 → 35247 [RST, ACK] Seq=1 Ack… |
| 231 | 10.408583684 | 172.16.168.229 | 172.16.168.173 | TCP | 60 | 80 → 36321 [RST, ACK] Seq=1 Ack… |
| 232 | 10.408616274 | 172.16.168.173 | 172.16.168.229 | TCP | 74 | 35152 → 80 [SYN] Seq=0 Win=2920… |

*Figure 5.* Snapshot of packets captured by Wireshark.

in Figure 6. At runtime, the input file instantiated the rules to create the attack paths shown in Figure 7.

Table 2 describes the notation used in Figure 7, which shows two attack paths. The attack path on the left $[7, 8] \rightarrow 6 \rightarrow [5, 9, 10] \rightarrow 4 \rightarrow [3, 11] \rightarrow 2 \rightarrow 1$ corresponds to the SQL injection attack on the web server that exploited the CWE89 vulnerability to steal user data. The attack path on the right $[8, 16] \rightarrow 15 \rightarrow [14, 17, 18] \rightarrow 13 \rightarrow 12$ corresponds to the DDoS attack on FileServer.

However, Snort and Wireshark failed to capture the DoS attack on FileServer that exploited the CVE-2015-3241 vulnerability in the OpenStack Nova service. Fortunately, the OpenStack Nova API logs, which record information about user operations on running instances, provided evidence related to the DoS attack on FileServer.

Figure 8 shows a snapshot of the Nova API logs pertaining to the instance migration caused by the DoS attack. The commands in bold font show that instance `bd1dac18-1ce2-44b5-93ee-967fec640ff3` representing the FileServer virtual machine was resized via the commands

```
//Initial attack status and final attack status
attackerLocated(internet).
attackGoal(serviceDown(fileServer, user)).
attackGoal(execCode(database, user)).

//Network topology and computer configuration
//"_" means any port
hacl(internet, webServer, tcp, 80).
hacl(internet, fileServer, tcp, _).
directAccess(webServer, database, modify, user).

//Evidence found in WebServer
vulExists(webServer, 'SQLInjection', httpd).
vulProperty('SQLInjection', remoteExploit, privEscalation).
networkServiceInfo(webServer, httpd, tcp, 80, user).

//Evidence captured by Wireshark
vulExists(fileServer, 'DDoS', httpd).
vulProperty('DDoS', remoteExploit, privEscalation).
networkServiceInfo(fileServer, httpd, tcp, _, user).
```

*Figure 6.*   Prolog predicates for the SQL injection and DDoS attacks.

mv (move) and `mkdir` (create new directory) issued by user `admin`. Table 3 shows that the instance ID was obtained by executing the `nova list` command on the Ubuntu host computer.

To combine the attack status and cloud system configuration, the related Nova API calls were manually aggregated and encoded as Prolog evidence predicates. This yielded the input file shown in Figure 9.

Running the Prolog-based forensic analysis tool on this input file produced the logical evidence graph shown in Figure 1, but with different node notation (shown in Table 4). The logical evidence graph shows an attack path that exploited the vulnerability CVE-2015-3241 and used the control dashboard Horizon to launch a DoS attack on the cloud.

Figure 7, which represents the SQL injection and DDoS attacks, and Figure 1, which represents the DoS attack, cannot be grouped together because the attacks originated from different locations. In addition, the DoS attack was on the Nova service instead of on a virtual machine, although it was launched from a virtual machine.

## 5.    Using System Calls for Evidence Analysis

Because system calls enable low user-level processes to request kernel level services such as storage operations, memory and network access, and process management, they are often used for intrusion detection and

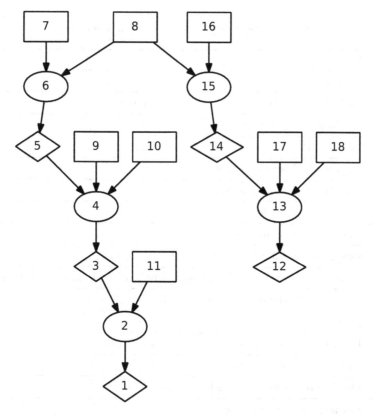

*Figure 7.* Attack path reconstruction for the SQL injection and DDoS attacks.

```
2016-09-18 07:52:00.237 DEBUG oslo_concurrency.processutils [req-f79c7911-04ed-
4a0c-adbe-0ae0a487c0f7 admin admin] Running cmd (subprocess): mv /opt/stack/data/
nova/instances/bd1dac18-1ce2-44b5-93ee-967fec640ff3 /opt/stack/data/nova/instan
ces/bd1dac18-1ce2-44b5-93ee-967fec640ff3_resize from (pid=41737) execute
/usr/local/lib/python2.7/dist-packages/oslo_concurrency/processutils.py:344

2016-09-18 07:52:00.253 DEBUG oslo_concurrency.processutils [req-f79c7911-04ed-
4a0c-adbe-0ae0a487c0f7 admin admin] CMD "mv /opt/stack/data/nova/instances/ bd1d
ac18-1ce2-44b5-93ee-967fec640ff3 /opt/stack/data/nova/instances/bd1dac18-1ce2-44b5-
93ee-967fec640ff3_resize" returned: 0 in 0.016s from (pid=41737) execute
/usr/local/lib/python2.7/dist-packages/oslo_concurrency/processutils.py:374

2016-09-18 07:52:00.254 DEBUG oslo_concurrency.processutils [req-f79c7911-04ed-
4a0c-adbe-0ae0a487c0f7 admin admin] Running cmd (subprocess): mkdir -p /opt/stack/
data/nova/instances/bd1dac18-1ce2-44b5-93ee-967fec640ff3 from (pid=41737) execute
/usr/local/lib/python2.7/dist-packages/oslo_concurrency/processutils.py:344

2016-09-18 07:52:00.271 DEBUG oslo_concurrency.processutils [req-f79c7911-04ed-
4a0c-adbe-0ae0a487c0f7 admin admin] CMD "mkdir -p /opt/stack/data/nova/instances/
bd1dac18-1ce2-44b5-93ee-967fec640ff3" returned: 0 in 0.017s from (pid=41737)
execute /usr/local/lib/python2.7/dist-packages/oslo_concurrency/processutils.py:374
```

*Figure 8.* Nova API call logs.

Table 2.   Descriptions of the nodes in Figure 7.

| Node | Notation |
|------|----------|
| 1 | execCode(database, user) |
| 2 | THROUGH 7 (attack by compromised computer) |
| 3 | execCode(webServer, user) |
| 4 | THROUGH 3 (remote exploit of a server program) |
| 5 | netAccess(webServer, tcp, 80) |
| 6 | THROUGH 9 (direct network access) |
| 7 | hacl(internet, webServer, tcp, 80) |
| 8 | attackerLocated(internet) |
| 9 | networkServiceInfo(webServer, httpd, tcp, 80, user) |
| 10 | vulExists(webServer, 'SQLInjection', httpd, remoteExploit, privEscalation) |
| 11 | directAccess(webServer, database, modify, user) |
| 12 | execCode(fileServer, user) |
| 13 | THROUGH 3 (remote exploit of a server program) |
| 14 | netAccess(fileServer, tcp, _) |
| 15 | THROUGH 9 (direct network access) |
| 16 | hacl(internet, fileServer, tcp, _) |
| 17 | networkServiceInfo(fileServer, httpd, tcp, _, user) |
| 18 | vulExists(fileServer, 'DDoS', httpd, remoteExploit, privEscalation) |

Table 3.   Virtual machine instances, names and IP addresses.

| ID | Name | Networks |
|----|------|----------|
| bd1dac18-1ce2-44b5-93ee-967fec640ff3 | FileServer | private = 10.0.0.13, 172.16.168.229 |
| c01d5e66-c20d-4544-867b-d3e2b70bfc60 | WebServer | private = 10.0.0.5, 172.16.168.226 |

forensic analysis [6]. When evidence cannot be obtained from forensic tools or system services to help recognize a known attack, system calls can be used to ascertain system behavior. Because it would be extremely rare to have an attack path in which every attack step is a zero-day

```
//Initial and final attack status
attackerLocated(controlDashboard).
attackGoal(execCode(nova, admin)).

//FileServer VM could be reached from control dashboard
hacl(controlDashboard, fileServer, http, _).

//Evidence of attack using CVE-2015-3241 that uses RESTful service
vulExists(nova, 'CVE-2015-3241', 'REST').
vulProperty( 'CVE-2015-3241', remoteExploit, privEscalation).
networkServiceInfo(nova, 'REST', http, _, admin).
```

*Figure 9.* Input file for the attack using CVE-2015-3241.

*Table 4.* Descriptions of nodes in the DoS attack.

| Node | Notation |
|------|----------|
| 1 | execCode(nova,admin) |
| 2 | THROUGH 3 (remote exploit of a server program) |
| 3 | netAccess(nova, http, _) |
| 4 | THROUGH 9 (direct network access) |
| 5 | hacl(controlDashboard, nova, http, _) |
| 6 | attackerLocated(controlDashboard) |
| 7 | networkServiceInfo(nova, 'REST', http, _, admin) |
| 8 | vulExists(nova, 'CVE-2015-3241', 'REST', remoteExploit, privEscalation) |

attack [17], system calls can help reconstruct the missing attack steps when other evidence is not available.

Five popular mechanisms are available to trace the system calls in a cloud-based virtual machine: (i) `ptrace` command that sets up system call interception and modification by modifying a software application; (ii) `strace` command that logs system calls and signals; (iii) auditing facilities within the kernel; (iv) system call table modification and the use of system call data writing wrappers to log the corresponding system calls; and (v) system call interception within a hypervisor [1]. Because OpenStack supports several hypervisors, including Xen, QEMU, KVM, LXC, Hyper-V and UML, no generic solution for intercepting system calls within a hypervisor exists. Hence, the `strace` command and system

```
Sep 25 00:15:49 FileServer sshd[829]:  Server listening on 0.0.0.0 port
22.
Sep 25 00:15:49 FileServer sshd[829]:  Server listening on ::  port 22.
Sep 25 00:28:15 FileServer sshd[1162]:  Accepted password for coco from
172.16.168.173 port 44842 ssh2
Sep 25 00:28:16 FileServer sshd[1162]:  pam_unix(sshd:session):  session
opened for user coco by (uid=0)
```

*Figure 10.*   SSH authentication log.

*Table 5.*   Important system calls.

| Tasks | System Calls |
| --- | --- |
| Process modifies file | write, pwrite64, rename, mkdir, linkat, link, symlinkat, symlink, fchmodat, fchmod, chmod, fchownat, mount |
| Process uses but does not modify file | stat64, lstat6e, fsat64, open, read, pread64, execve, mmap2, mprotect, linkat, link, symlinkat, symlink |
| Process uses and modifies file | open, rename, mount, mmap2, mprotect |
| Process creation or termination | vfork, fork, kill |
| Process creation | clone |

call table modification with system call data writing wrappers may be used to log relevant system calls.

An example attack launched from Kali Linux is used to demonstrate how system call sequences are used in attack reconstruction. In this attack, SSH was used to log into FileServer by supplying stolen credentials from a legitimate user named coco. In order to simulate the stealthy attack without triggering intrusion detection sytem alerts, the attacker was assumed to use shoulder surfing to obtain the (username, password) credentials. Figure 10 shows the SSH log from /var/log/auth.log in FileServer. The log entry shows that coco logged into FileServer from 172.16.168.173, which actually belonged to the attacker, indicating that the attacker stole the credentials belonging to coco.

A process typically issues many system calls; however, only some of the calls are important for ascertaining process behavior. The important system calls [17] are listed in the second column of Table 5.

Figure 11 shows the important system calls captured from the attack. The **read** and **write** calls (in bold font) indicate that the attacker

```
write(9, "v", 1) = 1
read(11, "v", 16384) = 1
write(3, "\0\0\0\20\331\255\275\264c\2173)z2j\32\255n\2007d\366m\21\316
\2648\240\207\31\211"..., 36) = 36
read(3,"\0\0\0\20\240\253\341\227\321xU\305\347\226\246\361\316\242S =
\30\341QT\231\n\343\314\343\307\f\361"..., 16384) = 36
write(9, "i", 1) = 1
read(11, "i", 16384) = 1
write(3,"\0\0\0\20\177\352\313\332\373yjM\3416l\230\215\10\220p\252g\375
\365
\1\f\335\361\r\273\374\357"..., 36) = 36
read(3, "\0\0\0\20\27\334?\201x\300\16\356\346, \0379\32\220{\372)\366\4\v\1
= \347\263\311\250k\353"..., 16384) = 36
write(9, " ", 1) = 1
read(11, " ", 16384) = 1
write(3,"\0\0\0\20ñ\321\344\220\313\322\254S\252o\201\225; 6v\243\205\10gŝ
\253\237\325\375\332v" ..., 36) = 36
read(3, "\0\0\0\20\5\27k; \254\301\24\n\\ZN\267\260\336\323ı\323\32\345\2b\
226 − \271|[B\21" ..., 16384) = 36
write(9, "t", 1) = 1
read(11, "t", 16384) = 1
read(3,"\0\0\0\20\325\261\7\254\211(\201\331\272\344[\355\200\\u4\357G\347
\232\276 : \201\376\342\202\201."..., 16384) = 36
write(3,"\0\0\0\20\320\254\#\312\211_\3022\n\227u\16I\372\202\347\37\252T
\257\220
\210E\343\222\342\24S" ..., 36) = 36
write(9, "e", 1) = 1
read(11, "e", 16384) = 1
write(3, "\0\0\0\20\334n}4\375Q\212o\353\375\262\342\316\334w − F\213\303
\277t\312\245\16\266\255B|" ..., 36) = 36
read(3, "\0\0\0\20\274\376\7J\214L\314OL\1c\22\364 − gvJ\%\21\344Jı, h\363
\261\36\10" ..., 16384) = 36
write(9, "\t", 1) = 1
read(11, "st.txt ", 16384) = 7
...
```

*Figure 11.* Traces of `read` and `write` system calls.

opened and modified a file named `test.txt`. In a `read` or `write` call, the first argument is the file descriptor where the process reads/writes data, the second is the buffer contents, the third is the number of bytes read/written by the system call; and = 1 or any number greater than 1 indicates that the system call was executed successfully.

The program behavior and the opening and modifying of a legitimate user's file were expressed in the form of the Prolog predicate: canAccessFile(fileServer, user, modify, _). This predicate states that the attacker as a legitimate user can modify the file located at _, which represents the home directory of the legitimate user. Using the evi-

```
//Initial attack status
attackerLocated(internet).
//Attacker was able to log into FileServer using stolen credentials
attackGoal(logInService(fileserver, tcp, 22).
attackGoal(principalCompromised(user)).
//Incompetent user
inCompetent(user).

//Attack status obtained by analyzing system call sequence
attackGoal(canAccessFile(fileServer, user, modify, _)).
//User could log into FileServer using the SSH protocol
networkServiceInfo(fileServer, sshd, tcp, 22, _).
//User who has the account on FileServer has file modification privileges
localFileProtection(fileServer, user, modify, _).
```

*Figure 12.*  Input file for modifying a file with stolen credentials.

dence obtained from the log in Figure 10, which shows that the attacker with stolen credentials (expressed by the predicates: (i) attackGoal(principalCompromised(user)); (ii) inCompetent(user); and (iii) attackerLocated(internet)) logged into FileServer using SSH (expressed by the predicate attackGoal(principalCompromised(user))), and the fact that user coco with an account on FileServer had the privileges to modify files (expressed by the predicate localFileProtection(fileServer, user, modify, _)), the input file shown in Figure 12 was created for the Prolog-based tool.

Figure 13 shows the reconstructed attack paths and Table 6 shows the associated node notation. The attack path [3, 4, 7] → 2 → 1 has three pre-conditions, which are represented by Nodes 3, 4 and 7. Node 3 expresses the fact that files in FileServer can be modified by FileServer users. Node 4 is obtained from the fact that FileServer can be accessed using SSH via TCP on port 22. Node 7 is obtained from the SSH authentication log in Figure 10, which indicates that the user's credentials were stolen by the attacker. Note that, without the evidence obtained from the system call sequence (Node 1), the attack path [3, 4, 7] → 2 → 1 would not have been established.

The two rule nodes (Node 5 and Node 2) in Figure 13 do not have rule descriptions because of the obvious correlation between Node 6 and Node 4 (if the network provides the SSH service for logging into FileServer via TCP on port 22, then any user or attacker with stolen credentials could log into FileServer); and Nodes 3, 4 and 7 collectively and Node 1 (if a user has privileges to modify a file in FileServer, then the attacker who has stolen a user's credentials could modify the file).

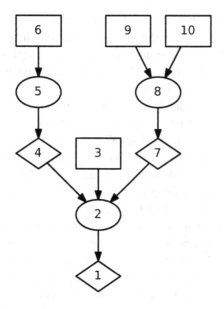

*Figure 13.* Attack path reconstruction using evidence obtained from system calls.

*Table 6.* Descriptions of the nodes in Figure 13.

| Node | Notation |
|------|----------|
| 1 | canAccessFile(fileserver, user, modify, _) |
| 2 | THROUGH 23 () |
| 3 | localFileProtection(fileserver, user, modify, _) |
| 4 | logInService(fileserver, tcp, 22) |
| 5 | THROUGH 18 () |
| 6 | networkServiceInfo(fileserver, sshd, tcp, 22, user) |
| 7 | principalCompromised(user) |
| 8 | THROUGH 16 (password sniffing) |
| 9 | inCompetent(user) |
| 10 | attackerLocated(internet) |

# 6. Conclusions

Cloud computing increases the efficiency and flexibility of enterprise operations. However, clouds present significant challenges to digital forensics. One challenge is the lack of customer control over the physical locations of data. Other challenges include the dependence of forensically-relevant data on the cloud deployment model, large volumes of data, proprietary data formats, multiple isolated virtual machine instances running on a single physical machine, and inadequate tools for conducting cloud forensic investigations.

This research has demonstrated that evidence from multiple sources can be used to reconstruct cloud attack scenarios. The sources include intrusion detection system and application software logs, cloud service API calls and system calls from virtual machines. To acquire evidence from the sources, a forensics-enabled cloud should support: (i) logging and retrieval of intrusion detection system and software service data; (ii) secure storage and retrieval of OpenStack service API call logs, firewall logs and snapshots of running instances; and (iii) storage and retrieval of system calls, especially when the first two sources are unavailable. The Prolog-based forensic analysis presented in this chapter demonstrates the effectiveness and utility of automating the correlation of evidence from multiple sources to reconstruct attack scenarios in digital forensic investigations.

Future research will implement extensions to the forensics-enabled cloud to preserve data integrity, reduce data volume and manage the diversity of digital forensic data stored in the cloud.

This chapter is not subject to copyright in the United States. Commercial products are identified in order to adequately specify certain procedures. In no case does such an identification imply a recommendation or endorsement by the National Institute of Standards and Technology, nor does it imply that the identified products are necessarily the best available for the purpose.

# References

[1] F. Beck and O. Festor, Syscall Interception in Xen Hypervisor, Technical Report no. 9999, INRIA Nancy – Grand Est, Villers-les-Nancy, France, 2009.

[2] D. Birk and C. Wegener, Technical issues of forensic investigations in cloud computing environments, *Proceedings of the Sixth International Workshop on Systematic Approaches to Digital Forensic Engineering*, 2011.

[3] J. Dykstra and A. Sherman, Acquiring forensic evidence from infrastructure-as-a-service cloud computing: Exploring and evaluating tools, trust and techniques, *Digital Investigation*, vol. 9(S), pp. S90–S98, 2012.

[4] J. Dykstra and A. Sherman, Design and implementation of FROST: Digital forensic tools for the OpenStack cloud computing platform, *Digital Investigation*, vol. 10(S), pp. S87–S95, 2013.

[5] B. Hay and K. Nance, Forensic examination of volatile system data using virtual introspection, *ACM SIGOPS Operating Systems Review*, vol. 42(3), pp. 74–82, 2008.

[6] S. Hofmeyr, S. Forrest and A. Somayaji, Intrusion detection using sequences of system calls, *Journal of Computer Security*, vol. 6(3), pp. 151–180, 1998.

[7] M. Hogan, F. Liu, A. Sokol and J. Tong, NIST Cloud Computing Standards Roadmap, NIST Special Publication 500-291, National Institute of Standards and Technology, Gaithersburg, Maryland, 2011.

[8] A. Jaquith, *Security Metrics: Replacing Fear, Uncertainty and Doubt*, Pearson Education, Boston, Massachusetts, 2007.

[9] K. Kent, S. Chevalier, T. Grance and H. Dang, Guide to Integrating Forensic Techniques into Incident Response, NIST Special Publication 800-86, National Institute of Standards and Technology, Gaithersburg, Maryland, 2006.

[10] C. Liu, A. Singhal and D. Wijesekera, A logic-based network forensic model for evidence analysis, in *Advances in Digital Forensics XI*, G. Peterson and S. Shenoi (Eds.), Springer, Heidelberg, Germany, pp. 129–145, 2015.

[11] C. Liu, A. Singhal and D. Wijesekara, A probabilistic network forensic model for evidence analysis, in *Advances in Digital Forensics XII*, G. Peterson and S. Shenoi (Eds.), Springer, Heidelberg, Germany, pp. 189–210, 2016.

[12] P. Mell and T. Grance, NIST Definition of Cloud Computing, NIST Special Publication 800-145, National Institute of Standards and Technology, Gaithersburg, Maryland, 2011.

[13] X. Ou, S. Govindavajhala and A. Appel, MulVAL: A logic-based network security analyzer, *Proceedings of the Fourteenth USENIX Security Symposium*, 2005.

[14] G. Palmer, A Road Map for Digital Forensic Research, DFRWS Technical Report, DTR-T001-01 Final, Air Force Research Laboratory, Rome, New York, 2001.

[15] A. Pichan, M. Lazarescu and S. Soh, Cloud forensics: Technical challenges, solutions and comparative analysis, *Digital Investigation*, vol. 13, pp. 38–57, 2015.

[16] K. Ruan, J. Carthy, T. Kechadi and M. Crosbie, Cloud forensics, in *Advances in Digital Forensics V*, G. Peterson and S. Shenoi (Eds.), Springer, Heidelberg, Germany, pp. 35–46, 2011.

[17] X. Sun, J. Dai, P. Liu, A. Singhal and J. Yen, Towards probabilistic identification of zero-day attack paths, *Proceedings of the IEEE Conference on Communications and Network Security*, pp. 64–72, 2016.

[18] W. Wang and T. Daniels, A graph based approach toward network forensic analysis, *ACM Transactions on Information and Systems Security*, vol. 12(1), article no. 4, 2008.

[19] S. Zawoad and R. Hasan, A trustworthy cloud forensics environment, in *Advances in Digital Forensics XI*, G. Peterson and S. Shenoi (Eds.), Springer, Heidelberg, Germany, pp. 271–285, 2015.

IV

# THREAT DETECTION AND MITIGATION

# Chapter 8

# DIGITAL FORENSIC IMPLICATIONS OF COLLUSION ATTACKS ON THE LIGHTNING NETWORK

Dmytro Piatkivskyi, Stefan Axelsson and Mariusz Nowostawski

**Abstract**    The limited size of a block in the Bitcoin blockchain produces a scaling bottleneck. The transaction scalability problem can be addressed by performing smaller transactions off-chain and periodically reporting the results to the Bitcoin blockchain. One such solution is the Lightning Network.

Bitcoin is employed by lawful users and criminals. This requires crimes against lawful users as well as the use of Bitcoin for nefarious purposes to be investigated. However, unlike Bitcoin, the Lightning Network enables collusion attacks involving intermediate nodes and recipients. In such an attack, regardless of a sender's actions, money is received by an intermediate node that colludes with a dishonest recipient. Since the dishonest recipient does not "actually" receive the money, it does not provide the goods/service to the sender. Thus, the sender pays for the unprovided goods/service, but the recipient can prove that the payment was not received.

This chapter discusses the forensic implications of collusion attacks with regard to lawful users because no discernible traces of attacks remain, as well as for law enforcement, where the attacks can target parties as a form of forfeiture, analogous to law enforcement "sting" operations. This chapter also discusses the potential of the Lightning Network to be used for money laundering activities.

**Keywords:** Bitcoin, Lightning Network, audit trail

## 1.    Introduction

Digital currencies are increasingly being leveraged by criminal entities. Therefore, it is important for digital forensic investigators to have

© IFIP International Federation for Information Processing 2017

Published by Springer International Publishing AG 2017. All Rights Reserved

G. Peterson and S. Shenoi (Eds.): Advances in Digital Forensics XIII, IFIP AICT 511, pp. 133–147, 2017.

DOI: 10.1007/978-3-319-67208-3_8

detailed knowledge of how these currencies work and how they can be exploited.

Bitcoin has emerged as the *de facto* standard for peer-to-peer value exchange in decentralized systems. However, a key problem with the Bitcoin blockchain technology is its scalability. Several solutions have been proposed to address the scalability problem. One solution is the Lightning Network, a peer-to-peer payment system that performs smaller transactions off-chain and periodically reports the results to the Bitcoin blockchain. This chapter discusses the design of the Lightning Network and demonstrates a fundamental flaw that facilitates collusion attacks. Such an attack enables money to go astray between a sender and a dishonest recipient who colludes with an intermediate to claim non-receipt of funds. This chapter discusses the forensic implications of collusion attacks with regard to lawful users and law enforcement, along with the potential of the Lightning Network to be used for money laundering activities.

## 2. Related Work

Decentralized crypto-currencies is a new research field. Off-chain transactions, as used in the Lightning Network, is an emergent trend that has not been investigated adequately. However, there is no published research on the security of the Lightning Network nor is there any discussion of the digital forensic implications of its use.

The concept of a collusion attack is not new. Conspiracies involving actors in a system have been investigated before. For reasons of space, it is not possible to discuss the topic in detail; instead, a few examples are presented from the literature.

Distributed systems such as wireless sensor networks rely heavily on their key management infrastructures. If the keys are not managed properly, network nodes can collude and reveal the keys [5].

In the case of fingerprinting digital data, when users collude, fingerprints can be removed and the data can be distributed freely [1]. Another example is a collusion attack on an Android device where two applications can collaborate to escalate their access rights [2].

In the financial sector, collusion can be used to manipulate stock prices or to secure loans despite having bad credit. With so many varied examples of collusion attacks, it is important that designers of new methods of collaboration, such as the Lightning Network, understand and guard against collusion.

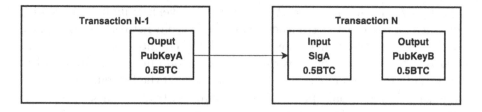

*Figure 1.* Bitcoin transaction.

## 3. Bitcoin Blockchain

Blockchain technology enables novel decentralized applications ranging from simple digital tokens that represent currency, through digital assets management and audit trails, to establishing decentralized institutions [7]. Decentralization eliminates the need for a trusted third party in many scenarios. The first large-scale deployment of blockchain technology was in the Bitcoin crypto-currency and peer-to-peer payment system [6].

Bitcoin allows fast cross-border monetary transfers, on average within ten minutes, for a low transaction fee. In addition to providing pseudonymity, the system offers several advantages. Since Bitcoin is decentralized, no one holds custody over it. Moreover, if its secret keys are kept secure, no entity can steal or seize money intended for another entity.

A payment in the Bitcoin blockchain is a transfer of a numerical value from one public address to another. Bitcoins, the crypto-currency, are just numbers that belong to a public address (i.e., a public key). The ownership of bitcoins is claimed by demonstrating the associated private key. An entity can generate as many public-private key pairs as desired. A good practice is to generate a new key pair for every new monetary transfer. Thus, the de-anonymization of an address to a user identity is difficult, albeit potentially possible; in any case, this is an active topic of research [11].

To make a payment, the sender creates a transaction – Transaction N in Figure 1. The transaction consists of two parts: (i) inputs; and (ii) outputs. There may be multiple inputs and multiple outputs in a transaction, but for the sake of simplicity, only one input and one output are illustrated in Figure 1. In the transaction, the sender references the output of a previous transaction (Transaction N-1) and can claim ownership of the coins from this output. The sender claims the ownership via a signature made with his private key. This particular signature must be specified in the input of the new transaction. In the output, the sender identifies the entity to whom ownership is transferred by specifying the public key of this entity (receiver). Finally, the sender broadcasts the created transaction to the Bitcoin network of validating nodes so that the transaction can be accepted into the system. The broadcasted transaction is verified by each node in the network and is eventually recorded in the shared database called the Bitcoin blockchain. The Bitcoin blockchain protocol timestamps all transactions, preventing double spending; the earliest transaction has precedence over more recent transactions.

The blockchain is a decentralized database that is secured from tampering and revision. It consists of blocks that are chained by embedding the hash of the previous block into the next block. The hash calculation is made intentionally difficult so that after a block is stamped with a hash it cannot be recomputed easily. This means that all the transactions that get on the blockchain remain on it forever because the blocks cannot be changed.

The Bitcoin scalability problem arises because Bitcoin blocks can carry a limited amount of transactions. Since the blocks have a fixed size and new blocks are generated at fixed times, the Bitcoin payment system can only sustain a fixed transaction rate. The current limit is around seven transactions per second.

The scalability problem has attracted the attention of the research community and a number of potential solutions have been proposed. The most promising solution is the Lightning Network [9], which uses off-chain transactions.

## 4.    Lightning Network

The Lightning Network [9] is a payment protocol built on top of the Bitcoin blockchain. It leverages off-chain transactions to provide a scalable solution to the problem of limited transaction throughput. The fundamental idea underlying the Lightning Network is not to log all the transactions directly on the blockchain, but to pass them between the participating nodes in a peer-to-peer fashion and log only the final balance of the accounts.

Transactions in the Lightning Network are processed within previously established payment channels. A channel is a set of two Bitcoin transactions created cooperatively by the channel participants. This work considers two participants to simplify the presentation. However, it is possible to emulate multi-party channels with slightly more elaborate protocols.

A funding transaction spends channel participants' funds while a commitment transaction returns funds to the channel participants. The

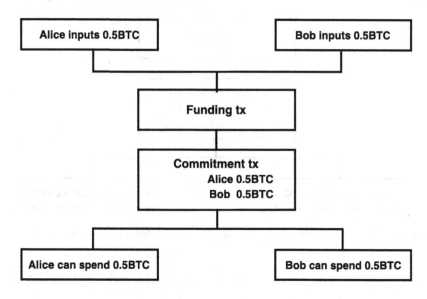

*Figure 2.* Funding and commitment transactions.

commitment transaction is kept off the blockchain during the time that the channel is open. After a channel is opened, the participants can send arbitrarily small payments to each other up to the channel capacity. The number of transactions possible in a channel is nearly infinite and the transaction speed is only limited by the direct connections between the channel participants, which typically means nearly instantaneous delivery.

The processed transactions are not broadcast to the Bitcoin network. Instead, the transactions are passed in a peer-to-peer fashion between the channel participants. The only transactions that get advertised and, consequently, recorded on the Bitcoin blockchain are channel funding and commitment transactions. At any time, the commitment transaction reflects the channel state. When a channel is to be closed, the commitment transaction is published on the blockchain, which returns the funds to the channel participants. The balance is established at the moment of channel closure. The commitment transaction is the guarantee that a channel participant can get the funds back at any point in time with the agreed balance.

Figure 2 shows funding and commitment transactions. In the case of a bi-directional channel, both channel participants create inputs to the channel funding transaction that define the channel capacity. A funding transaction has a single two-of-two multi-signature output. In other

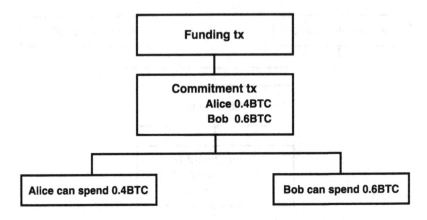

*Figure 3.*    Commitment transaction balances are updated after transacting 0.1BTC.

words, it takes two signatures, one belonging to each channel participant, to spend the output.

In contrast, a commitment transaction spends the output of the funding transaction and has two outputs. Each of these outputs returns back to an investor exactly the amount of funds invested in the channel. The benefit of establishing the channel is that funds can be moved within the channel capacity by simply updating the commitment transaction.

For example, if Alice wishes to send 0.1BTC to Bob, then the commitment transaction is updated so that it returns 0.4BTC to Alice and 0.6BTC to Bob (Figure 3). Within the updated channel Bob now can send to Alice up to 0.6BTC and Alice can send to Bob only up to 0.4BTC. Such payment channels allow nearly unlimited transactions within a channel. Note however, that this simple scheme requires that an entity has to open a channel with every entity with which it has ever interacted. This is an expensive proposition. A solution to this problem is to route payments through existing channels.

## 4.1    Payment Routing

The Lightning Network extends the idea of payment channels by routing payments over multiple entities that have pre-existing channels between them. For example, if Alice has a channel with Bob and Bob has a channel with Charlie, then Alice can send funds to Charlie through Bob. Because the two money transfers – from Alice to Bob and from Bob to Charlie – are independent, there must be a way to bind them so that the execution of one depends on execution of the other. Otherwise, Bob can send funds to Charlie, but Alice does not send funds to Bob, leaving Bob defrauded. Another scenario involves Alice sending funds

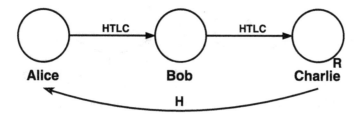

*Figure 4.* Chain of hashed timelock contracts in a channel.

to Bob, but Bob not sending funds to Charlie, leaving Alice defrauded. The binding has to account for the untrusted nature of Bitcoin and the Lightning Network. Specifically, network nodes do not know anything about their peers and do not rely on established trust relationships.

The Lightning Network protocol relies on a method for binding the execution of transactions without any custodial trust. This solution is called a hashed timelock contract (HTLC). A hashed timelock contract enables Bob to pull funds from Alice only after Charlie has pulled the funds from Bob. The basic idea is that Charlie, the recipient, tells Alice, the sender, a riddle. They agree that, in order to pull the funds, Charlie must give the answer to the riddle. Thus, Alice makes a contract with Bob that, if Bob knows the answer (i.e., the secret), then Alice pays the funds to Bob. Bob cannot know the secret unless Bob pays Charlie. Thus, two contracts are created – between Alice and Bob and between Bob and Charlie. Each contract says "'I will pay you if you give me the answer to the riddle." Only Charlie knows the answer, so he gives the answer to Bob and Bob gives the money to Charlie. Since Bob knows the answer, he can give the answer to Alice and Alice gives him the money.

The scheme works the same when there are more than three participants on the route. The answer to the riddle is passed through all the nodes from the recipient to the sender. At the end, the sender is the only node that does not pull the funds from any other node; the sender just spends the funds whereas everyone else along the path pulls the funds from their respective senders and pushes the funds to their respective recipients. The recipient is the only node that just pulls the funds, so it is the only entity to ultimately receive funds.

A hashed timelock contract riddle is "What value hashes to hash $H$?" Nobody knows the answer except the entity that generated the hash. Thus, Charlie, the recipient, generates a random secret value $R$ and calculates its hash $H = h(R)$. Then, he sends the hash $H$ to Alice. Based on the hash value $H$, Alice creates a hashed timelock contract with Bob and Bob creates a hashed timelock contract with Charlie (Figure 4).

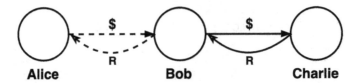

*Figure 5.*    All the hashed timelock contracts are executed after $R$ is revealed.

To complete the transaction, Charlie reveals $R$ to Bob, Bob checks that $R$ hashes to $H$ and Bob pays the promised funds. Then, Bob reveals $R$ to Alice and receives his funds from her (Figure 5).

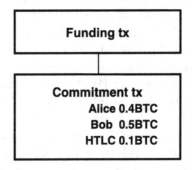

*Figure 6.*    Commitment transaction with a hashed timelock contract.

A hashed timelock contract is realized as one additional output in a commitment transaction (last output in Figure 6). There are two ways to spend the output. Bob can spend this output by providing $R$ (hashed timelock contract execution delivery). Alice can spend this output after some timeout $t$ (hashed timelock contract timeout). Needless to say, only one of these transactions can be published because they spend the same output. They are kept by the channel participants as guarantees that a counterparty will not misbehave analogous to the commitment transaction itself. Unlike the commitment transaction, which eventually gets recorded on the blockchain when the channel is closed, hashed timelock contract execution delivery and timeout transactions may never get on the blockchain. Before closing a channel the parties may cooperatively cancel or execute all the hashed timelock contracts in the channel.

In order to execute a hashed timelock contract, Bob sends $R$ to Alice. Alice knows that, if the commitment transaction gets on the blockchain, Bob will spend the hashed timelock contract output, so she agrees to update the commitment transaction, removing the hashed timelock contract output in Bob's favor. If Alice does not agree to update the commitment transaction, then Bob simply publishes it on the blockchain and right after it is confirmed, he publishes the execution delivery transaction that sends the hashed timelock contract output to himself. Bob does the same if Alice is unresponsive for any reason.

On the other hand, Alice may wish to cancel the hashed timelock contract if Bob does not provide the secret value $R$ for an extended period of time or Alice may simply wish to close the channel and release the funds. In this case, Alice asks Bob to cancel the hashed timelock contract in her favor. If Bob does not agree or does not respond, Alice publishes the commitment transaction on the blockchain and after the timeout $t$, she publishes the timeout transaction, which sends the hashed timelock contract funds to her. Note that, during the timeout $t$, Bob can get to know the secret value $R$ and publish the execution delivery transaction to get his funds. In such a case, Alice considers the payment completed. If Alice is an intermediate node on the route, she can execute the contract on the other side and pull her funds.

The Lightning Network uses hashed timelock contracts to provide a secure way to route payments through untrusted nodes. The problem is that the system relies on the recipient being honest and keeping $R$ secret. If the recipient is dishonest and colludes with a node along the route, it is possible to steal money from the sender or use the scheme for money laundering purposes.

## 4.2 Lightning Network Topology

Several researchers have speculated about the topology of the Lightning Network [8]. A Lightning channel keeps the funds locked within the channel. Unless an entity uses the channel, the time value of the money locked in the channel is wasted. Therefore, channel management is very important. The intuition is that it should dictate the topology taken by the Lightning Network.

Two likely topologies are the hub-and-spoke topology and the organic topology. A hub-and-spoke topology assumes the emergence of bank-like operators (hubs) that would process and route large numbers of transactions. The concerns regarding this topology are centralization, privacy and money locking. There is a fear of large hubs growing larger, which would lead to centralization. Since hubs process transactions, they could aggregate knowledge about many transactions and, thus, pose a threat to privacy (anonymity). Finally, although money locking is a contextual notion, hubs could lock the money in open channels because they do not intend to spend money, only route money. The vast amount of money locked in the topology could impact the viability of the topology and result in high transaction fees.

Organic routing may lock less money because channels are opened on demand. Two limitations with organic routing are route finding and supporting the needed route capacity in the network. Another problem is that the number of on-chain transactions are expected to be much higher than in the hub-and-spoke topology. Detailed evaluations of these topologies is a good topic for future research.

Onion routing has been proposed as a mechanism to alleviate the threat to anonymity in the Lightning Network [10]. It limits the knowledge about nodes in the network only to their neighbor nodes. While the principal advantage of onion routing is final destination masking, this type of routing can impede network analysis and hinder forensic investigations. The implications of onion routing are discussed later in this chapter.

## 5.    Collusion Attack on the Lightning Network

The Lightning Network design relies on the recipient being honest and keeping $R$ secret. At the same time, it is designed to operate in an absolutely untrusted environment and to provide a good level of anonymity to all its participants. The latter assumes an adaption of onion routing, where every node in the network only knows its neighbor nodes. In such conditions, the system must be perfectly secure and flawless. While the Lighting Network is cryptographically secure, it does not take into account the misbehavior of its users.

The original Lightning Network article [9] states that the only way of acknowledging successful transactions is "knowing $R$ is proof of funds sent." However, this does not necessary hold. The sender Alice considers a transaction to be completed when her hashed timelock contract is executed. The recipient Dave considers a transaction to be completed when he receives the funds (Dave is added to the channel for a more explanatory scenario). If the system is used as intended, these two events occur together.

However, there is a situation in which Alice executes her hashed timelock contract, but Dave does not receive the funds. This can only happen if a node on the route (e.g., Bob) knows the pre-image of the hash $H$ – the secret value $R$. It could be that Bob just guessed it; this is very unlikely, but it is still a possibility. A much more likely scenario involves Dave secretly sending $R$ to Bob, enabling Bob to defraud Alice.

Figure 7 illustrates the simple collusion attack. The recipient Dave generates a secret value $R$ upon which depends the execution of each hashed timelock contract on the route. Dave calculates the hash $H = h(R)$ and sends it to Alice. All this is according to the protocol.

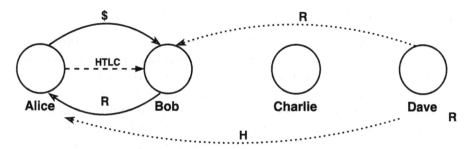

*Figure 7.* Simple collusion attack.

However, the attack occurs when Dave also shares the secret value $R$ with Bob, which is a breach of the protocol. Dave and Bob are now in collusion. Alice, who is unaware of the collusion against her, creates a hashed timelock contract with Bob promising to pay money upon him revealing $R$. At this point, Bob already knows $R$, so he executes the contract. Alice still does not suspect anything and considers the transaction to be completed. She expects Dave to deliver the goods/services for which she has paid. Dave "rightfully" claims not to have received the funds. As a result, Alice loses her money to Dave and Bob.

This collusion attack is due to a fundamental flaw in the Lightning Network. Poon and Dryja [9], the authors of the protocol, mention the problem, but do not analyze or attempt to mitigate it:

> "In the event that $R$ gets disclosed to the participants halfway through expiry along the path, then it is possible for some parties along the path to be enriched. The sender will be able to know $R$, so due to [the] Pay to Contract, the payment will have been fulfilled even though the receiver did not receive the funds. Therefore, the receiver must never disclose $R$."

This scenario described by Poon and Dryja has the same dependencies and consequences as the collusion attack discussed above. The entire operation of the system relies on the assumption that the receiver is not interested in revealing $R$. However, as discussed below, there are certain incentives for a receiver to prematurely reveal $R$.

## 6. Collusion Attack Implications

The collusion attack has several potential consequences for digital forensics. These consequences are passive or active. The entity making the payment is either the victim of criminal activity or a subject of interest to law enforcement.

## 6.1     Fraud

A straightforward use of the collusion attack is fraud. After the attack steps are performed as described above, the attacking nodes may become non-responsive. This attack requires the recipient to collude with a node on the route. Of particular interest are the traces left by the attack that remain in the Lightning Network. Unfortunately, the protocol does not impose a requirement to save any information of value. This is one of the fundamental points of the Lightning Network, namely to summarize many smaller transactions into a fewer large ones for communication with and entry into the shared ledger that is the Bitcoin blockchain. Because it is decentralized, the Lightning Network also cannot dictate a particular implementation with sound logging.

## 6.2     Money Laundering

Another possible use case is to pass money to a recipient on the route via a regular, apparently legitimate, payment system. In this scenario, the sender, the final recipient and an intermediary node collude in order to pretend that a legitimate payment has been made and lost to a rogue intermediary node along the route. The intention is to pass funds to an "unknown" intermediary node under the false pretext of making a legitimate payment. The sender can claim the loss of the funds that were paid but not received by the final intended recipient. This is analogous to the ever popular playing-poker-badly method of money laundering.

## 6.3     Forfeiture

It is possible for an illegal service to claim no wrongdoing and blame intermediary nodes for the loss of sender funds. For example, in the case of law enforcement sting operations, the police could use the mechanism to intercept illegal funds from a criminal at one of the intermediary nodes as a form of forfeiture [4]; the destination never receives the funds because they have been intercepted by law enforcement.

Although this may be problematic from the law enforcement jurisdictional and procedural law perspectives, it is by no means an impossible scenario. Specifically, an anonymous payment routing protocol renders a traditional sting operation, whose goal is to identify the perpetrator, impossible; as a result, law enforcement can only attempt to disrupt illegal activity instead of prosecuting a suspect. In this scenario the ability of a recipient to show "clean hands" by legitimately claiming that the funds never arrived provides plausible deniability and postpones the recipient from being flagged as a "fake" supplier by a reputation-based system.

# 7.    Attack Mitigation

A straightforward way to mitigate a collusion attack is to require (e.g., via a contract) that the knowledge of $R$ constitutes a proof of payment. One method is via a pay-to-contract scheme [3] that is mentioned by the inventors of the Lightning Network [9]. The obvious problem with this approach – which is not implemented in the Lightning Network at this time – is that it relies heavily on a public-key infrastructure. The same is true of all similar mitigation strategies.

Forensic readiness can be implemented by the verbose logging of transactions; the logs would serve as evidence if something goes wrong. However, logging Lightning Network transactions is not enough. Hashed timelock contracts only appear in commitment transactions and they are signed with temporary keys that are not bound to physical-world identities. This is where a public-key infrastructure is needed. If a Lightning Network node has a SSL certificate, it can sign the commitment transactions that it processes. This enables an entity to prove the obligations of its neighbor nodes. Specifically, the completion of a monetary transfer can be proven by following the route and checking the commitment transactions with the corresponding hashed timelock contracts. All the nodes on the route would have to follow forensically-sound logging procedures, which may be enforced by appropriate regulations. A regulated node can also check that all the neighbor nodes fall in the appropriate jurisdiction. However, this may require the network to be partitioned into regulated and unregulated segments. While the regulated segment would have the desired properties, the presence of an unregulated segment would raise the risk of abuse if the two network segments were to interact.

To conclude, a public-key infrastructure could solve a number of fundamental problems with the Lightning Network and crypto-currencies in general. An example problem is transaction acknowledgement in a decentralized environment. Unless the receiver is a legally recognized electronic entity, the receiver can always claim to have not received funds even if it did receive the funds. Such problems arise due to the nature of a virtual identity and the fact that it is distinct from a physical identity. A public-key infrastructure does bridge the gap between the virtual and physical worlds. However, in the domain of decentralized applications, anonymity and freedom are paramount. Therefore, the mitigations described in this section are not adequate and an appropriate solution remains elusive.

## 8.    Conclusions

Off-chain transactions in the Bitcoin-based Lightning Network increase the likelihood of collusion attacks. These attacks enable payment recipients or merchants to collude with intermediaries to ensure payments to the intermediaries, while claiming that payments were not received by the ultimate receivers. This does not meet the guarantee made by the Lightning Network, where the end state of an initiator of a transaction is that it should end up with no funds and the goods/services or with funds and no goods/services.

Collusion attacks have forensic implications because they enable fraud with very little traceability. Additionally, they enable law enforcement to intercept funds used in illegal transactions for the purpose of forfeiture. In the two scenarios, the fraudulent entities and law enforcement can claim innocence when the (unidentifiable) initiators of the transactions complain that their funds were lost and they did not receive any goods/services.

Digital currencies are increasingly becoming the targets of crime and vehicles for furthering criminal activities. It is hoped that this research will stimulate increased efforts in this new and important area of research.

## References

[1] D. Boneh and J. Shaw, Collusion-secure fingerprinting for digital data, *IEEE Transactions on Information Theory*, vol. 44(5), pp. 1897–1905, 1998.

[2] S. Bugiel, L. Davi, R. Dmitrienko, T. Fischer, A. Sadeghi and B. Shastry, Towards taming privilege-escalation attacks on Android, *Proceedings of the Nineteenth Annual Network and Distributed System Security Symposium*, 2012.

[3] I. Gerhardt and T. Hanke, Homomorphic Payment Addresses and the Pay-to-Contract Protocol, arXiv:1212.3257v1 [cs.CR], Cornell University Library, Cornell University, Ithaca, New York (`arxiv.org/pdf/1212.3257v1.pdf`), 2012.

[4] B. Hay, Sting operations, undercover agents and entrapment, *Missouri Law Review*, vol. 70(2), pp. 387–432, 2005.

[5] M. Moharrum, M. Eltoweissy and R. Mukkamala, Dynamic combinatorial key management scheme for sensor networks, *Wireless Communications and Mobile Computing*, vol. 6(7), pp. 1017–1035, 2006.

[6] S. Nakamoto, Bitcoin: A Peer-to-Peer Electronic Cash System (`bitcoin.org/bitcoin.pdf`), 2008.

[7] M. Nowostawski and C. Frantz, Blockchain: The emergence of distributed autonomous institutions, *Proceedings of the Sixth International Conference on Social Media Technologies, Communication and Informatics*, pp. 29–35, 2016.

[8] C. Pacia, Lightning Network skepticism (`chrispacia.wordpress.com/2015/12/23/lightning-network-skepticism`), December 23, 2015.

[9] J. Poon and T. Dryja, The Bitcoin Lightning Network: Scalable Off-Chain Instant Payments, Draft Version 0.5.9.2 (`lightning.network/lightning-network-paper.pdf`), 2016.

[10] P. Prihodko, S. Zhigulin, M. Sahno, A. Ostrovskiy and O. Osuntokun, Flare: An Approach to Routing in the Lightning Network, White Paper (`bitfury.com/content/5-white-papers-research/whitepaper_flare_an_approach_to_routing_in_lightning_network_7_7_2016.pdf`), 2016.

[11] F. Reid and M. Harrigan, An analysis of anonymity in the Bitcoin system, *Proceedings of the Third IEEE International Conference on Privacy, Security, Risk and Trust/Social Computing/Workshop on Security and Privacy in Social Networks*, pp. 1318–1326, 2011.

# Chapter 9

# INSIDER THREAT DETECTION USING TIME-SERIES-BASED RAW DISK FORENSIC ANALYSIS

Nicole Beebe, Lishu Liu and Zi Ye

**Abstract**     This research tests the theory that volitional, malicious computer use based on insider threat activity can be detected via a time-series-based analysis of data and file type forensic artifacts that reside on a raw disk. In other words, statistical profiling of allocated and unallocated space pertaining to the types of files accessed and the data browsed, acquired and processed incident to espionage, intellectual property theft, fraud or organizational computer abuse can help detect insider threats. The t-test approach is used to compare the means of two time windows using the split and sliding window methods along with first-order autoregressive modeling. Empirical testing against the nineteen-day snapshots of the M57-Patents case provides support for all three methods, but the results suggest that the first-order autoregressive modeling method is the most robust. Additionally, the autoregressive modeling approach is likely to generate more intuitive results for an analyst. Ground truth analysis confirms nearly all of the outliers that were detected. While the majority of the outliers were due to benign and easily explainable situations and system contexts and the minority were due to malicious activity, the approach does not yield an inordinate amount of search hits to examine and validate. This research thus provides a new computational approach for locating digital forensic evidence.

**Keywords:** Insider threat, anomaly detection, time series, profiling

## 1.     Introduction

The trusted insider remains one of the most critical cyber security threats to organizations [3, 7, 17, 23]. In fact, some contend that insiders present greater risks to organizations than external attackers [19, 22]. Insiders vary along two major dimensions – malice and volition [5, 11,

© IFIP International Federation for Information Processing 2017                     149
Published by Springer International Publishing AG 2017. All Rights Reserved
G. Peterson and S. Shenoi (Eds.): Advances in Digital Forensics XIII, IFIP AICT 511, pp. 149–167, 2017.
DOI: 10.1007/978-3-319-67208-3_9

24]. Malicious, volitional insiders are often characterized by their methods and motivation and placed into four categories: (i) espionage; (ii) intellectual property theft; (iii) fraud; and (iv) sabotage [1, 12]. Volitional, non-malicious insiders include users who knowingly subvert security measures to accomplish work goals and insiders who violate acceptable use policies for personal gain or satisfaction. This research focuses on volitional insiders with malicious intent, specifically those interested in espionage, intellectual property theft or fraud, as well as non-malicious, volitional insiders who abuse computing privileges for personal satisfaction (e.g., browsing pornography on the web). Both types of insiders often leverage institutional trust and system access privileges to facilitate their criminal or unauthorized computing activities [4, 24].

Current approaches for detecting insiders rely largely on behavioral heuristics based on past insider cases [18]. These approaches fall short in three important ways: (i) they fail to detect novel insider methodologies and attacks; (ii) they fail to detect large-scale data collection within the scope of authorized access permissions; and (iii) they fail to consider forensic traces of information-handling activity in unallocated space. Analyses of seven insider cases – Robert Hanssen (1979), Aldrich Ames (1985), Harold Nicholson (1994), Brian Reagan (1999), Leandro Aragoncillo (2004), Chelsea Manning (2010) and Edward Snowden (2013) – have revealed a single, common distinguishing characteristic: in preparing to exfiltrate data, an insider often browses, acquires and prepares data for exfiltration on a single system, typically his/her own workstation [1, 6, 8, 13, 15, 16].

This research posits that digital forensic traces of user activity, in both allocated and unallocated space, can signal impending exfiltration and unauthorized computer use for which information browsing, collection and/or handling are facilitating activities. Specifically, this research seeks to profile a workstation disk at the physical level based on the forensic artifacts that are left behind from user activity with respect to the types of data browsed, stored and handled. Following this, it attempts to detect statistical anomalies in the profile over time that signal nefarious user activity. Five types of features are considered, including file types, file classes, data types, email related features and string classes other than email-related strings. Table 1 shows examples of each feature type. In the case of string classes, the measures used include the total number of instances (hits) that match the type of string and the total number of unique instances (i.e., without repeated hits); in the case of email addresses and URLs, the measures used also include

*Table 1.* Feature types.

| Feature Type | Examples |
|---|---|
| File Types | JPEG, Email, PDF, EXE |
| File Classes | Text, Video, Audio, System |
| Data Types | Compressed, Encrypted, Allocated |
| String Classes | Email, CCN, SSN, URL |

the numbers of instances in specific most frequently occurring (high-frequency) domains (e.g., `gmail.com`).

## 2. Methodology

A time series analysis was conducted of four disks with a synthetic dataset (discussed below) that were snapshotted daily for nineteen days. Two classes of time series analysis were employed: (i) t-tests; and (ii) autoregressive analyses, both with varied set-ups and parameters. The t-tests involved two methods for establishing time series windows: (i) split window; and (ii) sliding window. A *post hoc* ground truth analysis was conducted to validate the statistically-detected anomalies by assessing the Type I error (false positives) and the Type II error (false negatives).

### 2.1 Sample Data

The sample data was taken from the M57-Patents dataset [9, 10] corresponding to a case involving four employees of a fictitious corporation, three of whom were involved in various types of criminal activity, including intellectual property theft, extortion and possession of illegal pornography. In producing the synthetic evidence, the scenario participants engaged in scripted and normal user activities every day for nearly three weeks. Researchers made forensic images of the user workstations at the end of each day. All the daily disk images from the case were analyzed using a data driven anomaly detection algorithm.

### 2.2 Data Driven Algorithm Development

In this context, a statistical outlier means that the outlier media (e.g., an employee workstation) has a storage profile that is different from a historical perspective. The mathematical definition of what constitutes an inlier versus an outlier varies from dataset to dataset, especially when the central distribution violates conditions such as normality. In such cases, the central distribution is ideally identified by removing outliers and then modeling the data. However, removing outliers may not be possible because they are not always known. Challenges to defining inlying user behavior include: (i) encompassing the full range of normality; (ii) normality that evolves over time; (iii) normality that varies across contexts; and (iv) difficulty in establishing a precise boundary between inlying and outlying behavior [21]. As a result, an outlier detection process cannot be easily separated from the process of identifying the normal storage profile.

Traditional statistical methods cannot be used when outliers cannot be eliminated from a dataset before determining the central distribution. Instead, robust statistical measures are required that are not significantly influenced by outliers. Otherwise, outlier masking occurs – the central distribution is skewed by outliers, causing failures in outlier detection [14, 20].

In a deployed application of this research, such as the ongoing monitoring of employees, an analyst would not know the ground truth *a priori* and would be unable to separate outliers before establishing a statistical profile of a workstation. Furthermore, the analyst would often be unable to ensure that outliers do not already exist when establishing a statistical profile. Accordingly, this research uses a robust data driven algorithm that is not as sensitive to outliers as traditional methods. The data distribution is characterized using a robust location parameter (center of the data) and a robust dispersion parameter (variability of the data around the center).

## 2.3    Time-Series-Based Anomaly Detection

In time-series-based anomaly detection, the storage profiles of daily disk snapshots are treated as time-ordered sequences. Anomalies are then detected by: (i) comparing means between two different time periods; or (ii) predicting future observations in a time series based on past values and declaring as outliers the actual values that deviate significantly from predicted values. The former is accomplished via unpaired t-testing whereas the latter is accomplished via autoregressive modeling.

**Unpaired t-Test Approach.**    Outliers are found in time series data by comparing two periods of time, $\Delta T1$ and $\Delta T2$, for statistical differences between the periods. Toward this end, unpaired t-tests were conducted – unpaired because $\Delta T1$ and $\Delta T2$ occur at different times and the observations are not paired in the sense of a repeated measures design.

The basic outlier detection approach involves the following steps:

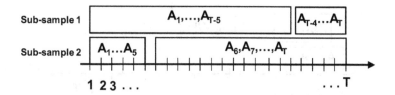

*Figure 1.* Unpaired t-test – Split window method.

- **Step 1:** From a complete time series $A_1, A_2, ..., A_T$, create several sub-samples where each sub-sample contains two sub-series, $X_{1i}, X_{2i}, ..., X_{Mi}$ and $Y_{1i}, Y_{2i}, ..., Y_{Ni}$, where $M, N < T$ and $i$ is the index of a sub-sample.

- **Step 2:** Perform an F-test to test for the equality of the variances of the two sub-series in each sub-sample. If the p-value of the F-test is greater than 0.1, then the variances are considered to be equal ($\sigma_X^2 = \sigma_Y^2$).

- **Step 3:** Perform the appropriate t-tests based on variance equality and obtain a p-value for each sub-sample $i$. If a p-value is larger than a certain significance level, then the null hypothesis that the means of the two sub-series are equal ($\mu_X = \mu_Y$) is not rejected.

- **Step 4:** For each time series division point (split point) at which the p-value meets a specified significance threshold, declare an outlier at the split point. When a time series exhibits multiple outlying points, order the split points in ascending order of p-value significance to rank order the outlying points for further analysis.

Two methods for defining sub-series samples were employed: (i) split window method; and (ii) sliding window method:

- **Split Window Method:** In the split window method, each sub-sample contains the entire time series sequence split into two sub-series. Different sub-samples have successively different split points in the time series continuum beginning at $t_2$ (first observation is $t_0$) and ending at $t_{n-2}$ because at least two points are needed in a sub-series sequence. In the example shown in Figure 1, the split point for sub-sample 1 ($i = 1$) occurs at the fifth to last time point $A_{T-5}$. The split point for the second sub-sample ($i = 2$) occurs at the sixth time point $A_5$. Continuing this procedure yields $T - 3$ sub-samples.

    As described above, $T - 3$ p-values $P_1, P_2, ..., P_{T-3}$ are computed. When the p-value is statistically significant, it can be concluded

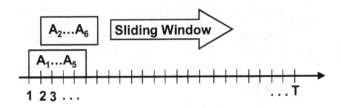

*Figure 2.* Unpaired t-test – Sliding window method.

that there is a difference between the means of the observations that occurred before and after the split point. This is referred to as a jump point or change point and the later observation is typically considered to be the outlying point (chronologically speaking). Using the terminology, the outlying observation for $P_i$ is $A_{i+2}$.

The limitations of the unpaired split window method are: (i) inability to detect outliers at the first two or last two time points in a time series because they cannot be split points; (ii) inability to conduct a t-test when there is no variance in the sub-series on either side of a split point (e.g., in the case of a step function); and (iii) sub-optimal level of robustness.

- **Sliding Window Method:** In the sliding window method, the entire time sequence in the composite of the two sub-series is no longer included in a single sub-sample. Furthermore, the window size $W$ is held constant for all the sub-series in a sub-sample. After setting $W$, the window is moved incrementally along the entire time series, creating $T - W + 1$ sub-series of length $W$. Each sub-series is then paired with its successive sub-series to obtain $T - W$ sub-samples. While $W$ remains fixed for an entire set of sub-samples, $W$ could vary for alternate sub-sample sets. For a time series $A_1, A_2, ..., A_T$, the range of $W$ is $2 \leq W \leq T - 2$. Small window sizes may bear too little information while large window sizes are limited from the standpoint of outlier detection sensitivity, similar to the split window method discussed above. Again, the p-values between sub-series within each sub-sample are computed and ranked outliers are considered based on statistically significant p-values. Figure 2 shows a graphical depiction of two sub-series in a single sub-sample using the sliding window method.

The limitations of the unpaired t-test sliding window method are: (i) inability to detect outliers at the first $W - 1$ points or the last $W - 1$ points in a time series because they cannot be split points (this is mitigated by a small window size); and (ii) inability to perform a t-test when there is no variance in the sub-series on either side of a split point (e.g., in the case of a step function). When there is a constant segment in the time series of length $\geq 2W$, the t-test cannot be performed for the segment because $s_X^2 = s_Y^2 = 0$ for the first $W + 1$ sub-samples. An anomaly detection system should test for constant segments and univariate step functions and the p-value should be set to one for these sub-samples because no outliers exist in constant value segments. Finally, this approach is not particularly robust because the sub-series means are influenced by outliers. However, the effect is less pronounced than in the split window method, especially when $W$ is sufficiently small.

**Autoregressive Model Method.** Instead of comparing means between two sub-series in a time series sequence, the autoregressive (AR) model method predicts successive observations in a time-varying sequence as a linear model of its previous values. $AR(p)$ ($p$ is the number of prior observations in the sequence) along with a noise term help predict the current observation. In an $AR(0)$ time sequence, the prior observation does not help predict the current observation. In an $AR(1)$ time sequence, the single prior observation helps predict the current observation, and so on. When a time series conforms to the autoregressive model assumptions and the model is $AR(p > 0)$, then outliers can be declared as the points whose actual values deviate statistically from the predicted values. An autoregressive model $AR(p)$ of order $p$ is given by:

$$A_t = c + \sum_{j=1}^{p} \phi_j A_{t-j} + \varepsilon_t \tag{1}$$

where $\theta = (c, \phi, \sigma_2)'$ is the parameter vector and the error terms $\varepsilon_t$ are independent and identically distributed and follow a normal distribution $\varepsilon_t = N(0, \sigma_2)$.

Since it is not possible to readily know the exact distribution of sub-series, it is necessary to first work with the simplest autoregressive model $AR(1)$, which is given by:

$$A_t = c + \phi A_{t-1} + \varepsilon_t \tag{2}$$

where $\theta = (c, \phi, \sigma_2)'$ is the parameter vector.

The parameters are estimated using the maximum likelihood estimation (MLE) method. Given an observed sample $a_1, a_2, ..., a_T$ of size $T$, the first step is to compute the joint probability density function:

$$f_{A_1, A_2, ..., A_T}(a_1, a_2, ..., a_T; \theta) \qquad (3)$$

This can loosely be considered to denote the probability of having observed the particular sample.

The maximum likelihood estimate $\hat{\theta}$ is the value for which the sample is most likely to have been observed. Specifically, it is the value of $\theta$ that maximizes the probability density function in Equation (3). Note that at least three observations are required to obtain an estimate using this approach.

Suppose that the three observations are $a_1$, $a_2$ and $a_3$, and the maximum likelihood estimate is:

$$\hat{\theta} = (\hat{c}, \hat{\phi}, \hat{\sigma}_2)' \qquad (4)$$

It is possible to predict the next observation using the equation:

$$\hat{a}_4 = \hat{c} + \hat{\phi} a_3 + \hat{\varepsilon}_4 \qquad (5)$$

and to compute the residual between the actual and predicted values as:

$$res_4 = a_4 - \hat{a}_4 \qquad (6)$$

Continued iteration yields $T - 3$ residuals $res_4, res_5, ..., res_T$.

Using a forward (chronologically speaking) autoregressive model approach, it is not possible to identify whether the first three observations are outliers; this is because they are required for model building. However, unlike the unpaired t-test approach, a work-around is available. This simply involves backward (chronologically speaking) autoregressive modeling. When using the reversed sequence $a_T, a_{T-1}, ..., a_3$ as the observed time series values, the maximum likelihood estimates are obtained in the same manner as before. Specifically, the next future value is given by:

$$\hat{a}_2 = \hat{c}^* + \hat{\phi}^* a_3 + \hat{\varepsilon}_2 \qquad (7)$$

and the residual is:

$$res_3 = a_2 - \hat{a}_2 \qquad (8)$$

Note that the residual for the third point is $a_2 - \hat{a}_2$ instead of $a_3 - \hat{a}_3$ because a reversed sequence is used. Also, if $a_3$ were an outlier, a very large difference between $a_2$ and $\hat{a}_2$ would be obtained by the backward procedure.

The residuals are $res_2, res_3, ..., res_T$. Defining the residual threshold for an outlier, however, is less straightforward than for unpaired t-tests because the magnitudes of the residuals can vary widely. Therefore, the residuals are standardized using the equation:

$$res_{sd(i)} = \frac{res_i - mean(res)}{var(res)} \qquad (9)$$

and an observation whose absolute standardized residual is larger than two is defined as an outlier:

$$|res_{sd(i)}| \geq 2 \tag{10}$$

The sensitivity of this procedure can be tuned by defining a larger absolute standardized residual value (e.g., $|res_{sd(i)}| \geq 3$). However, the experiments conducted in this research suggest that it is better to use a threshold of two.

The primary limitation of this approach is that white noise $\varepsilon_t$ is required to build a time series model. However, even in constant value segments, it is easy to add a small random noise term with the same mean as the sub-series and with very little variance to remove the constancy of the sub-series without modifying its underlying distribution.

## 3.  Experimental Results

The three time-series-based anomaly detection methods were evaluated using the nineteen observation time series for the users in the synthetic M57-Patents dataset. While the intervals between observations in this data set are not identical, they are approximately equal (daily) and, hence, the observations were treated as having equal intervals.

Thirty-three of the 88 features have constant and/or zero values across all nineteen time intervals and were, therefore, removed from the sample, leaving 55 univariate, time series samples for testing. The constant and/or zero valued features included twelve credit card number features, twelve social security number features and the following file/data types: active server page files (.asp/.aspx), base64, base85, base16, URL encoded, postscript (.ps), tagged image file format (.tif/.tiff), configuration files (.ini) and link files (.lnk).

## 3.1  Unpaired t-Test/Split Window Method

A p-value of 0.05 was selected as the significance threshold for outlier determination. The unpaired t-test with split window method was observed to work well for time series exhibiting sudden changes after sustained periods with low variance (Figures 3(a) and 3(b)) and for step functions (Figures 4(a), 4(b) and 5(a); the data type in Figure 4(a) is the top-third most frequent email domain). Note that all the experimental results described here pertain to user Charlie. Similar functions and outlier detection trends were realized for the other users in the dataset.

However, the t-test with the split window method can be misleading. This is seen in Figure 5(b) when the change is more gradual (i.e., gradual change function with misleading outlier detected using the split window

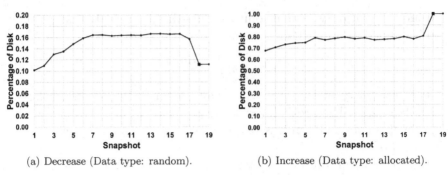

(a) Decrease (Data type: random).          (b) Increase (Data type: allocated).

*Figure 3.*   Time series exhibiting sudden changes.

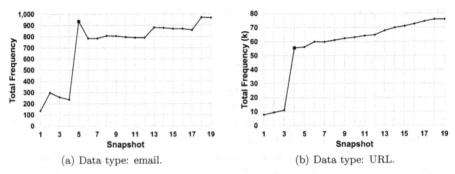

(a) Data type: email.                          (b) Data type: URL.

*Figure 4.*   Time series with pseudo-step function changes.

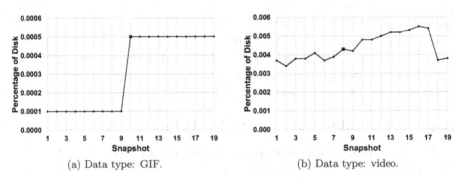

(a) Data type: GIF.                            (b) Data type: video.

*Figure 5.*   Time series with step function (left) and gradual function changes (right).

method) and also in Figure 6 when the change is a spike function (i.e., temporary change returning to the previous relative, steady-state condition where the data type is the top-third most frequent email domain). When the change is more gradual, an outlier would be declared in the midst of the gradual change, making it difficult for an analyst to understand why the snapshot was deemed an outlier. The gradual change

*Figure 6.* Time series with spike function change (Data type: email).

scenario is a concern because a patient and skilled insider may collect data gradually to specifically thwart detection efforts.

When the change is a spike function, the observation identified as an outlier is again misleading. The return to steady-state masks the true outlying observation point that occurs one or two intervals after the observation identified as the outlier. In this situation, without being alerted to the full nature of the time series, an analyst may only examine the identified outlying snapshot and erroneously declare it to be a false positive. A different conclusion may have been reached if the analyst had analyzed the snapshot(s) following the split point for a more complete context. The spike function scenario is a concern when an insider collects, exfiltrates and quickly wipes the collected data from the hard drive (i.e., allocated and unallocated space). A potential mitigation strategy is to design the system to detect significant changes in the wiped disk space.

In summary, using the unpaired t-test and split window method can identify outliers. However, an analyst would be able to make more informed analytical and investigative decisions if provided with the supporting time series function as a visualization aid.

## 3.2 Unpaired t-Test/Sliding Window Method

Once again, a p-value of 0.05 was selected as the significance threshold for outlier determination, although this could be changed akin to a sensitivity setting. The results indicate that an unpaired t-test with the sliding window method works reasonably well at detecting sudden changes and step functions; to some extent, the sliding window method may be more sensitive at detecting small changes than the split window method. Also, it may occasionally provide more intuitive results to an analyst by identifying the outlying observation at the end of the change period as in Figure 7(a) (for the video data type) rather than during the

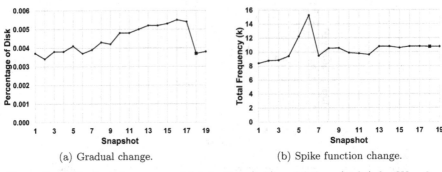

(a) Gradual change.                    (b) Spike function change.

*Figure 7.*   Sliding window successful detection (left) and failure (right) for $W = 2$.

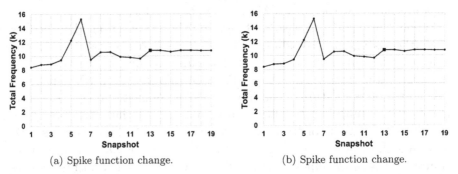

(a) Spike function change.            (b) Spike function change.

*Figure 8.*   Sliding window spike detection failure for $W = 3$ (left) and $W = 4$ (right).

change period as in Figure 5(b). However, the sliding window approach appears to be even less able to detect very short duration spikes regardless of $W$ as shown in Figures 7(b), 8(a) and 8(b) (for the top-third most frequent email domain data type).

Another problem with the sliding window approach is that a wide variety of results were obtained depending on the window size $W$. This is because there does not appear to be a single, universal objectively superior $W$ that could be used. Two example sets are shown in Figures 9(a) through 9(c) and in Figures 10(a) through 10(c).

The empirical results indicate that the split window method should be preferred over the sliding window method. However, the impact that the time aperture may have on the split window method is a concern. The empirical time aperture was approximately nineteen days. Further empirical research is needed to ascertain the impact of a larger time aperture on the results.

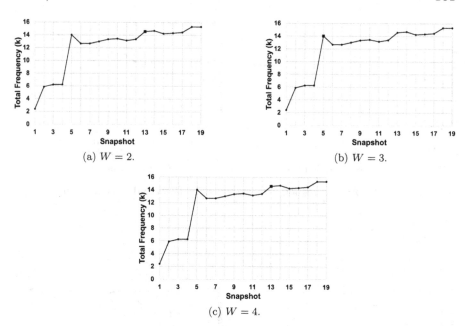

*Figure 9.* Outliers detected via sliding window (Data type: email).

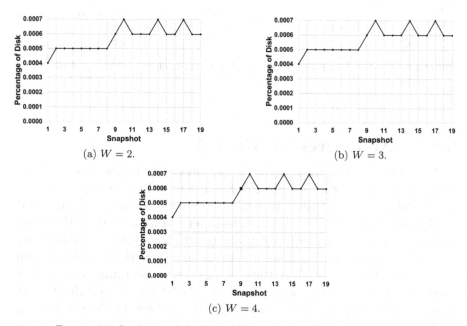

*Figure 10.* Outliers detected via sliding window (Data type: JPEG).

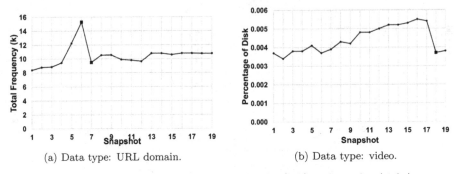

(a) Data type: URL domain.                    (b) Data type: video.

*Figure 11.*   Autoregression detection of spike (left) and at edge (right).

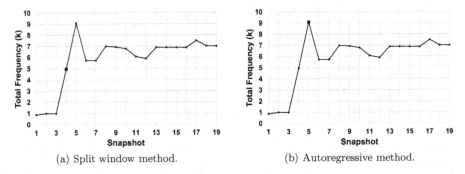

(a) Split window method.                    (b) Autoregressive method.

*Figure 12.*   Outlier detection (Data type: top-ninth most frequent URL domain).

## 3.3    Autoregressive Method

The first-degree autoregressive model proved to be the most reliable
of the three methods. It detected the most outliers, it was the most
consistent in rank ordering outliers based on statistical significance and
it does not appear to have some of the detection limitations of the other
methods. In particular, when compared with the other methods, especially the split window method, it was better able to detect spikes in the
time series (Figure 11(a)), outliers at the edges (beginning and ending
observations in the time series in Figure 11(b) for the top-third most
frequent URL domain data type). Also, it consistently identified as an
outlier the more intuitive, successive observation, rather than the less
intuitive, precipitory observation (Figures 12(a) and 12(b)). In both figures, the successive fourth and fifth observations are identified as outliers
compared with the precipitory third observation.

## 3.4 Ground Truth Analysis

To establish ground truth and thereby evaluate the validity of detected outliers and identify false negatives, investigative interrogatories pertaining to the detected outliers as well as general investigative interrogatories pertaining to the case scenario to identify false negatives were developed. A trained digital forensic investigator analyzed the disk images using the interrogatories. The forensic analysis, when compared against the anomalies detected via time series analysis, identified nine true positives and two false positives. A true positive occurred when the forensic analysis confirmed that the drive snapshot did indeed contain an anomalous number of data/files of a specified type – whether benign or nefarious in nature. A false positive occurred when the results of the forensic analysis suggested that the drive should not have been flagged as anomalous by the outlier detection system.

The two false positives were identified as a result of issues with the outlier detection system design. First, it was determined that the file extension list for video files was overly broad and included extensions that are not exclusively used for video file types. This resulted in a statistical anomaly that would not have been anomalous if the video file type was defined more narrowly and reliably. Second, the approach failed to detect recycle bin content. If the recycle bin content had been detected, the second false positive anomaly would not have been statistically anomalous because the forensic traces of the data still existed on the disk; they were reported as missing because recycle bin content was omitted from the analysis.

Of the nine true positives that were identified, forensic analysis revealed that seven were benign anomalies. In other words, the anomalous activity was explained by legitimate circumstances (e.g., job role/task change) and activity (e.g., system activity related to infrequent system logging during the period of analysis). Two true positive cases were confirmed to be (synthetic) illegal behavior, specifically: (i) possession of illegal graphic images; and (ii) installation of a keylogger.

False negatives are somewhat challenging to define in this context. On the one hand, no false negatives were encountered from a statistical perspective. However, from an investigative perspective, the outlier detection method failed to detect two pieces of evidence that could have been detected via time-series-based analysis, if not for two extenuating circumstances. First, the same unauthorized keylogger that was detected on user Pat's machine via time series analysis of file types was not detected on user Terry's computer through the same means. This is likely because the keylogger stored its log files in HTML and Terry's drive had a significant amount of HTML data as a result of much more web browsing activity than Pat. Second, Terry had a great deal of unauthorized screen captures of Pat's machine stored in the JPEG format, but these screen captures were missed by time-series-based anomaly detection. Again, this is likely because Terry's extensive web browsing activity masked this evidence from a time series perspective, given the large number of .jpg files stored in the web cache on the drive.

## 4.    Conclusions

Time-series-based analysis, specifically first-order autoregressive modeling, successfully identified statistical anomalies with a direct investigative payoff. The number of true positives exceeded the number of false positives (nine versus two) and the false negatives were due to outlier detection system design errors, not problems with the anomaly detection method. While only two of the nine true positives were malicious, meaning that the number of investigatively-irrelevant true positives exceeded the number of investigatively-relevant true positives, this is nothing new in digital forensics. Text string searches typically yield 95% or more irrelevant search hits from an investigative perspective. They are not false positives from a search perspective; they simply are not germane to the investigation. Similarly, the false positives were indeed statistically anomalous; they simply were not germane to the investigation. Not only is the 70% rate of benign statistical anomalies an improvement over what is typically experienced in text string search (>95%), but it is also important to note that the total number of anomalies that have to be assessed for benign or malicious intent is a very small fraction of what text string search and other digital forensic techniques encounter. It is also important to remind users of the proposed method that the outliers are associated with p-values, which could be rank ordered to enable analysts to examine the more outlying observations first and analyze the less outlying observations as resources permit. Indeed, the results demonstrate that a time-series-based method for statistical disk profiling can detect insider threat activity with a manageable ratio of benign to malicious root causes and the ability to rank order the outliers.

Two key limitations of the dataset used in this research impact the research findings. First, the dataset is synthetic, which limits the external validity and generalizability of the research findings. Second, the data is limited in the number of observations. Approximately nineteen time series observations were available for each synthetic user. More observations would have been better, but suitable test datasets in the digital forensics field are difficult to come by. Robust synthetic digital forensic cases are very rare and real-world datasets have access restrictions and the results are generally not reproducible by other researchers.

Note that the views expressed in this chapter do not necessarily reflect the official policies of the Naval Postgraduate School nor does the mention of trade names, commercial practices or organizations imply an endorsement by the U.S. Department of Homeland Security or the U.S. Government.

## Acknowledgement

This research was sponsored by the U.S. Department of Homeland Security Science and Technology Directorate, Cyber Security Division (DHS S&T CSD) via Contract No. N6600112WX01362 under a Cooperative Agreement No. N00244-13-2-0004 with the Naval Postgraduate School.

## References

[1] S. Band, D. Cappelli, L. Fischer, A. Moore, E. Shaw and R. Trzeciak, Comparing Insider IT Sabotage and Espionage: A Model-Based Analysis, Technical Report CMU/SEI-2006-TR-026, Software Engineering Institute, Carnegie Mellon University, Pittsburgh, Pennsylvania, 2006.

[2] V. Barnett and T. Lewis, *Outliers in Statistical Data*, John Wiley and Sons, New York, 1994.

[3] S. Boss, D. Galletta, P. Lowry, G. Moody and P. Polak, What do users have to fear? Using fear appeals to engender threats and fear that motivate protective security behaviors, *Management Information Systems Quarterly*, vol. 39(4), pp. 837–864, 2015.

[4] H. Chivers, J. Clark, P. Nobles, S. Shaikh and H. Chen, Knowing who to watch: Identifying attackers whose actions are hidden within false alarms and background noise, *Information Systems Frontiers*, vol. 15(1), pp. 17–34, 2013.

[5] D. Costa, M. Collins, S. Perl, M. Albrethsen, G. Silowash and D. Spooner, An Ontology for Insider Threat Indicators: Development and Application, *Proceedings of the Ninth Conference on Semantic Technology for Intelligence, Defense and Security*, pp. 48–53, 2014.

[6] D. Dishneau, Army general upholds Chelsea Manning's conviction, 35-year sentence in WikiLeaks case, *U.S. News and World Report*, April 14, 2014.

[7] F. Farahmand and E. Spafford, Understanding insiders: An analysis of risk-taking behavior, *Information Systems Frontiers*, vol. 15(1), pp. 5–15, 2013.

[8] J. Gallu, Snowden used "web crawler" to scrape NSA: New York Times, *Bloomberg Technology*, February 9, 2014.

[9] S. Garfinkel, M57-Patents Scenario, Digital Corpora (`digitalcorpora.org/corpora/scenarios/m57-patents-scenario`), 2017.

[10] S. Garfinkel, P. Farrell, V. Roussev and G. Dinolt, Bringing science to digital forensics with standardized forensic corpora, *Digital Investigation*, vol. 6(S), pp. S2–S11, 2009.

[11] K. Guo, Y. Yuan, N. Archer and C. Connelly, Understanding non-malicious security violations in the workplace: A composite behavior model, *Journal of Management Information Systems*, vol. 28(2), pp. 203–236, 2011.

[12] M. Hanley and J. Montelibano, Insider Threat Control: Using Centralized Logging to Detect Data Exfiltration Near Insider Termination, Technical Note CMU/SEI-2011-TN-024, Software Engineering Institute, Carnegie Mellon University, Pittsburgh, Pennsylvania, 2011.

[13] K. Herbig and M. Wiskoff, Espionage Against the United States by American Citizens 1947–2001, Technical Report 02-5, Defense Personnel Security Research Center, Monterey, California, 2002.

[14] P. Huber and E. Ronchetti, *Robust Statistics*, John Wiley and Sons, Hoboken, New Jersey, 2009.

[15] L. Kramer, R. Heuer and K. Crawford, Technological, Social and Economic Trends that are Increasing U.S. Vulnerability to Insider Espionage, Technical Report 05-10, Defense Personnel Security Research Center, Monterey, California, 2005.

[16] M. Maasberg, Insider espionage: Recognizing ritualistic behavior by abstracting technical indicators from past cases, *Proceedings of the Twentieth Americas Conference on Information Systems*, 2014.

[17] Mandiant, M-Trends 2015: A View from the Front Line, Threat Report, Alexandria, Virginia, 2014.

[18] A. Moore, D. McIntire, D. Mundie and D. Zubrow, The justification of a pattern for detecting intellectual property theft by departing insiders, *Proceedings of the Nineteenth Conference on Pattern Languages of Programs*, article no. 8, 2012.

[19] Ponemon Institute, 2015 Cost of Data Breach Study: Global Analysis, Ponemon Institute Research Report, Traverse City, Michigan, 2015.

[20] P. Rousseeuw and A. Leroy, *Robust Regression and Outlier Detection*, John Wiley and Sons, Hoboken, New Jersey, 2003.

[21] K. Singh and S. Upadhyaya, Outlier detection: Applications and techniques, *International Journal of Computer Science Issues*, vol. 9(1), pp. 307–323, 2012.

[22] Vormetric Data Security, 2015 Vormetric Insider Threat Report, San Jose, California, 2015.

[23] J. Wang, M. Gupta and R. Rao, Insider threats in a financial institution: Analysis of attack-proneness of information systems applications, *Management Information Systems Quarterly*, vol. 39(1), pp. 91–112, 2015.

[24] R. Willison and M. Warkentin, Beyond deterrence: An expanded view of employee computer abuse, *Management Information Systems Quarterly*, vol. 37(1), pp. 1–20, 2013.

# Chapter 10

# ANTI-FORENSIC THREAT MODELING

Bruno Hoelz and Marcelo Maues

**Abstract**     The role of a digital forensic professional is to collect and analyze digital evidence. However, anti-forensic techniques can reduce the availability or usefulness of the evidence. They threaten the digital forensic examination process and may compromise its conclusions. This chapter proposes the use of threat modeling to manage the risks associated with anti-forensic threats. Risk management is introduced in the early stages of the digital forensic process to assist a digital forensic professional in determining the resources to be invested in detecting and mitigating the risk. The proposed threat model complements the incident response and digital forensic processes by providing a means for assessing the impact and likelihood of anti-forensic threats, evaluating the cost of risk mitigation and selecting tools and techniques that can be used as countermeasures. This renders the digital forensic process more robust and less susceptible to the consequences of anti-forensic actions.

**Keywords:** Forensic examination, anti-forensics, threat modeling, risk management

## 1.     Introduction

In digital forensics, evidence can be found in computer systems and networks, and in devices ranging from cell phones to game consoles. Over the years, several digital forensic process models have been proposed to examine evidence. Some of these models deal with specific needs while others incorporate more general approaches. Most models, however, do not take into account the risks associated with anti-forensic actions (AFAs) [10].

An anti-forensic action attempts to reduce the availability or usefulness of digital evidence in the forensic process [6]. The anti-forensic result can be achieved via the use of a malicious tool or method, or through the use of legitimate protection mechanisms such as passwords and encryption.

© IFIP International Federation for Information Processing 2017
Published by Springer International Publishing AG 2017. All Rights Reserved
G. Peterson and S. Shenoi (Eds.): Advances in Digital Forensics XIII, IFIP AICT 511, pp. 169–183, 2017.
DOI: 10.1007/978-3-319-67208-3_10

The use of anti-forensic tools has increased, requiring greater attention to ensure the integrity of forensic results [3]. Despite the fact that anti-forensic actions constitute a threat to the digital forensic process, this concern is not reflected in the process models found in the literature. Overlooking these risks could compromise an entire investigation. The use of threat modeling during the digital forensic process can help address anti-forensic risks in a structured manner – mitigating the threats where possible or, at least, reducing their impact.

This chapter proposes an anti-forensic threat modeling process that complements the digital forensic processes suggested in the literature. The modeling process enables an expert to assess the risks posed by anti-forensic threats, providing an opportunity to devise strategies for handling the threats during forensic procedures ranging from collecting evidence to data analysis and reporting.

## 2.    Threats to the Digital Forensic Process

A threat is a potential cause of an unwanted incident that, if manifested, may harm the operations and/or resources of an organization. Stoneburner et al. [12] define a threat as the "potential for a threat-source to exercise (accidentally trigger or intentionally exploit) a specific vulnerability."

Anti-forensic actions are considered to be permanent threats to a digital forensic process because they can result in evidence loss that can compromise an investigation. In this case, the threat-source is an attacker or suspect who benefits from the successful execution of an anti-forensic action. These actions can be classified into four types: (i) evidence destruction; (ii) evidence source elimination; (iii) evidence hiding; and (iv) evidence counterfeiting [6].

## 2.1    Evidence Destruction

Evidence destruction seeks to delete or corrupt data, rendering it unusable in the investigative process [4, 6]. This technique may leave some evidence. For example, overwriting a file may destroy the content partially or completely, but the software used to destroy the file can leave traces [6]. Methods for evidence destruction include:

- **Wiping:** Deletes files by filling their clusters with random data.

- **File Attribute Modification:** Changes file attributes or replaces them with random data.

- **User Activity Artifact Destruction:** Removes user activity artifacts such as Internet history, recently accessed files, file downloads and chat logs.

## 2.2 Evidence Hiding

Hiding actions seek to reduce or eliminate the visibility of evidence so that it is not discovered during a forensic examination. In this case, evidence is not destroyed or modified [6]. The presence of data hiding tools on a system is an indicator that a technique has been used. Evidence hiding methods include:

- **Hiding File System Structures:** Hides structures such as the slack space of an NTFS filesystem.

- **Encryption:** Renders file content unreadable.

- **Steganography:** Hides digital data in another file (e.g., image file).

## 2.3 Evidence Source Elimination

The elimination of evidence sources prevents evidence from being created. Unlike the other techniques, there is no need to destroy or hide evidence because the evidence is simply not created. However, the evidence source elimination process itself could produce evidence [6]. Methods for eliminating evidence creation include:

- **Disabling Logs:** Ensures that activity information is not recorded.

- **Use of Portable Applications:** Reduces the amount of evidence because the applications avoid leaving traces in the system.

- **Use of Operating System on Removable Media:** Reduces the amount of evidence because the operating system runs from a CD or thumb drive.

## 2.4 Evidence Counterfeiting

Evidence counterfeiting is the act of creating false evidence or manipulating it to compromise the conclusions of a digital forensic investigation. Falsified evidence may mislead the investigation by pointing to individuals other than the threat agent [6]. Evidence counterfeiting techniques include:

- **File Attribute Modification:** Modifies or tampers with file attributes such as timestamps.

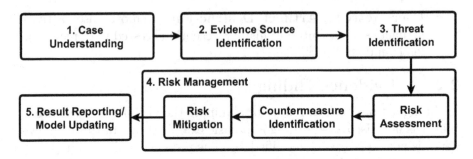

*Figure 1.* Threat modeling in the digital forensic process.

- **Spoofing:** Spoofs IP or MAC addresses.

- **Account Hijacking:** Creates fake evidence by impersonating the account owner.

## 3.        Threat Modeling Applied to Digital Forensics

Threat modeling is a widely discussed subject in the context of secure software development. It allows for the identification, quantification and treatment of risks associated with a system in a structured manner [9].

A number of threat modeling approaches are described in the literature [2, 7, 9, 11]. Each model is created according to the structure and needs of an organization. This prevents direct comparisons of their quality and effectiveness.

In general, threat modeling has three main steps: (i) system understanding; (ii) asset and access point identification; and (iii) threat identification [8]. The first step is to learn about the operation of the system and define usage scenarios in order to reveal the essential characteristics of the system. This is crucial to understanding the attacker objectives. Next, the assets must be identified. These correspond to the attacker's targets, which must be protected. Access points should also be identified because they enable the attacker to reach the targets. The final threat identification step uses the information gathered in the previous steps to evaluate the risks and propose countermeasures.

In this work, threat modeling is applied to the digital forensic process. As shown in Figure 1, threat modeling involves five steps. The first step involves the collection of information about the case or incident. The second step focuses on identifying evidence sources that may be targeted. The third step deals with the identification of anti-forensic actions that may compromise the previously-identified evidence sources. The fourth step manages the risk, which involves risk assessment, countermeasure identification and risk mitigation. The final step reports the results and uses the results to update the model.

## 3.1 Case Understanding

The purpose of this step is to gather information about the investigated case in order to assist decision making in the subsequent steps of the modeling process. This step is essential to the effectiveness of the proposed model. It involves the determination of the ability, motivation and financial profile of the suspect. A questionnaire is recommended to guide the collection of information. The questionnaire would feature questions such as:

- Are there reasons for the use of an anti-forensic method by the suspect?

- What are the suspect's technical skills?

- Does the suspect have the support of technically-skilled professionals?

- Are there reports of anti-forensic actions being employed in similar cases in the past?

With regard to the last question, the proposed model incorporates a catalog that records the occurrences of anti-forensic actions identified in previous investigations or actions reported in external sources such as research papers and security advisories.

## 3.2 Evidence Source Identification

This step attempts to identify the data storage media where evidence related to the investigation can be found. The identification of these resources is critical to identifying anti-forensic threats. Evidence can be obtained from various sources such as user files, operating system event logs, Internet browser history and file metadata. Sources also include devices such as digital cameras, game consoles and GPS devices. The more important the device is to the investigation, the more likely it is to be the target of an anti-forensic action.

## 3.3 Threat Identification

This step analyzes the evidence sources to see if any anti-forensic actions can be applied to compromise them. The classification of anti-forensic methods proposed by Harris [6] is used to categorize anti-forensic threats. As discussed above, anti-forensic methods can be classified as

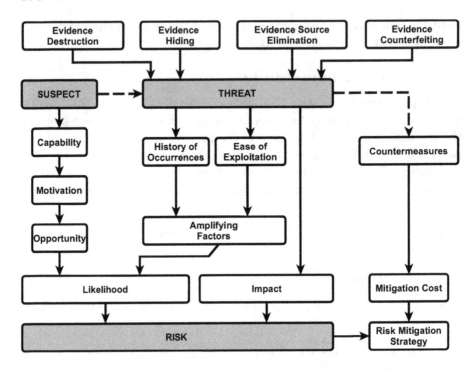

*Figure 2.* Risk management components.

evidence destruction, evidence hiding, evidence source elimination and evidence counterfeiting. For example, in a case where it is crucial to analyze the operating system logs (evidence source), the threat identification step should specify the actions that enable the logs to be modified or destroyed.

The proposed model incorporates a catalog of known anti-forensic threats to support threat identification. This catalog, which records anti-forensic methods, must be updated whenever a new anti-forensic method is reported or encountered.

## 3.4    Risk Management

This step estimates the risks that anti-forensic threats pose to the digital forensic process. It helps determine which risks should and should not be mitigated – dealing with every possible threat is not always feasible due to limited resources, including time. Risk management has three components: (i) risk assessment; (ii) countermeasure identification; and (iii) risk mitigation. Figure 2 summarizes the components involved in the risk management step.

*Table 1.* Capability assessment.

| Score | Capability Assessment |
| --- | --- |
| 5 | The suspect has technical and financial limitations to employ the anti-forensic action. |
| 15 | The suspect has technical or financial limitations to employ the anti-forensic action. |
| 25 | The suspect has extensive technical and/or financial abilities to employ the anti-forensic action. |

*Table 2.* Motivation assessment.

| Score | Motivation |
| --- | --- |
| 5 | The anti-forensic action does little to the criminal act. |
| 15 | The anti-forensic action contributes to the criminal act. |
| 25 | The anti-forensic action is essential to the criminal act. |

Risk assessment is performed by combining the threat likelihood and impact [12]. The threat likelihood is estimated by considering factors related to the suspect (threat agent) and factors related to the anti-forensic action, called amplifying factors. The likelihood is rated as low, medium or high, according to the total score assigned to each factor. The impact is estimated by the digital forensic professional's ability to recover potential evidence when facing an anti-forensic threat. The impact is also rated as low, medium or high. Finally, the risk is determined using a risk matrix that is generated by combining the likelihood and impact ratings.

The suspect's capability, motivation and opportunity are key factors in estimating the threat likelihood [13]. In the proposed model, the capability expresses suspect's technical and financial resources for executing the anti-forensic action. The motivation is related to the benefit of the anti-forensic action to the suspect. For example, the anti-forensic action may camouflage the criminal action; in credit card fraud cases, encryption is often used to hide stolen credit card data. Opportunity refers to the circumstances that favor the success of the anti-forensic action. The suspect may, for example, consider that an action will not be identified during the forensic examination. Tables 1 though 3 list scores that are used to assess a suspect's capability, motivation and opportunity.

*Table 3.*   Opportunity assessment.

| Score | Opportunity |
|-------|-------------|
| 0 | It is part of the routine of a digital forensic expert to treat the anti-forensic action and resources (software and hardware) and trained personnel are available to handle the anti-forensic action. |
| 10 | It is not part of the routine of a digital forensic expert to handle the anti-forensic action, but resources (software and hardware) and trained personnel are available to handle the anti-forensic action. |
| 20 | It is not part of the routine of a digital forensic expert to handle the anti-forensic action and/or resources are not available (software and hardware) or trained personnel are not available to handle the anti-forensic action and/or it is very difficult to handle the anti-forensic action. |

In addition to the suspect's capability, motivation and opportunity, certain other factors can increase the likelihood of an anti-forensic action. These amplifying factors [13] are:

- **History of Occurrences:** Whether or not the anti-forensic action has been used in other situations.

- **Ease of Exploitation:** The amount of resources necessary to execute the anti-forensic action. The existence of tools and documentation of the method and a vulnerability contribute to the ease of exploitation.

*Table 4.*   History of occurrences.

| Score | History of Occurrences |
|-------|------------------------|
| 0 | There is no record of the anti-forensic action in previous reports. |
| 5 | The anti-forensic action is rarely used. |
| 10 | The anti-forensic action is sometimes used. |
| 15 | The anti-forensic action is widely used. |

Tables 4 and 5 are used to determine the score of the amplifying factors. The final likelihood is estimated by adding the scores assigned to each factor (low, medium or high) as shown in Table 6. The score for each factor is set so that the factors related to the suspect (capability, motivation and opportunity) are adequate to yield a high likelihood of an anti-forensic action.

*Table 5.* Ease of exploitation.

| Score | Ease of Exploitation |
|-------|----------------------|
| 5 | Limited resources (no tools) exist for executing the anti-forensic action. |
| 10 | Some resources exist for executing the anti-forensic action. |
| 15 | Many resources (tools and documentation) exist for executing the anti-forensic action. |

*Table 6.* Likelihood of threat by score.

| Final Score | Likelihood |
|-------------|------------|
| Below 35 | Low |
| 35 to 60 | Medium |
| Above 60 | High |

The amplifying factors score increases the likelihood of occurrence, but on its own, it cannot establish a high likelihood for the anti-forensic action. However, in a scenario involving an anti-forensic action that is easily and often used, the amplifying factors score would increase the likelihood of the threat from low to medium and from medium to high.

The computation of the likelihood of a threat is illustrated for missing data hidden in the filesystem slack space. In this case, a medium likelihood is obtained as follows:

$$\begin{aligned}
\text{Likelihood} &= (\text{Capability} + \text{Motivation} + \text{Opportunity}) \\
&\quad + (\text{History} + \text{Ease of Exploitation}) \qquad (1) \\
&= (15 + 15 + 10) + (5 + 10) = 55 \text{ (Medium)}
\end{aligned}$$

Having determined the likelihood of the threat, it is necessary to determine its potential impact. The anti-forensic action could impact the recovery and presentation of evidence with probative value [5]. Table 7 shows the three impact levels, low, medium and high.

After calculating the likelihood and impact, the risk of the anti-forensic threat may be obtained by combining the results according to the risk matrix presented in Table 8.

The level of tolerance to risk is subjective and should be evaluated in the context of other threats. Some low-risk threats can be tolerated in the case of a simultaneous threat of medium risk if the resources to handle the threats are limited. Therefore, the risk level alone does not

*Table 7.*    Impact levels.

| Impact Level | Description |
|---|---|
| Low | Evidence will no longer be recovered. |
| Medium | Usable evidence will no longer be recovered. |
| High | Probative value of evidence is lost and can compromise the prosecution of the suspect. |

*Table 8.*    Risk level matrix adapted from [12].

| | | Likelihood | | |
| | | Low | Medium | High |
|---|---|---|---|---|
| Impact | **Low** | Low | Low | Low |
| | **Medium** | Medium | Medium | Medium |
| | **High** | Medium | High | High |

determine the obligation to take action. This depends on the available countermeasures and the cost of mitigating the risks.

After determining the risk level of a threat, it is necessary to identify the countermeasures that can minimize the impact and prevent evidence loss. The proposed model incorporates a catalog that records the countermeasures to threats. This catalog also specifies the techniques and tools that must be used in each situation. Of course, the catalog must be updated as and when new countermeasures are developed or reported.

*Table 9.*    Cost of implementing countermeasures.

| Cost | Conditions |
|---|---|
| Low | Requires little effort and time to employ. |
| Medium | Requires moderate effort and time to employ. |
| High | Requires a lot of effort and time to employ. |

After identifying the available countermeasures, the risk mitigation step evaluates the specific countermeasures that should be employed. This depends on the risk and the available resources, including the cost of implementing each countermeasure. The cost, which is classified as low, medium or high, is estimated by considering the time and effort involved, as shown in Table 9. Some countermeasures can be very costly and, depending on the risk, may be deemed unnecessary. Naturally, this

*Table 10.* Mitigation strategy matrix.

|  |  | Implementation Cost | | |
|---|---|---|---|---|
|  |  | **Low** | **Medium** | **High** |
| **Risk** | **Low** | Mitigate | Accept | Accept |
|  | **Medium** | Mitigate | Mitigate | Accept |
|  | **High** | Mitigate | Mitigate | Mitigate |

decision would vary according to the resources available to an organization.

As an example, consider a countermeasure for minimizing the risk of missing data that is hidden in the filesystem slack space. In this situation, the countermeasure does not require much effort or time because forensic tools are available for analyzing the slack space. Therefore, the cost of implementing the countermeasure is low.

Table 10 shows the mitigation strategy matrix that assists in deciding whether or not to mitigate the risk. The combination of risk and cost of the countermeasure in the matrix suggests one of two outcomes: (i) mitigate the risk; or (ii) accept the risk. Mitigation involves the application or implementation of the countermeasure. On the other hand, the risk is accepted if the cost of implementing the countermeasure is deemed too high or no countermeasure is available.

In the case of missing data hidden in the filesystem slack space, the best option is to mitigate the risk by applying the available countermeasure. This is because the risk level is considered to be medium and the cost of applying the countermeasure is low. Note, however, that the cost depends on the resources, including time, that are available to the digital forensic professional or the organization.

## 3.5 Result Reporting and Model Updating

In this step, a report is generated with the results of the previous steps. This report can be used to review the assessments made by the digital forensic professional and to register the threats that were not considered initially, but that were discovered during the examination process. Information from the report should also be used to update the model catalogs.

## 4. Applying the Threat Model

This section shows how the proposed threat model can be incorporated in a digital forensic process. The digital investigation process

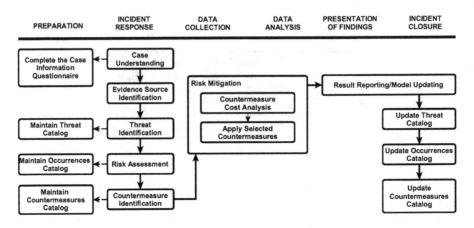

*Figure 3.* Threat model actions in the digital forensic process.

model proposed by Beebe and Clark [1] is employed because it covers the majority of the processes proposed in the literature. The model has six steps: (i) preparation; (ii) incident response; (iii) data collection; (iv) data analysis; (v) presentation of findings; and (vi) incident closure.

The preparation phase involves taking technical and administrative actions prior to an incident to maximize the collection of evidence. The incident response phase defines the strategy to be adopted in the subsequent data collection and analysis phases. The presentation of findings phase covers the presentation of results through the forensic report. Finally, the incident closure phase involves an assessment of the entire process to enhance future investigations.

The threat model actions are integrated in the various phases of the digital forensic process. Figure 3 shows that the first step of the threat model is executed during the incident response phase. However, before this, during the preparation phase, the case information questionnaire is completed and the catalogs are maintained; all this information is used in the incident response phase. The use of the threat model results in a list of countermeasures for treating anti-forensic threats that pose risks to the digital forensic examination. The countermeasures are applied during the data collection and/or data analysis phases, but after a cost analysis is performed. During the presentation of findings phase, the threats are articulated formally, the countermeasures are applied and the results are recorded. During the incident closure phase, the catalogs are updated with information pertaining to the incident. Note that, during the preparation phase, the catalogs are also updated with new threats, countermeasures and lessons learned from other incidents. Updating the

Table 11. Risk assessment.

| Threat | Likelihood | | | | | | Impact | Risk |
|--------|-----|-----|-----|-----|-----|-------|--------|------|
| | Mo | Ca | Op | Hi | Ea | Total | | |
| Full-disk encryption | 25 | 25 | 20 | 10 | 15 | 95 [H] | H | H |
| Steganography | 15 | 25 | 10 | 0 | 10 | 60 [M] | M | M |

H = High, M = Medium, Mo = Motivation, Ca = Capability, Op = Opportunity,
Hi = History of Occurrences, Ea = Ease of Exploitation

catalogs frequently enhances decision making during the threat modeling process.

An investigation of a child exploitation case is used to illustrate the application of the proposed model. In this case, the suspect, who has no criminal history, is known to possess advanced computer skills. This information is determined in the first case understanding step. In the second step – evidence source identification – potential sources of digital evidence are considered, such as the suspect's digital camera, mobile devices, computers and storage media. In the third step, threat identification, potential threats to the evidence are identified based on the information recorded in the threat catalog.

The example considers data hiding threats involving full-disk encryption and steganography. Table 11 shows the computation of the risk associated with each threat.

Table 12. Countermeasures and mitigation strategy.

| Threat | Risk | CM | Cost | Strategy |
|--------|------|-----|------|----------|
| Full-disk encryption | H | CM1 | M | Mitigate |
| Steganography | M | CM2 | H | Accept |

H = High, M = Medium, CM = Countermeasure

Two countermeasures are identified, CM1 and CM2. CM1 involves the acquisition of data while the computer system is running with its volumes mounted. CM2 involves searching for signs of steganography applications and artifacts. The mitigation strategy matrix shown in Table 12 considers the risks and the implementation costs of the countermeasures in order to decide which mitigation strategy should be adopted. In this case, the threat of full-disk encryption should be mitigated while the threat of steganography should be accepted. During the last step, a report is produced that contains the assessments of all the previous steps along with the decisions that were made. The occurrences catalog is updated after the threat is confirmed. Note that in some cases – as in the threat of encryption being used – countermeasures may have to be applied before confirming the existence of the threat.

## 5.     Conclusions

This research advocates the use of threat modeling to handle anti-forensic threats to the digital forensic process. The threat modeling process adapts and incorporates concepts and methods originally proposed for the software development domain. The threat modeling process has five steps: case understanding, evidence source identification, threat identification, risk management, and results reporting and model updating. The model complements the phases commonly used in the digital forensic process while systematically introducing anti-forensic risk management activities in the workflow.

Risk management is introduced in the early stages of the digital forensic process in order to assist forensic professionals in making decisions about investing resources to detect and mitigate risks due to anti-forensic actions. The proposed threat model complements the incident response and digital forensic processes by helping assess the impact and likelihood of anti-forensic threats, the cost of risk mitigation and the selection of techniques and tools that may be used as countermeasures. Consequently, the digital forensic process becomes more robust and less susceptible to the negative consequences of anti-forensic actions.

Future work will focus on the application and evaluation of the threat model in real investigations. Efforts will also be made to develop and disseminate threat and countermeasure catalogs that will enhance risk management in digital forensic investigations.

## References

[1] N. Beebe and J. Clark, A hierarchical, objectives-based framework for the digital investigation process, *Digital Investigation*, vol. 2(2), pp. 147–167, 2005.

[2] S. Burns, Threat Modeling: A Process to Ensure Application Security, InfoSec Reading Room, SANS Institute, Bethesda, Maryland, 2005.

[3] E. Casey (Ed.), *Handbook of Digital Forensics and Investigation*, Elsevier Academic Press, Burlington, Massachusetts, 2010.

[4] R. Chandran and W. Yan, A comprehensive survey of anti-forensics for network security, in *Managing Trust in Cyberspace*, S. Thampi, B. Bhargava and P. Atrey (Eds.), CRC Press, Boca Raton, Florida, pp. 419–447, 2013.

[5] R. de Beer, A. Stander and J. Van Belle, Anti-forensic tool use and their impact on digital forensic investigations: A South African perspective, *Proceedings of the International Conference on Information Security and Digital Forensics*, pp. 7–20, 2014.

[6] R. Harris, Arriving at an anti-forensics consensus: Examining how to define and control the anti-forensics problem, *Digital Investigation*, vol. 3(S), pp. S44–S49, 2006.

[7] J. Meier, A. Mackman, M. Dunner, S. Vasireddy, R. Escamilla and A. Murukan, *Improving Web Application Security: Threats and Countermeasures*, Microsoft, Redmond, Washington, 2003.

[8] S. Myagmar, A. Lee and W. Yurcik, Threat modeling as a basis for security requirements, *Proceedings of the Symposium on Requirements Engineering for Information Security*, 2005.

[9] Open Web Application Security Project, Application Threat Modeling, Columbia, Maryland (`www.owasp.org/index.php/Applica tion_Threat_Modeling`), 2015.

[10] J. Sachowski, *Implementing Digital Forensic Readiness: From Reactive to Proactive Process*, Elsevier, Cambridge, Massachusetts, 2016.

[11] A. Shostack, *Threat Modeling: Designing for Security*, John Wiley and Sons, Indianapolis, Indiana, 2014.

[12] G. Stoneburner, A. Goguen and A. Feringa, Risk Management Guide for Information Technology Systems, Special Publication 800-30, National Institute of Standards and Technology, Gaithersburg, Maryland, 2002.

[13] S. Vidalis and A. Jones, Analyzing threat agents and their attributes, *Proceedings of the Fourth European Conference on Information Warfare and Security*, pp. 369–380, 2005.

# V

# MALWARE FORENSICS

# Chapter 11

# A BEHAVIOR-BASED APPROACH FOR MALWARE DETECTION

Rayan Mosli, Rui Li, Bo Yuan and Yin Pan

**Abstract**    Malware is the fastest growing threat to information technology systems. Although a single absolute solution for defeating malware is improbable, a stacked arsenal against malicious software enhances the ability to maintain security and privacy. This research attempts to reinforce the anti-malware arsenal by studying a behavioral activity common to software – the use of handles. The characteristics of handle usage by benign and malicious software are extracted and exploited in an effort to distinguish between the two classes. An automated malware detection mechanism is presented that utilizes memory forensics, information retrieval and machine learning techniques. Experimentation with a malware dataset yields a malware detection rate of 91.4% with precision and recall of 89.8% and 91.1%, respectively.

**Keywords:** Malware, memory forensics, machine learning, handles

## 1. Introduction

The threat of malware is growing. The proliferation of electronic devices and the ever-increasing dependence on information technology have led to malware becoming an attractive tool for conducting criminal activities. Kaspersky Lab [10] reports that almost 250 million new and unique malware instances were detected during the second quarter of 2016 alone. Although substantial, the report was only able to present the amount of malware detected by anti-viral tools; it was not possible to estimate the total number of malware instances in the wild.

Current malware detection approaches focus on extracting unique signatures from captured malware samples and using the signatures in subsequent sightings of the same malware. This detection strategy is fast and has low false positive rates, but it is easily defeated by modifying

© IFIP International Federation for Information Processing 2017

Published by Springer International Publishing AG 2017. All Rights Reserved

G. Peterson and S. Shenoi (Eds.): Advances in Digital Forensics XIII, IFIP AICT 511, pp. 187–201, 2017.

DOI: 10.1007/978-3-319-67208-3_11

the malware code via encryption or packing [15]. Another strategy is to use a machine learning model to detect malware based on static malware features [24]. Although this malware detection strategy is more robust than signature-based detection, it can still be defeated [15].

The path to improving the detection of unknown malware started with the shift from signature-based detection to behavior-based detection. Behavior-based detection, which focuses on the activities of malware when it infects a system, can be implemented in two ways. The first involves extracting behavioral traits from the malware code statically; these traits are called malware semantics [6]. The second approach involves running malware in a sandbox environment and dynamically monitoring its behavior. System calls constitute an example of malware behavior that can be monitored dynamically and subsequently leveraged in malware detection [17, 21, 26]. Other behavioral features include file activity [22], registry activity [1] and API calls [27]. Behavior-based detection certainly improves the detection of unknown malware, but it is often slow and resource intensive because it requires running the malware in a sandbox. Furthermore, false positives are often a concern due to the misclassification of benign software that exhibits behavior similar to malware.

Several researchers have applied memory forensics to capture artifacts of malicious behavior that reside in memory [9, 23, 35, 36]. Memory forensics involves the analysis of a memory dump to extract evidence of malicious activity. An investigation using memory forensics has two stages: (i) memory acquisition; and (ii) memory analysis. In the memory acquisition stage, a digital forensic professional obtains a memory image via an acquisition tool such as Memoryze or Winpmem. The memory analysis stage attempts to find evidence of malicious activity using a tool such as Volatility or Rekall. This research employs memory forensics to extract information from memory images that is subsequently analyzed to detect malware.

The malware detection approach discussed in this chapter focuses on handles, abstraction pointers that are used to identify and access system objects without knowing their exact locations in memory. A resource such as a file, registry key or mutant requires a handle to be opened before it can be accessed. The handle must be closed when the resource is no longer required. Failing to release a handle may cause a handle leak, which can result in reaching the upper limit on the number of handles permitted by an application [29]. More than 30 resource object types can be identified using handles. Whenever a process requires such a resource, it must open a handle to the resource. The proposed approach uses the number of handles opened by a process to determine if it is potentially malicious. After dynamically obtaining the handle data by running the software in a sandbox, machine learning is used to discriminate between benign and malicious uses of handles and to generalize handle usage behavior to detect previously-unknown malware.

## 2. Related Work

Research in malware detection can be categorized according to how malware analysis is conducted. Static analysis involves dissecting malware code and analyzing the instructions, imported libraries, metadata, and program functionality and structure. However, challenges arise if the malware is packed or encrypted. Nonetheless, this type of analysis offers the advantage of observing all the execution flows of the code regardless of the environment. Dynamic analysis, on the other hand, involves running the malware in a sandbox and monitoring its behavior. Although this analysis is not affected by encryption or packing, the malware behavior might differ according to the runtime environment.

### 2.1  Static Analysis

Santos et al. [32] used opcode sequences to train a support vector machine (SVM) classifier with a normalized polynomial kernel; features were extracted using term frequency to count the occurrences of opcodes in malware code. Saxe and Berlin [33] used byte entropy, portable executable (PE) imports and metadata to train deep neural networks to detect malware with dropout to prevent overfitting. Markel and Bilzor [20] also used metadata as features; they trained and compared different classifiers and found that a decision tree classifier outperformed naive Bayes and logistic regression classifiers on the particular data and feature sets. Nath and Mehtre [24] studied the performance of machine learning classifiers trained on static features; they concluded that using static features in malware detection faces several challenges such as encryption and packing, $k$-ary code and multistage loaders.

### 2.2  Dynamic Analysis

Pirscoveanu et al. [27] used the Cuckoo automated malware analysis tool to execute and monitor malware. They trained a random forest classifier using behavioral features (DNS requests, accessed files, mutexes, registry keys and API calls) and used INetSim to simulate an Internet connection for malware. Berlin et al. [3] used an $n$-gram bag of words with a sliding window to extract malware behavioral features from Windows audit logs and trained a logistic regression classifier on data generated by running and monitoring malware samples using Cuckoo.

Mohaisen et al. [22] developed AMAL, a malware detection and classification system. AMAL comprises two subsystems: (i) AutoMal, which runs malware samples and extracts features related to memory, filesystem, registry and network activity; and (ii) MaLabel, which vectorizes features and trains the classifiers. Park et al. [26] derived behavioral graphs from malware samples by running them in a sandbox and monitoring their system calls using Ether. They then created a graph for each malware family by observing a common sub-graph for malware instances belonging to the same family. In the detection phase, a matching process is used to determine the maliciousness of a file and the malware family to which it belongs (if the file is found to be malicious).

In a previous study, the authors of this chapter [23] examined registry activity, imported DLLs and called APIs to determine their potential as features for discriminating between benignware and malware. The most distinguishing features were determined, following which, machine learning models that utilize the features were trained to classify activity (processes) as benign or malicious. A detection rate of 96% was achieved by training a support vector machine classifier through the optimization of a hinge loss function. The support vector machine classifier was trained on registry activity data generated by software from both classes.

The use of handles in malware detection is relatively uncommon. Galal et al. [11] used handles to categorize different API calls according to their actions; the APIs either created handles, passed handles as arguments, released or closed handles or were handle-independent. Naval et al. [25], however, explicitly ignored handles along with all system call parameters. Park et al. [26] used handles to express dependencies between different kernel objects and their attributes. This chapter discusses the potential of handles to provide insightful views of program behavior based on the resources that are used. These insights are used to train a model to distinguish between benign software and malicious software based on the number of handles used for each resource.

## 3.     Windows Handles and Objects

A handle is a pointer or reference to a Windows object [16]. Objects are managed by the Windows object manager, which is in charge of creating, deleting, protecting and tracking objects [31]. Every EPROCESS structure in memory contains a pointer in its *ObjectTable* member that points to a handle table, which contains pointers to all open objects used by the owning process. Each table has a *TableCode* that specifies the base address of the table and the number of levels in the table. A handle table may contain up to three levels that, in theory, can carry up to $2^{29}$ handles. When more than one level exists in a handle table, only the last level points to objects. Otherwise, each entry in the preceding levels points to other tables.

A table also contains a member that holds the number of handles in the table. When a process calls an API such as `CreateFile`, a pointer to the created file is added to the process handle table and the index of the entry is returned. This index is the handle to the file, which is used by the process whenever the file is accessed. The *HandleCount* member of the handle table is incremented whenever a handle is added. Each entry in the handle table contains a pointer to the object header of the referenced object and a bit mask that expresses the access rights provided to the owning process. A subset of objects allow handles to be inherited by child processes from parent processes; an inherited handle has a unique value, but it points to the same object as the parent handle.

More than 30 object types are referenced by handles; observing the number of handles to each object type provides valuable insights into the resources that are used. The handles used by a process can be enumerated in several ways. One way is to do this programmatically by calling `NtQuerySystemInformation` with `SystemHandleInformation`. Alternatively, the Sysinternals *Handle* command line tool displays handle information about all processes, or about a single process if a process id (PID) is specified by the user [30]. Another approach is to use the Application Verifier tool from Microsoft to track process handle activity from start to finish. The proposed approach uses the Volatility `handles` plugin to extract handle information. This approach walks the handle table for a given process and displays its content. The `handles` plugin provides several options to filter the results: process id, EPROCESS structure offset, object type and object name. The process id was used to obtain the necessary data for processes known to be benign or malicious. Figure 1 shows a portion of a Volatility `handles` plugin output.

## 4. Malware Detection Using Handles

This section discusses malware detection using handles. The steps include collecting data, extracting features and training the machine learning models.

## 4.1 Experimental Setup

The dataset comprised 3,130 malware samples from the VirusShare malware repository [28]. Additionally, 1,157 benign software samples

```
Offset (V)    Pid Handle    Access Type        Details
----------   ----- ------   ---------- ----------  -------
0x891cfea8   3104   0x4         0x3 Directory  KnownDlls
0x8439ff80   3104   0x8    0x100020 File       \Device\HarddiskVolume2\Users\
                                                   victim\AppData\Local\Temp
0x84335368   3104   0xc    0x100020 File       \Device\HarddiskVolume2\Windows\
                                                   winsxs\x86_microsoft.windows
0x8917fbd8   3104   0x10    0x20019 Key        MACHINE\SYSTEM\CONTROLSET001\
                                                   CONTROL\NLS\SORTING\VERSIONS
0x85e0b778   3104   0x14   0x1f0001 ALPC Port
0x95cf1db8   3104   0x18        0x1 Key        \MACHINE|SYSTEM|CONTROLSET001\
                                                   CONTROL\SESSION MANAGER
```

*Figure 1.*  Output of the Volatility **handles** plugin.

were collected from various locations such as the Windows System32 directory and from software websites such as FileHippo.

The environment used for the analysis comprised a Ubuntu virtual machine that hosted four Windows 7 SP1 virtual machines using VirtualBox. The Ubuntu virtual machine was hosted on a Windows 10 machine using VMWare. Each Windows machine was set to have 1 GB RAM and one core.

Cuckoo [8] was used to automate the analysis process on the Ubuntu machine. The four Windows virtual machines were run concurrently, each with an instance of benign or malicious software. During the analysis task, a memory dump was produced of each Windows virtual machine along with a report with content and behavioral information about the sample. Furthermore, VirusTotal was used to scan each sample to ensure that the sample was labeled correctly as benign or malicious, and then determine the malware family to which it belonged. The majority of the samples were Trojans, but worms, viruses, backdoors and adware were also encountered. A portion of the dataset was classified as being malware, but no consensus was reached by VirusTotal about the families to which all the samples belonged. These samples were included in the malware dataset, but were labeled as unclassified instead of as a malware family.

INetSim [14] was used to simulate an Internet connection to increase the chances of the malware behaving correctly. However, due to their anti-virtual-machine functionality, 668 malware samples terminated instantly after being launched; this left 2,462 malware samples to be used in the experiments. Although discarding malware with anti-virtual-machine functionality from the dataset omits such behavior from the classifiers, the increasing popularity of virtualization in the information technology sector is making malware with anti-virtual-machine functionality less common [18].

Handle data was extracted from the memory dumps of machines with benignware or malware using Volatility. Every EPROCESS structure in memory contains a pointer to a handle table specific to the owning process. Volatility outputs the handle information by walking the handle table of a specified process or of all processes if no process id was specified when running the `handles` plugin [16]. The process ids used to filter the results were provided by Cuckoo; the main process id in addition to the process ids of spawned processes were included in the Cuckoo report. The Volatility `handles` plugin outputs a table with six columns: (i) virtual offset of the handle in memory; (ii) process id of the owning process; (iii) handle offset in the process handle table; (iv) access granted to each object with a handle; (v) type of object pointed to by the handle; and (vi) details about the object, if available. All the Volatility results were stored in text files, where each text file contained information about the handles used by a single process.

## 4.2    Vectorizing the Handle Data

The term frequency-inverse document frequency (TF-IDF) [19] was used to extract measurable features from the Volatility `handles` output; the extraction and model training was implemented using scikit-learn [5]. A vocabulary was created comprising the handle types to be extracted from the handle text files. A list of all the possible terms in the vocabulary was obtained from Schuster [34]. Subsequently, the term frequency-inverse document frequency, which counts the occurrence of each vocabulary term in each text file, and then weights the importance of the term according to the number of times the term occurs across all the documents, was computed for all the handles data. This yielded a $3,619 \times 31$ matrix, each row representing a sample and each column representing a term. A total of 58,652 non-zero entries were present in the matrix, making the matrix 52.28% dense. To avoid division by zero, the `smooth_idf` option was set to true; this option adds one document to the corpus with every term in the vocabulary appearing once. Zero entries appearing in the matrix were largely the result of ten terms that did not appear in any document. These terms were discarded before training the models, resulting in a $3,619 \times 21$ matrix with a density of 77.17%.

## 4.3    Model Training

For evaluation purposes, the dataset was divided into two subsets, one for training and one for testing. A total of 724 samples were used for testing (20% of the dataset) and 2,895 samples were used for training.

A stratified split was used to generate the test set, which resulted in a balanced representation of both classes.

Three machine learning models were compared: (i) $k$-nearest neighbor (KNN) [2]; (ii) support vector machine (SVM) [7]; and (iii) random forest [12]. The $k$-nearest neighbor approach classifies each data point according to its neighbors; a number of options must be considered when training this classifier, including the number of neighbors to be evaluated and the method for assigning weights to the neighbors. The support vector machine is a discriminative model that searches for a hyperplane with maximum separation between the data points from different classes; the hyperplane is then used to classify new data points according to the side of the hyperplane where they fall. Random forest is an ensemble approach that trains multiple decision trees and outputs a decision according to the predictions of all the trees.

Accuracy, precision and recall were used as evaluation metrics for the three machine learning models. The exhaustive grid search approach was employed to determine the parameter values that produced the highest detection rates for the models. To perform the exhaustive grid search, a parameter space was created for each model that was populated with the values to be searched. Table 1 lists the parameter values tested for each machine learning model.

The $k$-nearest neighbor approach achieved the highest accuracy using three neighbors, the ball tree algorithm to find neighbors and distances as weights. In the case of the SVM, a radial basis function (RBF) kernel gave the highest accuracy; the numbers of support vectors used were 527 for the benign class and 625 for the malicious class. The random forest approach performed best with 25 decision trees. After determining the best parameter values for each model, the precision and recall were calculated to measure the model performance with regard to false positives and false negatives. Table 2 summarizes the performance of the three machine learning models.

Table 3 shows the confusion matrix for the random forest classifier with the predicted and true labels.

## 5.    Results and Analysis

Observations of the use of handles by benign and malicious software can reveal their potential for helping discriminate between the two classes. For example, section handles are used differently by benignware and malware. A section is a region of memory that can be shared by multiple processes. It is used by the Windows loader when loading a module into process address space [4]. A section is also used for inter-

*Table 1.* Exhaustive grid search parameter space.

| Model | Parameter | Value |
|---|---|---|
| KNN | Algorithm for finding neighbors | Ball tree<br>KDtree<br>Brute force |
| | Number of neighbors | 3<br>4<br>5<br>6<br>7 |
| | Weights of neighbors | Uniform<br>Distance |
| SVM | Penalty term | 1<br>0.75<br>0.50<br>0.25 |
| | Kernel type | Linear<br>Polynomial<br>RBF<br>Sigmoid |
| | Degree of polynomial | 1<br>2 |
| Random Forest | Max feature split algorithm | Auto<br>Square root<br>Logarithmic<br>None |
| | Number of decision trees | 5<br>10<br>15<br>20<br>25 |

*Table 2.* Performance of the KNN, SVM and random forest models.

| Learning Model | Accuracy | Precision | Recall |
|---|---|---|---|
| KNN | 0.910 | 0.892 | 0.899 |
| SVM | 0.911 | 0.899 | 0.920 |
| Random Forest | 0.914 | 0.898 | 0.911 |

*Table 3.*   Confusion matrix for the random forest classifier.

|         |     | Predicted | |
|---------|-----|-----------|--------|
|         |     | 0         | 1      |
| True    | 0   | 29.5%     | 3.1%   |
|         | 1   | 5.3%      | 61.8%  |

process communication (IPC), where a memory-mapped file is shared by two or more processes. When used with malicious intent, sections provide a means for injecting code into the address spaces of other processes. The different usage of sections by benign and malicious software explains the difference in the numbers of handles used by the two types of software. In the experiments, the average number of section objects used by benignware was 8.48 whereas the average number for malware was 27.12. Therefore, when training the random forest classifier, section features were at the top of the decision trees; this affected the largest fraction of sample predictions.

The number of process handles used by software is another indicator of maliciousness. A process handle is often obtained when a new process is created using the **CreateProcess** function. Furthermore, a handle to a process can also be retrieved by passing a process id to the **OpenProcess** function. Malware uses process handles to gain access to other victim processes with the goal of injecting, hollowing, terminating or hooking [13]. In the experiments, the average number of process handles used by legitimate software was 0.81 whereas the average number used by malware was 2.43. Consequently, process handles became the second most prominent term when training the random forest classifier.

Mutants are objects that can also help distinguish between benignware and malware. Mutants are used for mutual exclusions; specifically, to control access to shared system resources. A mutant handle is acquired by calling the function **OpenMutex** and is released by calling the function **ReleaseMutex**. Mutants are often used by legitimate software to avoid conflicts between multiple threads. However, malware samples use them to prevent the re-infection of already-infected resources, which could result in undesirable results. In the experiments, the average number of mutant objects used by benignware was 11.35 whereas the average number used by malware was 21.84. Table 4 shows the use of handles by benignware and malware.

To determine the effects of an imbalanced dataset (benignware: 1,157 and malware: 2,462) on the machine learning model, the experiments

Table 4. Use of handles by benignware and malware.

| Object Type | Benignware | | Malware | |
|---|---|---|---|---|
| | Average | Variance | Average | Variance |
| Desktop | 1.92 | 3.73 | 1.85 | 0.54 |
| Device | 22.8 | 710.38 | 25.34 | 148.42 |
| Directory | 2.21 | 0.25 | 2.35 | 0.25 |
| Event | 70.58 | 7468.62 | 94.92 | 2516.89 |
| File | 22.80 | 710.44 | 25.34 | 148.42 |
| IOCompletion | 1.06 | 1.36 | 2.31 | 0.93 |
| Job | 0.01 | 0.01 | 0.38 | 0.23 |
| Key | 32.79 | 873.35 | 49.66 | 277.51 |
| KeyedEvent | 0.56 | 0.26 | 0.93 | 0.06 |
| Mutant | 11.35 | 227.5 | 21.84 | 97.71 |
| Port | 7.51 | 57.27 | 12.76 | 25.36 |
| Process | 0.81 | 61.78 | 2.43 | 16.71 |
| Section | 8.48 | 70.13 | 27.12 | 156.99 |
| Semaphore | 10.91 | 173.83 | 12.59 | 43.01 |
| Thread | 14.38 | 668.91 | 20.61 | 98.75 |
| Timer | 2.01 | 4.30 | 2.85 | 0.75 |
| Token | 0.45 | 6.63 | 0.09 | 0.94 |
| WindowStation | 2.01 | 0.01 | 2.01 | 0.01 |
| WmiGuid | 0.18 | 0.14 | 0.02 | 0.02 |

were performed multiple times with a balanced dataset. This was accomplished by randomly discarding malware samples to reduce the number to 1,157. During each run, a different subset of malware samples was discarded. The performance of the classifiers trained on the balanced datasets was only slightly lower than the classifiers trained on the original dataset. This leads to the conclusion that significant behavior from the malware dataset can be captured using a smaller dataset.

# 6.    Conclusions

This research has demonstrated that handles, which capture the behavioral activity of software, can be used to detect malware. Specifically, malware uses resources differently from benignware and this fact can be used to train classifiers to categorize processes as malicious or benign. In the experiments, Cuckoo was used to automate the execution and monitoring of malware and benignware and to dump memory images. Volatility was used to extract the handle information from the memory dumps, which was then analyzed to determine the different uses of handles by the two classes of software. Three machine learning models,

$k$-nearest neighbor, support vector machine and random forest, were used to train the classifiers. Random forest outperformed the $k$-nearest neighbor and support vector machine models with a detection rate of 91.4%, precision of 89.8% and recall of 91.1%.

The experimental results demonstrate the efficacy of using handles to detect malware. However, the approach is reactive in that it is applied after the system has been infected. Nevertheless, one use case for the approach is as a second layer of defense if signature-based detection fails. The second use case is in forensic investigations, where malware detection and analysis are routinely performed. In fact, the approach can be applied to alleviate the cumbersome task of detecting malware in a large number of seized machines.

This research has focused on the types of objects referenced in handle tables. Information provided in the access rights and details columns of the Volatility `handles` plugin output was not considered. The details column provides in-depth information about objects, such as the registry key accessed by the process and the file path to which a handle is opened. File objects, in particular, may not be actual files – they may be devices treated as files due to similar read and write operations. Such granular details could significantly improve the performance of the classifiers. This exploration is a topic of future research.

Another topic for future research is the identification of other behavioral artifacts that may be used to distinguish malware from benignware. Zaki and Humphrey [37], who studied kernel-level artifacts left by rootkits, discovered that callbacks are more suspicious than other artifacts such as SSDT hooks. Future research will investigate the use of callbacks and other artifacts in developing classifiers with improved malware detection rates, precision and recall.

# References

[1] M. Aghaeikheirabady, S. Farshchi and H. Shirazi, A new approach to malware detection by comparative analysis of data structures in a memory image, *Proceedings of the First International Congress on Technology, Communication and Knowledge*, 2014.

[2] N. Altman, An introduction to kernel and nearest-neighbor nonparametric regression, *The American Statistician*, vol. 46(3), pp. 175–185, 1992.

[3] K. Berlin, D. Slater and J. Saxe, Malicious behavior detection using Windows audit logs, *Proceedings of the Eighth ACM Workshop on Artificial Intelligence and Security*, pp. 35–44, 2015.

[4] B. Blunden, *The Rootkit Arsenal: Escape and Evasion in the Dark Corners of the System*, Jones and Bartlett Learning, Burlington, Massachusetts, 2013.

[5] L. Buitinck, G. Louppe, M. Blondel, F. Pedregosa, A. Mueller, O. Grisel, V. Niculae, P. Prettenhofer, A. Gramfort, J. Grobler, R. Layton, J. VanderPlas, A. Joly, B. Holt and G. Varoquaux, API design for machine learning software: Experiences from the scikit-learn Project, *Proceedings of the European Conference on Machine Learning and Principles and Practice of Knowledge Discovery in Databases Workshop: Languages for Data Mining and Machine Learning*, pp. 108–122, 2013.

[6] M. Christodorescu, S. Jha, S. Seshia, D. Song and R. Bryant, Semantics-aware malware detection, *Proceedings of the IEEE Symposium on Security and Privacy*, pp. 32–46, 2005.

[7] C. Cortes and V. Vapnik, Support-vector networks, *Machine Learning*, vol. 20(3), pp. 273–297, 1995.

[8] Cuckoo Foundation, Cuckoo Sandbox (www.cuckoosandbox.org), 2016.

[9] B. Dolan-Gavitt, A. Srivastava, P. Traynor and J. Giffin, Robust signatures for kernel data structures, *Proceedings of the Sixteenth ACM Conference on Computer and Communications Security*, pp. 566–577, 2009.

[10] D. Emm, R. Unuchek, M. Garnaeva, A. Ivanov, D. Makrushin and F. Sinitsyn, IT Threat Evolution in Q2 2016, Kaspersky Lab, Moscow, Russia, 2016.

[11] H. Galal, Y. Mahdy and M. Atiea, Behavior-based features model for malware detection, *Journal of Computer Virology and Hacking Techniques*, vol. 12(2), pp. 59–67, 2016.

[12] T. Ho, The random subspace method for constructing decision forests, *IEEE Transactions on Pattern Analysis and Machine Intelligence*, vol. 20(8), pp. 832–844, 1998.

[13] G. Hoglund and J. Butler, *Rootkits: Subverting the Windows Kernel*, Pearson Education, Upper Saddle River, New Jersey, 2006.

[14] T. Hungenberg and M. Eckert, INetSim: Internet Services Simulation Suite (www.inetsim.org), 2007.

[15] B. Klein and R. Peters, Defeating machine learning – What your security vendor is not telling you, presented at *Black Hat USA*, 2015.

[16] M. Ligh, A. Case, J. Levy and A. Walters, *The Art of Memory Forensics: Detecting Malware and Threats in Windows, Linux and Mac Memory*, John Wiley and Sons, Indianapolis, Indiana, 2014.

[17] Y. Lin, Y. Lai, C. Lu, P. Hsu and C. Lee, Three-phase behavior-based detection and classification of known and unknown malware, *Security and Communication Networks*, vol. 8(11), pp. 2004–2015, 2015.

[18] J. Luttgens, M. Pepe and K. Mandia, *Incident Response and Computer Forensics*, McGraw Hill Education, New York, 2014.

[19] C. Manning, P. Raghavan and H. Schutze, *An Introduction to Information Retrieval*, Cambridge University Press, Cambridge, United Kingdom, 2008.

[20] Z. Markel and M. Bilzor, Building a machine learning classifier for malware detection, *Proceedings of the Second Workshop on Anti-Malware Testing Research*, 2014.

[21] M. Masud, S. Sahib, M. Abdollah, S. Selamat and R. Yusof, Analysis of features selection and machine learning classifier in Android malware detection, *Proceedings of the International Conference on Information Science and Applications*, 2014.

[22] A. Mohaisen, O. Alrawi and M. Mohaisen, AMAL: High-fidelity, behavior-based automated malware analysis and classification, *Computers and Security*, vol. 52, pp. 251–266, 2015.

[23] R. Mosli, R. Li, B. Yuan and Y. Pan, Automated malware detection using artifacts in forensic memory images, *Proceedings of the IEEE Symposium on Technologies for Homeland Security*, 2016.

[24] H. Nath and B. Mehtre, Static malware analysis using machine learning methods, *Proceedings of the Second International Conference on Recent Trends in Computer Networks and Distributed Systems Security*, pp. 440–450, 2014.

[25] S. Naval, V. Laxmi, M. Rajarajan, M. Gaur and M. Conti, Employing program semantics for malware detection, *IEEE Transactions on Information Forensics and Security*, vol. 10(12), pp. 2591–2604, 2015.

[26] Y. Park, D. Reeves and M. Stamp, Deriving common malware behavior through graph clustering, *Computers and Security*, vol. 39(B), pp. 419–430, 2013.

[27] R. Pirscoveanu, S. Hansen, T. Larsen, M. Stevanovic, J. Pedersen and A. Czech, Analysis of malware behavior: Type classification using machine learning, *Proceedings of the International Conference on Cyber Situational Awareness, Data Analytics and Assessment,* 2015.

[28] J. Roberts, VirusShare Project (`virusshare.com`), 2017.

[29] M. Russinovich, Pushing the limits of Windows: Handles, *Mark's Blog* (`blogs.technet.microsoft.com/markrussinovich/2009/09/29/pushing-the-limits-of-windows-handles`), September 29, 2009.

[30] M. Russinovich, Sysinternals Suite, Microsoft TechNet, Redmond, Washington (`technet.microsoft.com/en-us/sysinternals/bb842062.aspx`), 2017.

[31] M. Russinovich, D. Solomon and A. Ionescu, *Windows Internals,* Microsoft Press, Redmond, Washington, 2012.

[32] I. Santos, F. Brezo, X. Ugarte-Pedrero and P. Bringas, Opcode sequences as representation of executables for data-mining-based unknown malware detection, *Information Sciences,* vol. 231, pp. 64–82, 2013.

[33] J. Saxe and K. Berlin, Deep neural network based malware detection using two dimensional binary program features, *Proceedings of the Tenth International Conference on Malicious and Unwanted Software,* pp. 11–20, 2015.

[34] A. Schuster, Enumerate Object Types, *Computer Forensic Blog* (`computer.forensikblog.de/en/2009/04/enumerate-object-types.html`), April 7, 2009.

[35] J. Stuttgen and M. Cohen, Anti-forensic resilient memory acquisition, *Digital Investigation,* vol. 10(S), pp. S105–S115, 2013.

[36] T. Teller and A. Hayon, Enhancing automated malware analysis machines with memory analysis, presented at *Black Hat USA,* 2014.

[37] A. Zaki and B. Humphrey, Unveiling the kernel: Rootkit discovery using selective automated kernel memory differencing, presented at the *Virus Bulletin Conference,* 2014.

Chapter 12

# CATEGORIZING MOBILE DEVICE MALWARE BASED ON SYSTEM SIDE-EFFECTS

Zachary Grimmett, Jason Staggs and Sujeet Shenoi

**Abstract**    Malware targeting mobile devices is an ever increasing threat. The most insidious type of malware resides entirely in volatile memory and does not leave a trail of persistent artifacts. Such malware requires novel detection and capture methods in order to be reliably identified, analyzed and mitigated. This chapter proposes malware categorization and detection techniques based on measurable system side-effects observed in an exploited mobile device. Using the Stagefright family of exploits as a case study, common system side-effects produced as a result of attempted exploitation are identified. These system side-effects are leveraged to trigger volatile memory (i.e., RAM) collection by memory acquisition tools (e.g., LiME) to enable analysis of the malware.

**Keywords:** Mobile malware, memory-resident, categorization, system side-effects

## 1.    Introduction

Critical vulnerabilities that affect large families of mobile devices make it imperative to develop new techniques for securing these devices against increasingly sophisticated attacks as well as for conducting forensic investigations. Investigating attacks on mobile devices requires the capture and analysis of evidence pertaining to attacks. However, the most insidious malware resides entirely in memory and does not create persistent artifacts. Memory-resident malware that removes itself from a mobile device after performing its malicious activities can evade capture and analysis by malware investigators, even after its presence has been detected by a user. Live memory acquisition is the only way to recover memory-resident malware from exploited devices.

© IFIP International Federation for Information Processing 2017

Published by Springer International Publishing AG 2017. All Rights Reserved

G. Peterson and S. Shenoi (Eds.): Advances in Digital Forensics XIII, IFIP AICT 511, pp. 203–219, 2017.

DOI: 10.1007/978-3-319-67208-3_12

This chapter introduces a taxonomy for categorizing mobile device malware based on observable system side-effects in an effort to stimulate the development of new methods for memory-resident malware detection, capture and analysis. The Stagefright family of vulnerabilities and exploits is used as a case study to assess the system side-effects that occur as a result of exploitation attempts of the `libstagefright` Android library. The chapter also describes how system side-effects produced by this malware can be used to trigger volatile memory captures for subsequent malware analysis efforts.

## 2.    Live Memory Analysis of Mobile Devices

Live memory analysis refers to the capture and analysis of data stored in the volatile memory of a computer system or device. Numerous situations exist where important information only resides in volatile memory. These circumstances demand the application of techniques that can reliably and safely extract the information for forensic analysis.

Note that mobile devices have many more variations than computer workstations in their design and architecture. Beyond the obvious differences in design requirements due to their size and power constraints, mobile devices perform other unique tasks that require special consideration. Radio communications are highly sensitive to timing and poorly suited to sharing processing time with user applications. Moreover, user applications are equally ill-suited to execute on a real-time operating system that could enable reliable radio communications. As a result, most mobile devices contain two processors – an applications processor that handles user applications and a baseband processor that independently handles cellular communications (e.g., GSM, UMTS and LTE).

## 2.1    Information in Volatile Memory

The physical memory of a device essentially contains a snapshot of the recently-used information on the device. Recent web searches, text messages and session keys can all be recovered with access to physical memory [19]. This is why many devices now deny access to physical memory and restrict applications to their own allocated memory. Legitimate uses for physical memory dumps, such as debugging application crashes, are arbitrated by the operating system.

While a mobile device contains many types of evidence of interest in digital forensic investigations, some artifacts or data are unrecoverable if they are lost from volatile memory. These artifacts include cryptographic keys for unlocking encrypted containers and private messages sent via secure messaging applications. Digital forensic investigators

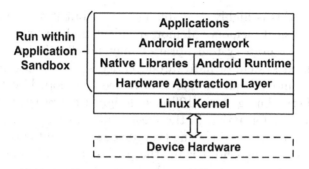

*Figure 1.* Android security architecture [1].

face a challenging trade-off – leaving a device powered on increases the risk of deleted data being overwritten while turning the device off risks losing evidence stored in volatile memory [13].

Another important use case for live memory analysis is malware detection and analysis. There are numerous examples of seemingly benign applications having malicious add-ons, including compromised applications that were pre-installed on some devices (e.g., Huawei G510 and Lenovo S860 smartphones) [9]. These applications do not require live memory analysis to detect and analyze. However, many of them act as Trojans that download and execute malicious code that may only exist in volatile memory. Understanding the threats posed by sophisticated mobile device malware requires deep analysis of the targeted hardware and operating system [7].

## 2.2 Memory Capture Techniques

Mobile devices have been developed with connectivity as the primary goal and have benefited from the lessons learned about the importance of securing connected devices. Mobile operating systems restrict user privileges to protect the devices and the network carriers.

Android uses long-standing Unix security concepts to provide application security – an application is limited to a "sandbox" and is assigned a unique UID that is used to apply and enforce user permissions. This ensures that only the Linux kernel has access to the process memory of more than one application.

Figure 1 presents the Android security architecture. The architecture limits software access to physical memory, a security improvement that prevents malicious applications from compromising other applications. For example, this prevents an infected social media application from having unfettered access to the memory of a banking application that may contain user account information and credentials. Under most circumstances, this is highly desirable behavior, but it also limits forensic access to physical memory. Memory-resident malware running in other applications or even system libraries may be effectively impossible to detect without system or hardware-level access to physical memory.

Several memory acquisition tools have been developed by digital forensic researchers. Thing et al. [19] have designed the `memgrab` tool, which parses process information in the filesystem (`/proc`) in order to locate process memory. Process tracing (via `ptrace`) is used to attach to a running process and suspend it while the process memory is being copied.

Sylve et al. [18] have developed the `Linux Memory Extractor` (LiME), a loadable kernel module that locates system memory and copies it to local storage or exfiltrates the memory over a TCP/IP network connection. LiME relies on parsing the kernel resource structure `iomem_resource` to identify physical memory locations in system RAM.

Stuttgen and Cohen [16] have attempted to create an even more general solution for creating forensically-sound images of live memory. Their solution leverages a minimal kernel module that can use other kernel modules to capture live memory. Another memory acquisition tool is TrustDump, which uses the ARM TrustZone to capture device memory in a manner that is completely transparent to the operating system [17].

## 3.  Android Exploitation Techniques

Mobile devices have access to sensitive information (e.g., bank accounts, saved passwords and medical data), which has motivated the development and use of mobile device malware by criminals and hackers. Mobile operating systems prioritize reliability and availability so much that system processes restart as quickly as possible after a crash. The information saved when a process crashes is useful for debugging, but it is often insufficient to identify exploits. This section introduces exploitation techniques that impact how malware interacts with and resides in memory.

No single software solution can be expected to combat all potential malware on a mobile device. However, it is possible to design solutions that capture specific types of malware. Understanding how security mechanisms are defeated by malware is integral to a long-term effort to improve device security. In the short term, it enables researchers to discover and defend against current exploitation efforts. This short-term view of security is focused on finding and fixing existing vulnerabilities and benefits directly from efforts to capture previously-unidentified malware for analysis.

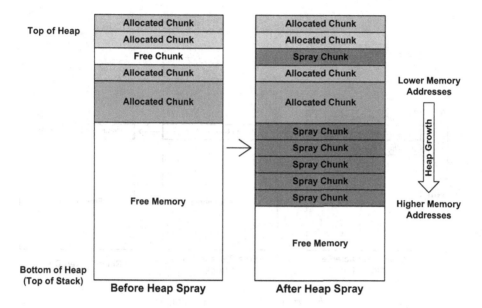

*Figure 2.* Heap spray example.

## 3.1    Heap Exploitation

Heap memory, or dynamic memory, enables a program to access and use memory as needed instead of requiring the program to request all the memory it will need at startup. Memory is allocated to a program in discrete chunks and is deallocated (freed) when it is no longer necessary. An attacker can manipulate the heap by performing specific allocations and deallocations that enable a vulnerability to be exploited. Heap exploitation leverages the control of heap memory to subvert a system. A program that does not properly verify or validate the use of dynamic memory is often vulnerable to multiple types of attacks.

Two common heap exploitation (or manipulation) techniques are: (i) heap spraying: and (ii) heap grooming:

- **Heap Spraying:** A heap spray involves a (generally large) number of allocations to place a designated chunk of memory into a specific location for later use (Figure 2). This leverages the tendency of a system to reuse and reorganize chunks in dynamic memory to avoid memory fragmentation. The specific location targeted by a heap spray is generally selected to be as reliable as possible while requiring no knowledge of the current dynamic memory layout.

  Programs routinely use dynamic memory to store user-controlled data – this only becomes a problem when the data is misused by

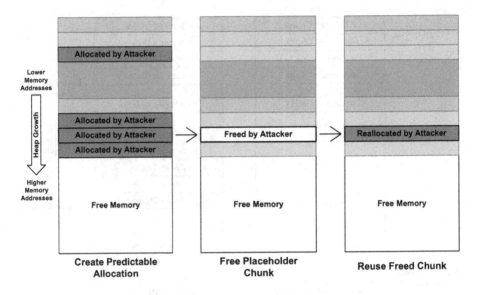

*Figure 3.* Heap groom example.

an exploit. A heap spray relies on an allocation of more memory than a system is expected to use. Such an allocation is noticeable because it involves an unusually large amount of memory. Several techniques have been developed to identify and prevent the anomalous use of dynamic memory [5, 11].

- Heap Grooming: Heap grooming uses allocations and deallocations to control an unspecified portion of the heap (Figure 3). When a program deallocates a chunk of memory and subsequently attempts to allocate another chunk of the same size, it is most efficient for the operating system to allocate the same piece of memory to the program. This behavior limits the impact of memory fragmentation without performing costly defragmentation techniques. Heap grooming takes advantage of the optimization by allocating a sequence of chunks and freeing a chunk in the middle of the sequence [15].

  Heap grooming uses far less memory than heap spraying and may display the behavior of a normal target program; this is because dynamic memory is intended to be allocated and deallocated as needed. Thus, heap grooming is more difficult to detect and prevent than heap spraying.

Heap manipulation techniques are not perfectly reliable. Systems with unexpected memory usage limit the probability of a heap spray or a heap

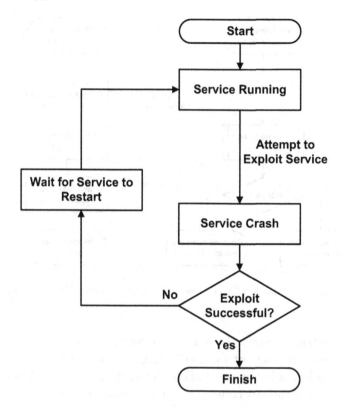

*Figure 4.* Brute-force execution.

groom succeeding. A heap exploit can be designed to maximize the chances of successful exploitation, but an alternative is to crash or reset a target process before attempting an exploit. In the case of a system that performs garbage collection after a process exits (or crashes), an attacker can assume that the process is in its initialized state and has predictable memory usage after it is restarted. Intentionally crashing a target process also serves another purpose – for attacks that require per-device or per-model adaptation (e.g., Stagefright), the presence of a vulnerability can be confirmed before any effort is made to develop an exploit for a particular model of device.

## 3.2    Defeating ASL Randomization

This section discusses techniques for defeating address space layout (ASL) randomization.

**Brute-Force Execution.** A brute-force execution attacks the same vulnerability repeatedly until the desired result occurs (Figure 4). The

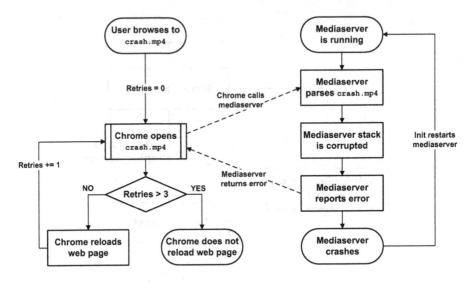

*Figure 5.* Google Chrome execution while parsing a crash vector.

initial Stagefright exploit (discussed below) repeatedly tries the exploit until address space layout randomization is defeated [6]. When the random offset address is not guessed correctly, the service crashes instead of executing the malicious code. Not all examples of brute-force execution either succeed or crash; it is possible for a program to merely return an error. The only requirement for brute-force execution is that the target returns to a vulnerable state after a failed exploit attempt.

The ability to mitigate brute-force exploitation attempts varies according to the system under attack. If reliability and availability are high priorities, rejecting or refusing to process information after a number of failed attempts may not be acceptable. It is worth noting that this mitigation is built into many applications to avoid getting stuck in an infinite loop. For example, as shown in Figure 5, Google Chrome stops the loading of a web page after four failed attempts. Unfortunately, a mitigation that is based on counting the number of failures could be subverted if an attacker succeeds before the maximum number of failures is exceeded.

**Information Leaking.** A memory leak involves the unintentional disclosure of information to an attacker. If the leaked information is sensitive, the leak itself may be the goal of an exploit. When memory address registers (e.g., stack pointer, heap pointer and program counter) are leaked, an attacker may gain useful information for exploiting the system [14]. Non-register addresses can enable an attacker to identify the locations in memory where a system library has been loaded. Address space layout randomization can be subverted if an attacker leaks information and determines where the targeted libraries are loaded in memory.

Exploit developers often look for arbitrary read and write operations in vulnerable software to enable the development of reliable malware. These operations, also called primitives, are generic and useful; they are named after the read/write primitives that form the foundation of programming languages. The heap manipulation techniques discussed above can be used to leak information from memory in addition to enabling remote code execution. Limiting how a program handles sensitive information can mitigate memory leaks.

## 4.     Stagefright Exploits

Stagefright is a family of exploits that target the `libstagefright` Android media-processing library [20]. Note that `libstagefright` refers to the media processing library and Stagefright refers to the family of vulnerabilities.

By exploiting integer overflow and memory corruption (heap overflow) vulnerabilities, a Stagefright exploit can be sent to an Android device and executed without the user's knowledge. The exploit triggers during preprocessing performed by `libstagefright` whenever a multimedia file is accessed, enabling it to be transmitted via text message, e-mail, web browsing or even when attempting to load a thumbnail of a malicious image saved on a device. The disclosure of the Stagefright exploits in conjunction with revelations that very few Android devices were receiving timely security patches resulted in new security update policies being released by Google [10] and Samsung [12]. This also prompted vulnerability researchers to focus on Android libraries, resulting in the discovery of additional vulnerabilities.

Multiple researchers have released proof-of-concept exploits for `libstagefright`. These exploits were generally released only after the exploited vulnerabilities were patched on applicable Android devices. The exploits frequently built on previous exploits by adding new capabilities or finding ways around the mitigation mechanisms. An examination of one of these exploits can reveal the nature of the vulnerability, but examining all of them can reveal how exploits evolve over time to combat mitigation efforts. A disclosed exploit can be used to demonstrate that the proposed modifications are successful at capturing malicious activity; however, a proposed solution should be resilient to changes in malware over time.

## 4.1    Zimperium zLabs

Drake [6] focused on the vulnerabilities in `libstagefright` because it is a privileged process (privileges inherited as a `mediaservice` process) that parses untrusted data. Additionally, `mediaserver` is started by the Android `init` process and is restarted whenever it crashes.

Drake chose to focus exclusively on MPEG4 file processing for fuzzing efforts; MPEG4 files are constructed in "chunks" that can be embedded inside each other. Parsing chunk code is complicated by the recursive MPEG4 file format and requires memory interactions that create vulnerabilities when unexpected sequences of chunks occur. An exploit developed for the CVE-2015-1538 vulnerability demonstrated that large Android frameworks incorporate assumptions that present significant risks to devices. The changes to the Android update policies discussed above occurred in response to this exploit, but before the details of the exploit were released to the public.

The initial Stagefright vulnerabilities presented by Drake [6] demonstrated that exploitation is possible through any vector that triggers media processing. This includes multimedia messages (MMS) that are automatically processed on receipt. Drake confirmed that the exploitation occurs before an alert is generated and displayed to a user. Effectively, an attacker could send a malicious multimedia message to a user and exploit the phone without any user interaction or notification.

The vulnerabilities were disclosed to Google before their public release, but most devices had not yet received the security updates for mitigating the exploits. Drake submitted patches to Google, but one patch introduced another vulnerability (CVE-2015-3864) that subsequent Stagefright efforts would exploit [8]. The proof-of-concept exploit [20] targeted an unspecified Nexus device (likely Nexus 5) running Android 4.0.4. It did not include an address space layout randomization defeat, but it achieved 100% reliability through repeated efforts because the `mediaserver` process is automatically restarted after it crashes due to a failed exploit.

## 4.2    Google Project Zero

Brand [4] leveraged the new vulnerability as the basis of a Stagefright exploit that targeted more recent versions of Android. Android versions 5.0 and later use a different memory allocation technique than older versions; the new allocation is based on `jemalloc` and necessitated changes to the heap grooming techniques used by the exploit [2]. Additionally, the address space layout randomization changes implemented in Android 5.0 made exploitation attempts less likely to result in remote code execution. However, a proof-of-concept exploit revealed that these vulnerabilities were still present in newer Android devices.

Address space layout randomization successfully prevents an attacker from knowing exactly where shared libraries are loaded in memory, but this can be circumvented if the attacker can leak enough information to determine the memory layout. Alternatively, an attacker could guess where a library is loaded. The address space layout randomization implementation on Android devices only provides eight bits of entropy when the shared library (`libc.so`) is loaded; thus, an attack has a one in 256 chance of succeeding. Once again, because an unsuccessful attack crashes `mediaserver` and it automatically restarts, repeatedly trying the exploit eventually results in remote code execution. Brand [4] experimented with the exploit and discovered that successful exploitation took 30 seconds to a little over an hour.

## 4.3    NorthBit

Metaphor [3] is a Stagefright implementation that incorporates improved heap grooming capabilities and an address space layout randomization defeat. This exploit still targets the CVE-2015-3864 vulnerability added by Drake's patch, but it requires JavaScript execution to leak information and bypass address space layout randomization. This reduces the set of vectors vulnerable to the attack, but the exploit is more reliable and less dependent on predetermined library locations. This makes the exploit easier to adapt to other devices and it does not rely on any additional Stagefright vulnerabilities.

MPEG4 media files can include metadata (e.g., title, duration, copyright and lyrics) that is accessible by JavaScript. The same heap overflow vulnerability used to overwrite a function pointer for code execution can be leveraged to overwrite pointers in memory and enable access to arbitrary locations in memory. This primitive read operation overwrites the pointer to the duration value (an 8-byte integer) before returning metadata to the browser. However, because the browser requires the duration to be a signed 64-bit integer, negative or degenerate values are set to zero before they are reported to the browser. This limits the readable value to 32-35 bits of useful information after it is converted from microseconds to milliseconds.

The Metaphor exploit relies on the same address space layout randomization limitations as previous exploits – shared library modules are limited to a maximum address range of 256 memory pages. By iterating over these pages and performing a memory leak, an attacker could, in theory, identify the exact location of the targeted library. However, the limitation on returned values prevents the reading of information that is normally used to identify a library (e.g., ELF header). Metaphor works around this limitation using p_memsz and p_flags as identifiers. These fields are relatively unique and are at known locations, so a lookup table can be created to match the read value to an expected value for the target module libc.so.

A proof-of-concept implementation includes server code that performs a memory leak until it determines the base address for libc.so; following this, it crafts and delivers the malicious media file. The media file performs the necessary heap grooming and overwrites a function pointer with an address controlled via heap overflow. Adapting the exploit to run on a new target is straightforward if an attacker has access to the version of libc.so running on the target device. This library can be extracted from a downloaded factory image or any device running the same version of the Android operating system.

These exploits demonstrate how quickly a discovered vulnerability can transition from a low-threat proof-of-concept to a sophisticated attack. Vulnerability researchers are paying much closer attention to Android frameworks, but the fear remains that a similar vulnerability could go unnoticed and result in large-scale compromise. The trade-off between a wide attack surface (initial Stagefright exploit) and a more sophisticated attack vector (Metaphor) is important from an attacker's perspective. It also plays a role in how mitigation mechanisms are developed and applied to resolve security problems.

## 5.     Categorizing Malware by Behavior

This section presents a novel approach for capturing malware on an Android device for future analysis. A simple taxonomy is introduced that classifies malware based on the crash behavior of the exploited services.

Exploits that leverage brute-force techniques are designed with the expectation that a targeted service will crash multiple times. An attacker can intentionally cause a target service to crash in order to reset the memory of the service and create more predictable memory usage. Memory corruption exploits rely on sophisticated techniques (e.g., information leakage and heap grooming), but they may not be very reliable.

If an attacker designs an exploit to be as stealthy and as reliable as possible, it may not create side-effects that are detectable by the underlying system. A highly-reliable and well-hidden exploit could still be detected and captured on the rare occasion that it causes a crash. The best method for capturing the most sophisticated exploits is persistent and continuous monitoring of volatile memory. However, no simple solution exists for finding an unknown malware sample in the large amount of data collected during a continuous data capture.

## 5.1 Malware Categories

Malware can be classified according to its intended and designed behavior. This classification enables the development of capture techniques that leverage the characteristics of each malware category.

- **User-Detectable Malware:** Not all malware is designed to avoid user detection – malware designed to intimidate or extort users intentionally disrupts and inconveniences victims. Mobile devices are now being targeted by "ransomware" that encrypts important files or locks users out of their devices until ransoms are paid. This category of malware is straightforward to detect and identify, but its disruptive behavior can make memory capture for malware analysis difficult.

- **System-Detectable Malware:** Malware can exhibit side-effects that are not obvious to a user, but can be detected by the underlying operating system. It is important to note that the focus is on side-effects that are explicit and well-defined. The side-effects include unreported service crashes, inappropriate application behavior and unexpected network connections. This category is not mutually exclusive with user-detectable malware; in most cases, the effects visible to a user are also apparent at the system level.

- **Inconspicuous Malware:** Inconspicuous malware does not create easily identifiable side-effects. This category includes malware that may be detectable through advanced analysis techniques (e.g., behavioral analysis and anomaly detection). Capturing this class of malware typically involves the collection of large amounts of data and eliminating the false positives.

## 5.2 Benefits of Malware Categorization

Categorizing malware according to observable side-effects facilitates the development of specialized detection techniques. These techniques are similar to heuristic analysis, but they rely on the results of attempted exploitation instead of analysis of the malware itself.

The Stagefright exploits demonstrate that mobile devices may hide side-effects (e.g., crash notifications and excessive memory paging) that are more noticeable on traditional computer workstations. The proposed categorization enables the capture and study of malware that relies on the differences remaining undetected. More importantly, the categorization can also enable the detection of unknown malware that relies on similar assumptions.

Some exploitation mechanisms are tailored specifically to a target device – the Stagefright exploits leverage the same malicious media files to trigger vulnerabilities across multiple devices, but they require model-specific techniques to achieve code execution. Detecting device-specific exploitation mechanisms requires the development and deployment of solutions at the device model level. However, exploitation mechanisms (and their side-effects) that can be detected at the operating system level can be applied across multiple models of devices that run the same operating system.

## 5.3    Detecting Malware Side-Effects

As mentioned above, kernel-level access is necessary for a tool to arbitrarily dump memory that belongs to the operating system or other processes. LiME [18] is a loadable kernel module that can dump an image of the entire physical memory of a device with minimal impact. This makes LiME a useful tool for capturing malicious activity that cannot be precisely located in memory. LiME is well-suited to capturing large amounts of memory at one time, but not for consistent or continuous memory monitoring. This makes it useful in situations where suspicious activity can be detected (e.g., a service freezes or crashes unexpectedly), but its effectiveness against undetected attacks is limited.

System libraries (e.g., libstagefright) can be modified so that certain types of media are collected and saved before media parsing is performed. The number of captured files that are stored and the length of time they are maintained can be modified to suit the needs of researchers. If a device is monitored consistently, the files may be stored until they are analyzed. Conversely, if a device is only investigated in the event of a suspected compromise, then the stored files have to be managed because limited space is available on the device. However, changes made to system libraries increase the risk that an exploit that targets the libraries will no longer behave as expected. Consequently, this research has focused on modifications that do not alter common services.

Some libraries on Android devices are designed to support system and application developers. The debugging daemon (debuggerd) creates "tombstones" when an application or library crashes; these tombstones contain useful system information and program backtraces from the time of the crash. Figure 6 demonstrates how debuggerd is associated with every dynamically-linked executable. The executables specify the linker

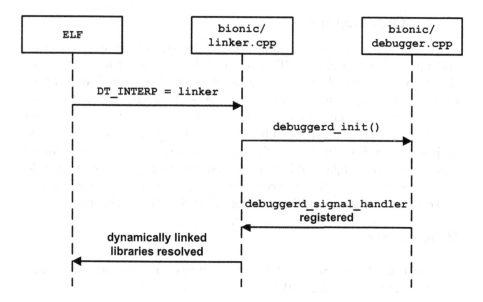

*Figure 6.* `debuggerd` handler setup.

DT_INTERP used to interpret the included symbols. Following this, the linker ties handlers for each signal to **debuggerd** before returning with the library symbols resolved.

The signal handlers are responsible for generating crash information. System properties can be configured to enable or disable additional debugging capabilities. The property `debug.db.uid` causes **debuggerd** to suspend a crashing process and attach **gdb** to the process – this enables a user to connect using **gdb** and actively debug the process before it crashes. (Note that the **uid** property is replaced with `wait_for_gdb` in newer Android devices.) The process remains suspended until the user depresses the "volume down" button or uses **gdb** to resume the process.

The **debuggerd** daemon is a useful tool for debugging Android platform code, but its backtrace and memory dump functionalities are poorly suited to analyzing exploits. Corrupted addresses in stack memory and unexpected register values can cause **debuggerd** to miss portions of memory that are relevant to malware analysis. To overcome this limitation, **debuggerd** may be modified to support additional functionality when a crash occurs. The limited memory capture functionality of **debuggerd** can also be enhanced with support for automatically launching the LiME capture process when crashes occur. The stated requirement that modifications to common libraries should be avoided can be overlooked for **debuggerd** because it is explicitly prevented from attempting to debug itself by design.

## 6.    Conclusions

Combating sophisticated malware requires novel detection, capture and mitigation techniques. This research has proposed malware detection techniques based on measurable side-effects in an exploited device. Categorizing malware to identify common side-effects enables the automated capture of memory-resident malware using digital forensic tools for live memory acquisition. The automated capture technique enables digital forensic investigators to discover and analyze previously-unknown exploitation techniques and to implement new mitigation strategies for vulnerable devices. Most importantly, the proposed modifications that make the technique possible are minimal and device-independent.

## References

[1] Android Open Source Project, Security (`source.android.com/security`), May 22, 2017.

[2] P. Argyroudis and C. Karamitas, Exploiting the `jemalloc` memory allocator: Owning Firefox's heap, presented at the *Black Hat USA Conference*, 2012.

[3] H. Be'er, Metaphor: A (Real) Real-Life Stagefright Exploit, Revision 1.1, NorthBit, Herzliya, Israel (`raw.githubusercontent.com/NorthBit/Public/master/NorthBit-Metaphor.pdf`), 2016.

[4] M. Brand, Stagefrightened? Project Zero, Google, Mountain View, California (`googleprojectzero.blogspot.com/2015/09/stagefrightened.html`), September 16, 2015.

[5] M. Cova, C. Kruegel and G. Vigna, Detection and analysis of drive-by-download attacks and malicious JavaScript code, *Proceedings of the Nineteenth International Conference on World Wide Web*, pp. 281–290, 2010.

[6] J. Drake, Stagefright: Scary code in the heart of Android, presented at the *Black Hat USA Conference*, 2015.

[7] J. Edmonds, Cell Phone Reverse Engineering and Malware Analysis, Ph.D. Dissertation, Tandy School of Computer Science, University of Tulsa, Tulsa, Oklahoma, 2012.

[8] Exodus Intelligence, Stagefright: Mission Accomplished? Austin, Texas (`blog.exodusintel.com/2015/08/13/stagefright-mission-accomplished`), August 13, 2015.

[9] G Data Software, G Data Mobile Malware Report, Threat Report: Q2/2015, Bochum, Germany, 2015.

[10] A. Ludwig and V. Rapaka, An Update to Nexus Devices, Google, Mountain View, California (officialandroid.blogspot.com/2015/08/an-update-to-nexus-devices.html), August 5, 2015.

[11] P. Ratanaworabhan, B. Livshits and B. Zorn, NOZZLE: A defense against heap-spraying code injection attacks, *Proceedings of the Eighteenth USENIX Security Symposium*, pp. 169–186, 2009.

[12] Samsung Electronics, Samsung Announces an Android Security Update Process to Ensure Timely Protection from Security Vulnerabilities, Press Release, Suwon, South Korea, August 5, 2015.

[13] Scientific Working Group on Digital Evidence, SWGDE Best Practices for Mobile Phone Forensics, Version 2.0, 2013.

[14] F. Serna, The info leak era of software exploitation, presented at the *Black Hat USA Conference*, 2012.

[15] A. Sotirov, Heap feng shui in JavaScript, presented at the *Black Hat Europe Conference*, 2007.

[16] J. Stuttgen and M. Cohen, Robust Linux memory acquisition with minimal target impact, *Digital Investigation*, vol. 11(S1), pp. S112–S119, 2014.

[17] H. Sun, K. Sun, Y. Wang, J. Jing and S. Jajodia, TrustDump: Reliable memory acquisition on smartphones, *Proceedings of the Nineteenth European Symposium on Research in Computer Security*, Part I, pp. 202–218, 2014.

[18] J. Sylve, A. Case, L. Marziale and G. Richard, Acquisition and analysis of volatile memory from Android devices, *Digital Investigation*, vol. 8(3-4), pp. 175–184, 2012.

[19] V. Thing, K. Ng and E. Chang, Live memory forensics of mobile phones, *Digital Investigation*, vol. 7(S), pp. S74–S82, 2010.

[20] Zimperium zLabs, The Latest on Stagefright: CVE-2015-1538 Exploit is Now Available for Testing Purposes, San Francisco, California (blog.zimperium.com/the-latest-on-stagefright-cve-2015-1538-exploit-is-now-available-for-testing-purposes), September 9, 2015.

# VI

# IMAGE FORENSICS

# Chapter 13

# SEMANTIC VIDEO CARVING USING PERCEPTUAL HASHING AND OPTICAL FLOW

Junbin Fang, Sijin Li, Guikai Xi, Zoe Jiang, Siu-Ming Yiu, Liyang Yu, Xuan Wang, Qi Han and Qiong Li

Abstract    Video files are frequently encountered in digital forensic investigations. However, these files are usually fragmented and are not stored consecutively on physical media. Suspects may logically delete the files and also erase filesystem information. Unlike image carving, limited research has focused on video carving. Current approaches depend on filesystem information or attempt to match every pair of fragments, which is impractical. This chapter proposes a two-stage approach to tackle the problem. The first perceptual grouping stage computes a hash value for each fragment; the Hamming distance between hashes is used to quickly group fragments from the same file. The second precise stitching stage uses optical flow to identify the correct order of fragments in each group. Experiments with the BOSS dataset reveal that the approach is very fast and does not sacrifice accuracy or overall precision.

Keywords: Digital forensics, video carving, perceptual hashing, optical flow

## 1. Introduction

The amount of video encountered in digital forensic investigations has increased significantly over the past decade. The digital evidence includes surveillance camera and mobile device video files, forged video files and erotic video files [15, 16]. However, video files are usually broken into segments due to large file sizes and filesystem storage mechanisms such as file scattering and wear leveling [10]. Additionally, criminals may attempt to erase the files that may have recorded their actions. Indeed, it is common for digital forensic investigators to only obtain (deleted) raw video fragments extracted from storage media. In such instances,

© IFIP International Federation for Information Processing 2017
Published by Springer International Publishing AG 2017. All Rights Reserved
G. Peterson and S. Shenoi (Eds.): Advances in Digital Forensics XIII, IFIP AICT 511, pp. 223–244, 2017.
DOI: 10.1007/978-3-319-67208-3_13

223

video carving is needed to reassemble the fragments to create the original video files for further investigation, especially when filesystem information related to file organization is lost [6].

In principle, video carving should only consider the content of video fragments instead of the filesystem structure or other metadata [13]. However, most research assumes that video fragments are stored sequentially or some type of metadata is available to help reorder file fragments [3, 9, 11, 18, 19]. Without these assumptions, the only option is to apply an exhaustive matching method, which compares the content of every pair of fragments and concatenates one fragment to another when the two fragments have the highest adjacency likelihood. This procedure is analogous to assembling a jigsaw puzzle using brute force.

The computational effort for the brute force content-based video carving grows quadratically with the total number of fragments. Specifically, for $n$ fragments, the algorithm requires $O(n^2)$ steps for reassembly [11]. Garfinkel [6] notes that many video files are typically recovered from storage devices during a digital investigation and these files are often very large, resulting in a massive number of fragments and, thus, significant computational costs. Therefore, an automated semantic video carving approach with high efficiency and precision is sorely needed to support digital forensic investigations.

Content-based video carving is complicated because fragmentation shuffles the constituent parts of a video file; additionally, the fragments from multiple video files are mixed together. The approach described in this chapter is designed to semantically carve video fragments from multiple video files, especially in the case of surveillance videos, which are commonly encountered in digital forensic investigations. The novel approach involves two stages that reduce the computational complexity while maintaining high precision. Instead of performing pairwise matching of all the fragments, the proposed approach employs perceptual grouping to collect fragments that originate from the same video file. This step is followed by content-based precise stitching that restores the video file by assembling the out-of-order fragments from a group corresponding to a single video file.

The proposed approach first calculates the perceptual hash (P-hash) value [12] (i.e., compressed digest) of each video fragment, following which the Hamming distances between pairs of hashes are computed. Two fragments whose Hamming distance is within a threshold are clustered into the same group and are deemed to originate from the same video file. The second stage precisely evaluates the adjacency likelihoods of the raw content of fragments in each group using optical flow; this enables the fragments to be reordered correctly based on their motion feature.

The overall computational complexity of semantic video carving is reduced significantly because the scale of the precise stitching computations is decreased by the perceptual grouping stage. For example, if all $n$ fragments from $m$ different video files are mixed together, the proposed approach requires $O(mn)$ grouping computations plus $O(m(n/m)^2)$ computations to compare fragments for reassembly instead of $O(n^2)$ computations required by the brute force method. Note also that the computational cost for perceptual grouping is much less than the cost for content-based precise stitching.

Experimental results obtained for the BOSS dataset [2] reveal that increasing the number of video files captured by the same camera from one file to ten files yields a final precision rate greater than 96%. Moreover, increasing the number of cameras from one to nine, all of them recording the same scenario, yields a final precision rate greater than 98%. The execution times range from two seconds to 15 minutes (for 10 to 100 fragments), demonstrating that the proposed approach is practical.

## 2. Related Work

File carving approaches can be classified as: (i) file-signature-based carving [17]; (ii) mapping function carving [5]; and (iii) graph theoretic-carving [10]. Graph-theoretic carving, which is often referred to as semantic carving, exhibits better performance than the other two approaches, especially for text carving and image carving [13].

However, while graph-theoretic carving approaches have constantly improved, they are not as effective on video images; this is because relatively little research has focused on semantic video carving. Most research has leveraged file signatures, file headers of video formats, codec specifications, etc. Additionally, the direct application of graph-theoretic carving to video fragments has high computational complexity. Table 1 lists the principal video carving methods described in the literature.

Poisel et al. [14, 16] have proposed file carving approaches for carving fragmented multimedia files. The approaches involve preprocessing, collating and reassembly. However, their work only focuses on image fragments.

Yoo et al. [19] have developed a file carving approach for multimedia AVI, WAV and MP3 files compressed by NTFS. The main contribution is a recovery method for deleted NTFS compressed files. The approach assumes that multimedia files are continuously allocated and that the files can be carved based on file header signatures.

*Table 1.* Comparison of video carving methods.

| Method | Auxiliary Information Used |
| --- | --- |
| AVI Carver [19] | NTFS compressed signature |
| Lewis Method [9] | Cluster boundaries in storage media |
| Robust Video Carver [18] | Frame and sequence headers |
| NFI Defraser [3] | MPEG structure and semantic checks |
| DC3carver [3] | File format characteristics |
| Frame-Based Recovery [11] | Codec specifications and STSZ box information |

Lewis [9] has proposed an improved video fragment reassembly method that leverages the cluster boundaries in storage media. Because files are generally saved on storage media by cluster, all the data in a single cluster belongs to a single file, except for the last cluster of a file, which may also contain data from other files in its slack or uninitialized space. The method relies on cluster configuration information. However, it is challenging to reliably detect clusters that contain video file data. Another challenge is to connect clusters that belong to the same fragmented file.

Yannikos et al. [18] have proposed the combination of two forensic techniques – video file carving and robust hashing – to automate the identification and recovery of video content. Their video frame carving approach analyzes frame information in order to extract and decode single intracoded frames (I-frames); this results in more robust recovery than traditional header/footer identification. However, the method carves video slices by searching for I-frame headers backwards and forwards, assuming that all the video fragments are allocated in sequence.

Casey and Zoun [3] have compared the Defraser and DC3Carver carving tools. They also discuss the trade-offs of using carving tools in digital forensic examinations.

Na et al. [11] have proposed a frame-based video carving approach that leverages codec specifications for surveillance video. Their approach restores corrupted video files at the frame level. However, it essentially performs extended signature-based file restoration because it relies on sample-to-size (STSZ) box data in MPEG-4 files, which records the length of each frame set. Without STSZ information, the approach has to match frames one by one, resulting in a significant time complexity of $O(n^2)$.

## 3.     Proposed Video Carving Approach

A successful reassembly of video fragments implies that all the fragments are placed in the same sequence as in the original video file. Fig-

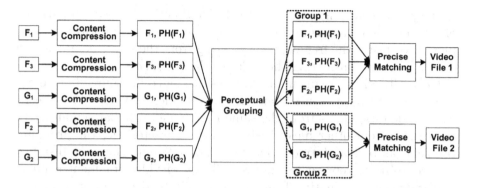

*Figure 1.* Proposed video carving approach.

ure 1 illustrates the proposed video carving approach using a simple example. Let $F_1$, $F_2$, $F_3$, $G_1$ and $G_2$ be video fragments that must be carved. Assume that $F_1$, $F_2$ and $F_3$ originate from one video file while $G_1$ and $G_2$ originate from a second file. Note that, in general, data fragments are extracted from physical storage using a digital forensic tool and the video fragments are identified via data type classification.

In the proposed video carving approach, each fragment is pre-processed via content compression to produce a P-hash value. Next, the video fragments (e.g., $F_1$) and their P-hash values (e.g., $PH(F_1)$) are input to the perceptual grouping stage. This stage clusters the fragments based on the Hamming distances between their P-hash values. For example, the grouping stage clusters the fragments $F_1$, $F_3$ and $F_2$ into Group 1, and the fragments $G_1$ and $G_2$ into Group 2.

Next, each group (now with a substantially smaller number of fragments) is input to the precise stitching stage to calculate the adjacency likelihoods of fragments in the group. Note that no effective measure exists for this step. In the proposed approach, optical flow is used to estimate the similarity of the frames around the fragmentation points of video fragments in same group. Based on the motion vectors computed for the image frames, an improved graph-theoretic carving algorithm is used to position the fragments in a group correctly to reconstruct the original video file. For example, fragments $F_1$, $F_3$ and $F_2$ are reordered in the correct sequence $(F_1, F_2, F_3)$ and are subsequently concatenated to produce Video File 1. Likewise, fragments $G_1$ and $G_2$ are reordered as $(G_1, G_2)$ and concatenated to produce Video File 2.

## 3.1    Perceptual Grouping

Since the video carving input is a large number of video fragments from different video files, exhaustively matching the fragments is an extremely time-consuming task. Instead of conducting precise comparisons of all the video fragments directly, a coarse grouping algorithm is employed to cluster the fragments originating from the same file in a single group, without considering the order of the fragments.

Generally, video fragments from the same video file source have more common features or scenes than those from different video files. Specifically, video fragments from the same file are more similar semantically than those from other files. Utilizing this characteristic, the grouping problem can be transformed to a clustering problem, where the distance between objects represents the dissimilarity of video fragment content and fragments originating from the same file tend to gather around a cluster center. The nearer the objects, the more similar the fragments and the greater the grouping likelihood. Centroid-based clustering is used to divide the video fragments into groups. Note that the cluster center can be initialized as the first fragment of a video file, which is easily identified because it usually contains a number of specific codes. For example, the two popular codecs, MPEG-4 [7] and H.264 [8], have the header codes 0x000001 and 0x00000001 or 0x000001, respectively, which help identify the header fragment.

Three techniques are employed to implement this approach efficiently. The techniques are described in the following paragraphs.

**Perceptual Evaluation.** The first technique helps choose an appropriate measure to evaluate the similarities or dissimilarities of video fragments with low computational complexity and a high recall ratio. Figure 2 demonstrates this grouping technique. Start Fragment 0 indicates the first fragment of a video file, which is obtained by simply searching for the unique magic number of a file in the storage media [11]; this fragment is marked as the initial cluster center. Next, the image frames around the fragmentation points of Start Fragment 0 and Candidate Fragment are compressed into binary descriptors (i.e., P-hash values corresponding to the white and black square patterns in the figure) through perceptual hashing as described below. The clustering distance is measured as the Hamming distance between two P-hash values. In the example, because the Hamming distance between Start Fragment 0 and Candidate Fragment is lower than the threshold, Candidate Fragment is assigned to Group 0, which contains the best available fragments that originate from the same video file as Start Fragment 0.

P-hashing is used to compress the contents of all the fragments before running the clustering algorithm. A number of hashing functions have been proposed based on histogram, discrete cosine transform (DCT), singular value decomposition (SVD), local color features and random

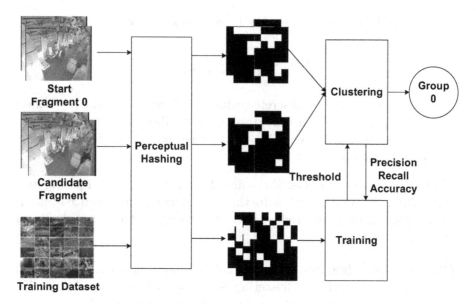

*Figure 2.* Perceptual grouping stage.

transformation methods [12]. The proposed approach generates P-hash values using a discrete cosine transform hashing function, which involves four steps:

- **Step 1 (Grayscale Transformation):** A color frame contains redundant information for processing. The grayscale transformation reduces the information content and, thus, the subsequent computational effort.

- **Step 2 (Resizing):** Resizing reduces the computational cost of discrete cosine transform hashing. In this case, video frames are resized to a fixed resolution of 32×32 pixels via linear interpolation.

- **Step 3 (Discrete Cosine Transformation):** This transformation converts video content from the spatial domain to the frequency domain, causing the primary information of a frame to converge to the low-frequency area, which means that the magnitudes of the low-frequency discrete cosine transform coefficients are robust to slight/invisible changes to video frames. Experimentation revealed that the first 64 coefficients are suitable for computing hash values that enable robust comparisons.

- **Step 4 (Hashing):** Binary hash values are computed as:

$$H(i) = \begin{cases} 1, & c[i] > c_{threshold} \\ 0, & otherwise \end{cases} \quad (1)$$

where $c[i]$ is the $i^{th}$ discrete cosine transform coefficient ($i = 1..64$) and $c_{threshold}$ is a threshold value for the discrete cosine transform coefficients; it is typically the average of the 64 discrete cosine transform coefficient values.

This processing reduces the computational cost of comparing two $1024 \times 768$-pixel video frames to the cost of comparing two 64-bit binary values, a dramatic reduction in the computational complexity of the grouping stage.

**Cluster Optimization.** The second technique involves optimal and self-adaptive clustering. Clustering is formulated as a multi-objective optimization problem. A training module shown in Figure 2 is employed to optimize the output groups. Since the Hamming distance between a pair of P-hash values is chosen as the weighting parameter in cluster analysis, adjusting the cluster radius affects the clustering performance when the inter-member distances are small.

An optimized threshold for the clustering radius is significant to the performance of the algorithm. If the threshold value is too small (i.e., too strict), then some candidate fragments may be excluded (false reject or false negative errors). On the other hand, a large threshold may lead to the addition of outliers (false accept or false positive errors). Therefore, before the clustering process is initiated, a training dataset must be input to the clustering algorithm to determine the optimal threshold by adjusting the clustering radius until optimal groups are produced that maximize the true positives and minimize the false positives in each group. To accomplish this, clustering performance metrics such as precision, recall ratio and accuracy are fed back to the training module in order to self-adjust the clustering radius threshold.

Note that if the fragments are restricted to being in exactly one group, then when a fragment is assigned incorrectly to a group, the precise stitching stage performance deteriorates because the correct group and the incorrect group both have the wrong output. Therefore, fragments are permitted to belong to multiple groups. This reduces the number of false negatives while increasing the number of false positives. Thus, more computations are performed during the precise stitching stage than in theory, but they are still much less than those required by the exhaustive matching algorithm with an optimal threshold setting.

**Fissile Clustering.** The third technique seeks to improve the traditional clustering algorithm to fit the characteristics of the video fragments. One problem with directly performing traditional clustering is that after the starting fragment is set as a fixed cluster center, when the video file is highly fragmented, the clustering radius – Hamming distance in this case – should be large enough to include all the video fragments (e.g., fragments around the end of the file). This occurs because of the inherent "chain-like" property of file carving. However, the larger the clustering radius threshold, the greater the number of incorrect fragments from other files included in each group. To address this problem, a "fissile clustering" algorithm is employed that compares the front-end frames of candidate fragments and the back-end frames of current fragments in similarity evaluations.

The fissile clustering algorithm involves the following steps:

- **Step 1:** For each group, begin with the start fragment and set it as the current fragment.

- **Step 2:** Calculate the Hamming distance between P-hash values of the back-end frame(s) of the current fragment(s) and the front-end frames of all the remaining fragments.

- **Step 3:** Compare the similarity likelihoods based on the Hamming distances. If the distance is below the threshold, then the candidate fragments are collected into a group and become the current fragment(s).

- **Step 4:** Select all the clustered fragments one by one, and repeat Steps 1 through 3 until there are no more available fragments.

## 3.2 Precise Stitching

After all the video fragments have been clustered into smaller groups, the second stage of the proposed approach evaluates the adjacency likelihoods or similarities of the fragments in each group and attempts to stitch them together in the correct order. For each group, a graph-theoretic carving algorithm can be applied with an appropriate weight function. The idea is to find the shortest path for the Hamilton path problem (i.e., optimal order of the fragments in a group). Compared with the original graph-theoretic carving method [10, 13], the scale of the proposed algorithm is reduced to the number of candidates in a group instead of the total number of fragments. The smaller scale also reduces the numbers of false positives in the groups, excluding outliers from the final restored video file.

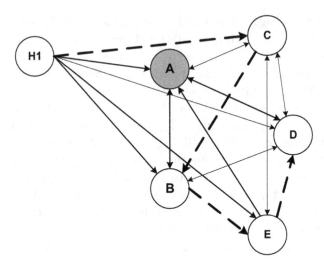

*Figure 3.*   Graph of six video fragments with a disjoint path and rejected outlier A

Consider two possible situations in which the algorithm mistakenly concatenates an outlier in the restored video file. First, if the content of an outlier fragment has a higher adjacency likelihood than those of the other candidate fragments, it may be mistakenly chosen as the best adjacent fragment. Since this erroneous concatenation occurs due to the high similarity between the outlier fragment and preceding fragment, it cannot be distinguished by a graph-theoretic algorithm, including the proposed precise stitching stage and the original graph-theoretic carving method. In this case, a double-check procedure may be needed.

On the other hand, even if the outlier fragments have lower adjacency likelihoods than other candidate fragments, the algorithm may still keep appending them to the end of the video file if the exhaustive method is not terminated based on some other constraint. Therefore, an additional constraint is required to identify the ending vertex of the optimal path and terminate the algorithm.

Figure 3 shows a simple example. A group with six fragments is represented as a complete graph of six vertices, where each edge has a weight corresponding to the adjacency likelihood between the fragments. The header fragment in the group is the vertex H1 and assume that fragment (vertex) A is an outlier that is mistakenly clustered during the previous stage. The problem of reconstructing the original video file is equivalent to finding the optimal path (i.e., shortest path in the graph). Thus, the algorithm should attempt the best adjacent fragment for each fragment and also try to avoid passing through the outlier vertex A.

Otherwise, the restored video file would contain incorrect content. In the example, the complete disjoint path is H1-C-B-E-D while the outlier vertex A is rejected.

Since a video is a series of frames (images) in time sequence and the objects in the video have spatial consistency between frames, the motion field between two frames can be leveraged as a similarity measure by the precise stitching algorithm. In the proposed method, the optical flow is selected for the relative motion analysis of frames at the fragmentation point of two candidate video fragments.

Suppose that two pixels from the frames of a preceding fragment $F_P$ and a candidate fragment $F_C$ have same pixel value, although the pixel positions may be different. In other words, $p_{preceding}(x, y) = p_{candidate}(x + \Delta x, y + \Delta y)$. Then, the motion distance is calculated as:

$$D(F_P, F_C) = \frac{\sum_{i=0}^{n_{pixels}} \sqrt{\Delta x^2(i) + \Delta y^2(i)}}{n_{pixels}} \qquad (2)$$

where $n_{pixels}$ is the number of pixels in each frame, $p_{preceding}(x, y)$ is the pixel value of the point $(x, y)$ in a preceding frame, $p_{candidate}(x + \Delta x, y + \Delta y)$ is the pixel value of point $(x + \Delta x, y + \Delta y)$ in the adjacent candidate frame and $D(F_P, F_C)$ is the average distance between the preceding frame $F_P$ and the candidate frame $F_C$; this is used to evaluate the adjacency likelihoods of the available candidate fragments to the preceding fragment.

Stitching processing is the straightforward application of a greedy approximation algorithm that is commonly used to solve edge- and vertex-disjoint problems [10]. To start with, the header fragment is chosen as the current fragment and its adjacency likelihoods with the remaining fragments in the current cluster group are computed. The best available fragment is stitched to the current fragment and this best available fragment is set as the current fragment. This process is repeated until the entire video is reassembled.

## 4. Experimental Results

The performance of the proposed video carving approach is evaluated using the BOSS public surveillance dataset [2].

The BOSS dataset has fifteen scenarios: two no-incident scenarios, three specific-incident detection scenarios and ten incident scenarios, such as "cell phone theft," "disease," "harassment" and "panic." Each scenario was concurrently recorded by nine surveillance cameras installed in a single train car (from nine different angles). Therefore, each scenario should have nine video clips. However, five scenarios do not have nine

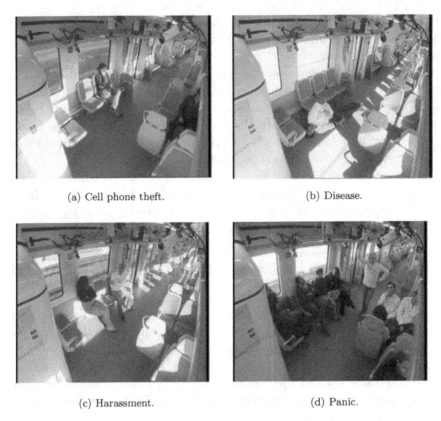

(a) Cell phone theft.                    (b) Disease.

(c) Harassment.                          (d) Panic.

*Figure 4.*   Four video scenarios recorded by Camera 1.

video clips; therefore, the other ten scenarios for which nine video clips exist were used in the experiments. Figure 4 shows images from video clips taken by Camera 1 for four scenarios. The parameters of the video clips in BOSS dataset are:

- **Frame Rate:** 25 fps interlaced.

- **Resolution:** 720×576 pixels.

- **Video Container:** AVI.

- **Codec:** MJPEG 4:2:2 (Cameras 1 through 9).

- **Bit Rate:** 30 Mbps.

To evaluate the proposed approach, all the video files were randomly sliced into video fragments, which were then mixed. The set of mixed video fragments was used as the experimental input. Since the proposed

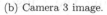

(a) Camera 2 image.

(b) Camera 3 image.

(c) Camera 5 image.

(d) Camera 8 image.

*Figure 5.* A single video scenario recorded by different cameras.

video carving approach focuses on the efficiency of reassembling video fragments, all the fragments were present in the input.

The following three metrics were used to evaluate the performance of the video carving approach:

- **Recall:** $TP/(TP + FN)$.

- **Precision:** $TP/(TP + FP)$.

- **Accuracy:** $(TP+TN)/(TP+TN+FP+FN)$ where $TP, TN, FP$ and $FN$ are the numbers of true positives (inliers), true negatives, false positives (outliers) and false negatives, respectively, and $n = (TP + TN + FP + FN)$ is the total number of video fragments.

Note that the dataset is quite challenging for the video carving algorithm because some of original video files recorded for the same scenario are extremely similar. For example, as shown in Figure 5, the same scenario recorded by Cameras 2, 3, 5 and 8 generates four different video frames, but the images are very similar, especially the images from Cameras 2 and 5. The great similarities of the video files increase the difficulty of video carving when the files are fragmented and the fragments are mixed together.

A series of experiments under different conditions were conducted to optimize the clustering threshold of the first stage and to investigate the performance of the proposed approach. The computing platform used in the experiments was a desktop computer with an Intel I5-3317U 2.60 GHz CPU and 6 GB memory.

**Optimizing the Clustering Threshold.** As discussed above, the clustering threshold has a significant impact on the performance of the perceptual grouping stage and the overall video carving approach. If the threshold is set too large, each group could include several outliers, increasing the recall ratio of the grouping while decreasing its precision and accuracy. In contrast, a small threshold could reject some inliers from each group, increasing the precision and accuracy, but decreasing the recall ratio. Therefore, the threshold should be selected carefully to optimize the overall performance.

The clustering threshold was optimized by training. Two public datasets were used for this purpose, the CAVIAR surveillance dataset [4] and the crowd segmentation dataset provided by the Center for Research in Computer Vision at the University of Central Florida [1].

Forty video clips from the two training datasets were randomly sliced into fragments to create training samples that were input to the perceptual grouping algorithm. Each video clip was divided into two to 30 fragments randomly. Figure 6 shows the relationships between recall, precision and accuracy versus the clustering threshold for the training datasets. When the threshold is larger than 16, the recall ratio of grouping reaches 100% while the accuracy drops to about 30% and precision is only 10%, meaning that the number of false positives is about nine times the number of true positives. At the other extreme, when the threshold is set to below 2, the recall ratio of grouping is less than 50%, meaning that about half the fragments are clustered in the correct group.

As mentioned above, video fragments are allowed to belong to multiple groups; this relaxes the restrictions on the precision and accuracy of a grouping. However, if the grouping precision is too low, the increase in the number of false positives contributes to increased computations in the subsequent precise stitching stage. According to the curves in Figure 6, the optimal threshold should be in the range 7 to 11 because the recall ratio and accuracy have high values and are flat within this range. Moreover, the recall ratio of grouping reaches 98% when the

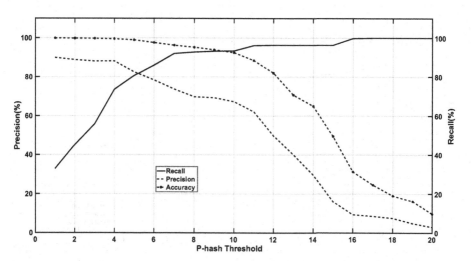

*Figure 6.* Performance metrics versus clustering threshold for the training datasets.

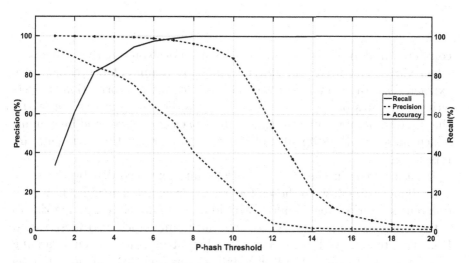

*Figure 7.* Performance metrics versus clustering threshold for the BOSS dataset.

threshold is 11 and only increases slightly after this value. Therefore, since all the datasets involve surveillance videos, a Hamming distance of 10 was chosen as the clustering threshold, which turns out to be adequate for the BOSS dataset to yield a 100% recall ratio. This is confirmed in the experimental results obtained with the BOSS dataset (Figure 7).

**Carving Fragments from the Same Camera.** An experiment investigated the performance of the proposed approach for video fragments originating from the same camera. Such a situation is commonly en-

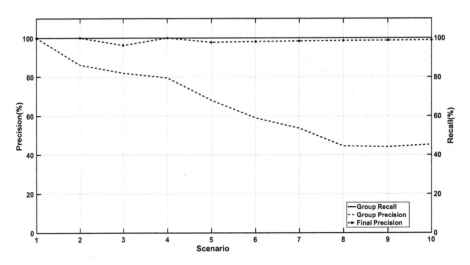

*Figure 8.*    Video file carving performance for the same camera.

countered in digital forensic investigations. For example, this may occur when videos captured and stored locally by a surveillance camera are extracted as fragments due to the lack of filesystem information or over-writing by the storage mechanism. Because the videos were recorded by the same camera at different times, their backgrounds should be similar, which increases the difficulty of video carving when the fragments are mixed together.

Digital videos in the BOSS dataset that were recorded by the same surveillance camera were chosen for this experiment. The video files with different scenarios were randomly divided into four pieces, giving rise to a total of $4n_f$ fragments, where $n_f$, the number of video files, varied from two to ten, yielding a total number of mixed fragments ranging from eight to 40. Since the BOSS dataset has nine surveillance cameras (recording sources), the experiment was performed on nine sets of video files. Figure 8 shows the average video file carving performance for the experiment.

Since the clustering threshold was set to 10 to achieve a 100% re-call ratio in the perceptual grouping stage, all the fragments could be grouped correctly with some outliers. The graph of final precision versus the number of scenarios in Figure 8 shows that more than 96% of the video fragments were correctly reassembled by the proposed approach even when the number of scenarios (i.e., video files) was increased to ten. The 4% error rate for $n_{scenarios} = 3$ is due to the fact that the video file of the No_Event scenario has almost stationary pictures, which makes

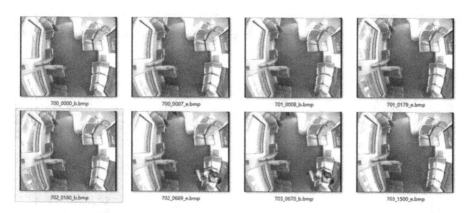

*Figure 9.* Frames shot in the No_Event scenario.

it very difficult to judge the order between fragments because all the frames are almost the same as shown in Figure 9.

An interesting point is that the perceptual grouping precision has less impact on the final precision. Although the grouping precision drops to 50% when the number of scenarios (video files) is increased to ten, the final precision is still greater than 96%. This is because the relaxed requirement for grouping precision is compensated for by the precise stitching stage. Of course, an increased number of outliers in the grouping stage increases the computational cost of the stitching algorithm.

**Carving Fragments from Different Cameras.** This experiment investigated the performance of the proposed approach when the mixed video fragments come from different cameras, although the scenario in the video files may be the same because the nine cameras monitored the same spot concurrently. This situation is frequently encountered in the real world because videos from surveillance cameras are usually uploaded to central servers or the cloud for storage, backup or analysis. When the servers are involved in a digital forensic investigation, it is common to recover a huge number of mixed video fragments.

In another experiment, digital videos of the same scenario that were recorded synchronously by different surveillance cameras were selected for analysis. In particular, video files of a scenario recorded by each of the nine cameras were chosen. Each video file was randomly divided into four pieces. Ten scenarios in the BOSS dataset were selected; therefore, ten sets, each with nine camera videos, were used in the experiment.

Figure 10 shows the average video file carving performance for the experiment. The results reveal that the grouping precision is much better than in the previous experiment; the final precision, which is higher than

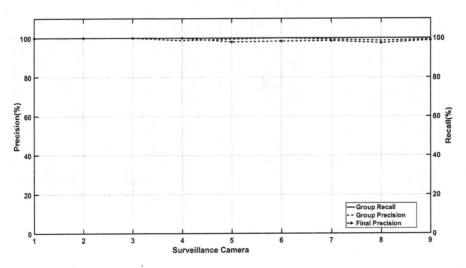

*Figure 10.*   Video file carving performance for different cameras.

98%, is also much better. The principal reason is that the video files from different cameras have similar, but slightly different backgrounds, which can be distinguished more robustly by the video carving approach, contributing to the good results.

**Carving Fragments with Various Fragmentation Degrees.**   This experiment investigated the impact of the fragmentation degree on the proposed video carving approach. Five video recordings of different scenarios recorded by the same camera were selected for analysis; each video file was randomly divided into two to 20 pieces. Since the BOSS dataset has nine surveillance cameras, the experiment was performed on nine sets of video files.

Figure 11 shows the average video file carving performance. When the fragmentation degree and number of video fragments increase, the performance in both stages drops, especially the final precision of the precise stitching stage. When the number of fragments in each video file is not greater than four, the grouping precision is greater than 76% while the final precision of the video carving approach, the final restored rate, is 100%. Despite the fact that the number of fragments goes up to 20 per video, the final restored rate is still as high as 67%.

**Computational Time.**   Since computational cost is positively correlated with the number of fragments, the computational time for the two stages was measured versus the number of fragments. Table 2 shows the results. As expected, the computational time $T_{grouping}$ for the percep-

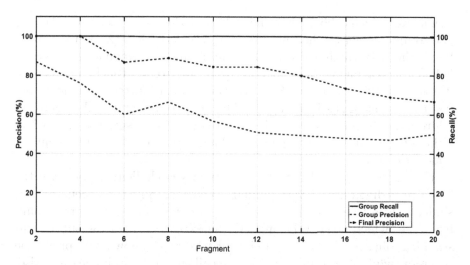

*Figure 11.* Video file carving performance versus fragmentation degree.

*Table 2.* Average time required to carve varying numbers of video fragments.

| Fragments | $T_{grouping}$ (ms) | $T_{stitching}$ (ms) |
|-----------|---------------------|----------------------|
| 10 | 2.8 | 2,281.0 |
| 20 | 16.1 | 18,214.5 |
| 30 | 40.1 | 45,889.6 |
| 40 | 79.7 | 109,242.1 |
| 50 | 127.5 | 195,378.6 |
| 60 | 197.5 | 329,275.1 |
| 70 | 245.2 | 402,303.9 |
| 80 | 304.0 | 562,519.6 |
| 90 | 451.0 | 863,913.9 |
| 100 | 584.3 | 946,265.4 |

tual grouping stage is very small while the time $T_{stitching}$ for the precise stitching stage is much larger. However, the total time for video carving is still reasonable – ranging from two seconds to 15 minutes as the number of fragments increases from 10 to 100.

## 5. Conclusions

The proposed semantic reassembly approach for video files with mixed video fragments yields good results in a reasonable amount of time. Experimental results show that most of the videos were correctly reassembled using the novel coarse-to-fine technique. In particular, for one to ten very similar videos originating from the same camera, the final precision was at least 96%. For the videos of the same scenario taken by one to nine cameras, the final precision was at least 98%. On the other hand, the performance drops when the number of fragments increases. When the fragments per file vary from two to 20, the final precision drops from 100% to about 67%. However, with fourteen fragments per file, the precision is still as high as 80%. Future research will attempt to address the drop in precision that occurs with increasing fragmentation, although the number of fragments seldom goes beyond 20 fragments in real-world scenarios.

The dataset selected for the experiments is challenging because the video recordings are of very similar scenarios. Since the scenarios are similar, more fragments exist in multiple clusters after the first grouping stage, which negatively impacts the effectiveness of the subsequent stitching phase. Future research will investigate how to improve the precision while maintaining a 100% recall in the grouping stage. Also, techniques will be developed to reassemble fragmented video files without any knowledge of the header fragments.

## Acknowledgements

This research was partially supported by the China State Scholarship Fund (Grant No. 201506785014), National Natural Science Foundation of China (Grant Nos. 61401176 and 61361166006), Natural Science Foundation of Guangdong Province (Grant No. 2014A030310205), Science and Technology Projects of Guangdong Province (2014B010120002 and 2016A010101017), Project of Guangdong Higher Education (YQ2015018) and NSFC/RGC Joint Research Scheme (N_HKU 72913), Hong Kong.

## References

[1] S. Ali and M. Shah, A Lagrangian particle dynamics approach for crowd flow segmentation and stability analysis, *Proceedings of the IEEE Conference on Computer Vision and Pattern Recognition*, 2007.

[2] BOSS Project, BOSS Dataset (`www.multitel.be/BOSS`), 2012.

[3] E. Casey and R. Zoun, Design tradeoffs for developing fragmented video carving tools, *Digital Investigation*, vol. 11(S2), pp. S30–S39, 2014.

[4] CAVIAR Project, CAVIAR: Context Aware Vision using Image-Based Active Recognition, School of Informatics, University of Edinburgh, Edinburgh, United Kingdom (`homepages.inf.ed.ac.uk/rbf/CAVIAR`), 2017.

[5] M. Cohen, Advanced carving techniques, *Digital Investigation*, vol. 4(3), pp. 119–128, 2007.

[6] S. Garfinkel, Carving contiguous and fragmented files with fast object validation, *Digital Investigation*, vol. 4(S), pp. S2–S12, 2007.

[7] International Organization for Standardization, Information Technology – Coding of Audio-Visual Objects – Part 2: Visual, ISO/IEC Standard 14496-2:2004, Geneva, Switzerland, 2004.

[8] International Organization for Standardization, Information Technology – Coding of Audio-Visual Objects – Part 10: Advanced Video Coding, ISO/IEC Standard 14496-10:2010, Geneva, Switzerland, 2010.

[9] A. Lewis, Reconstructing Compressed Photo and Video Data, Technical Report No. 813, UCAM-CL-TR-813, Computer Laboratory, University of Cambridge, Cambridge, United Kingdom, 2012.

[10] N. Memon and A. Pal, Automated reassembly of file fragmented images using greedy algorithms, *IEEE Transactions on Image Processing*, vol. 15(2), pp. 385–393, 2006.

[11] G. Na, K. Shim, K. Moon, S. Kong, E. Kim and J. Lee, Frame-based recovery of corrupted video files using video codec specifications, *IEEE Transactions on Image Processing*, vol. 23(2), pp. 517–526, 2014.

[12] A. Neelima and K. Singh, A short survey of perceptual hash functions, *ADBU Journal of Engineering Technology*, vol. 1, 2014.

[13] A. Pal and N. Memon, The evolution of file carving, *IEEE Signal Processing*, vol. 26(2), pp. 59–71, 2009.

[14] R. Poisel and S. Tjoa, Roadmap to approaches for carving of fragmented multimedia files, *Proceedings of the Sixth International Conference on Availability, Reliability and Security*, pp. 752–757, 2011.

[15] R. Poisel and S. Tjoa, A comprehensive literature review of file carving, *Proceedings of the Eighth International Conference on Availability, Reliability and Security*, pp. 475–484, 2013.

[16] R. Poisel, S. Tjoa and P. Tavolato, Advanced file carving approaches for multimedia files, *Journal of Wireless Mobile Networks, Ubiquitous Computing and Dependable Applications*, vol. 2(4), pp. 42–58, 2011.

[17] G. Richard and V. Roussev, Scalpel: A frugal, high performance file carver, *Proceedings of the Digital Forensic Research Workshop*, 2005.

[18] Y. Yannikos, N. Ashraf, M. Steinebach and C. Winter, Automating video file carving and content identification, in *Advances in Digital Forensics IX*, G. Peterson and S. Shenoi (Eds.), Springer, Heidelberg, Germany, pp. 195–212, 2013.

[19] B. Yoo, J. Park, S. Lim, J. Bang and S. Lee, A study on multimedia file carving method, *Multimedia Tools and Applications*, vol. 61(1), pp. 243–261, 2012.

# Chapter 14

# DETECTING FRAUDULENT BANK CHECKS

Saheb Chhabra, Garima Gupta, Monika Gupta and Gaurav Gupta

**Abstract**     Bank checks have been subjected to fraud for centuries. Technological advancements enable criminal actors to perpetrate innovative frauds that are very difficult to detect. One example is the use of erasable ink that allows alterations to be made to a bank check without raising suspicion. Another example is the misuse of a victim's handwritten signature by scanning it and then printing on a check. Since most banking systems accept scanned copies of checks for clearance, identifying erasable ink alterations and printed signatures on digital images can be very challenging. This chapter describes automated, low-cost, efficient and scalable solutions to these problems. A solution is proposed for determining whether or not a check is genuine or merely printed. A solution for detecting erasable ink alterations localizes the erased regions in the visible light spectrum. A solution for detecting printed signatures focuses on the high-density noise introduced by scanners and printers.

**Keywords:** Bank check fraud, check alteration, check forgery, image processing

## 1.     Introduction

Rapid advances in modern scanning technology have greatly simplified the task of converting documents to a digital format. Some digitized documents are very important and their unauthorized use could result in monetary, organizational, social or individual losses. Criminal entities often alter or counterfeit documents for malicious purposes. The wide availability of high-resolution scanners and printers has made it very easy for criminals to carry out alterations and produce high-quality counterfeits. It is very difficult for an ordinary person – sometimes, even document experts – to distinguish between genuine and counterfeit specimens with the naked eye. Bank checks are examples of high-value

© IFIP International Federation for Information Processing 2017                                         245
Published by Springer International Publishing AG 2017. All Rights Reserved
G. Peterson and S. Shenoi (Eds.): Advances in Digital Forensics XIII, IFIP AICT 511, pp. 245–266, 2017.
DOI: 10.1007/978-3-319-67208-3_14

documents that have been leveraged in a variety of frauds for centuries, but more so in recent years due to the availability of high-resolution scanners and printers and the acceptance of scanned copies of checks for clearance by banks.

Document fraud can be classified as static document fraud or dynamic document fraud. A static document holds the same information that was recorded on it at the time it was proclaimed usable, until the time it is declared invalid. A static document contains a combination of fixed and unique information. Examples of static documents are academic transcripts, banknotes, printed invoices, birth certificates, marriage certificates, driver's licenses and passports. A common way of perpetrating fraud involving a static document – aside from tampering – is to scan the original, make changes using a software tool and print a high-quality fraudulent copy.

A dynamic document is similar to a static document, except that it has a provision for the issuing party to write in or mark additional information (using a pen or a stamp) before the document is declared usable. Examples of dynamic documents are bank checks, examination forms and visas. A dynamic document fraud typically involves an alteration of the content generated by the issuing party for malicious reasons. A fraudster could generate a base document (i.e., dynamic document before the issuing party writes on it) using a technique for counterfeiting a static document and then write the desired content before the document is declared usable. Alternatively, a fraudster could write the desired content on a genuine base document. Yet another method of conducting dynamic document fraud is to alter the content created by the issuing party using physical means such as erasing, chemical washing or overwriting. Dynamic document fraud detection is a much more complex problem than static document fraud detection.

According to the Australian Payment Clearance Association [2], losses due to fraudulently-altered checks in 2015 were 80% more than the losses in 2013. Moreover, losses due to non-originated counterfeit checks in 2015 (i.e., fakes produced on counterfeit paper via laser printing or desktop publishing) registered a three-fold increase over 2013. Meanwhile, the Reserve Bank of India [15] reports that 1,197.2 million bank checks were cleared during the 2015-2016 fiscal year. In another report, the Reserve Bank of India [14] estimates that losses due to bank fraud nearly doubled from INR 10.071 billion during the 2013-14 fiscal year to INR 19.361 billion during the 2014-15 fiscal year.

Technological advancements in printing and scanning have enabled fraudsters to perpetrate innovative frauds that are difficult to detect. One example is the use of erasable ink that enables a variety of alterations to bank checks. Another example is forging a handwritten signature by scanning it and printing it on a check. Most banks accept scanned copies or digital photographs of customer checks for rapid and convenient online clearance. Identifying check alterations that leverage erasable and printed signatures in digital images of checks received by a bank can be very challenging. In addition to being accurate, check fraud detection solutions should be fast and inexpensive.

This chapter proposes efficient, inexpensive and scalable methods for detecting bank check fraud. One method determines if a check is genuine or printed. Another method detects check alterations by focusing on erased regions using the visible light spectrum. A third method distinguishes printed signatures from real handwritten signatures based on high-density noise introduced by scanners and printers.

## 2. Related Work

Counterfeit documents are typically detected by human experts who manually analyze suspect documents using a microscope and video spectral comparator, a process that is time-consuming, inefficient and non-scalable. Several automated methods have been developed to identify counterfeit documents. Gupta et al. [6] have identified several characteristics of printed documents that distinguish them from genuine documents. They discovered that the unique color count in a printed document is much larger than that in a genuine document. They also analyzed variations in intensity and the use of the gray level co-occurrence matrix to identify printed documents; this work has indirectly helped develop the proposed method for identifying printed checks. Furthermore, after a check is identified as a printed copy, the approach presented in [7] may be used to forensically link it to a source printer.

Garain et al. [4] have proposed a general framework for authenticating security documents. Their approach extracts color features and statistical features from check images and uses them to distinguish fake documents from genuine documents. Kumar et al. [9] have developed a method for authenticating bank checks. This approach uses color features such as the 2-D histogram of hue-saturation as well as texture features.

Other researchers [10, 16, 17] have proposed techniques for distinguishing counterfeit (primarily printed) documents from genuine documents. Rajendar et al. [13] have focused on the manipulation of digital information during the check clearing process. However, their approach differs from the current work in that they do not address the task of detecting physically-altered checks on which erasable ink has been used.

Abd-ElZaher et al. [1] have deciphered information written in erasable ink that was removed using the eraser attached to a magic pen. They use a chemical solution (NaOH) and infrared radiation from a VSC-600 scan converter to detect alterations. However, their approach, which requires manual human analysis, is expensive, time-consuming and non-scalable.

Deng et al. [3] have studied trace copy forgery detection of hand-written signatures. Their efficient approach uses wavelet transforms for offline handwritten signature verification. Other researchers [8, 11, 12, 18] have developed methods for detecting and/or verifying forged and imitated signatures. However, the current work is unique because no published research has specifically addressed the problem of analyzing handwritten signatures versus printed signatures on scanned checks.

## 3.    Experimental Setup

This research has sought to identify credible image processing features from scanned bank check samples that could help determine whether or not the checks are genuine. Interviews with experts provided valuable information about the types and nature of check frauds. Four features were considered: (i) pantograph; (ii) microline; (iii) user-written content; and (iv) signature. In the experiments, counterfeit checks were replaced with printed checks that were generated by printing high quality scanned blank checks using laser and inkjet printers. Also, fraudulent checks, which are referred to as altered checks in this work, were created using a magic pen to write information such as the payee name, amount (of money) in words and amount (of money) in numbers. A magic pen is a pen whose ink can be removed from a piece of paper using the eraser provided with the pen.

Additionally, the experiments evaluated checks that had printed signatures instead of handwritten signatures. Genuine and printed signature checks from four Indian banks, two public banks (SBI and PNB) and two private banks (AXIS and HDFC), were used in the experiments. An important point is that some premium customers receive permission from banks to print their signatures on checks (e.g., corporate executives who sign company checks). All other checks with printed signatures are potentially fraudulent. Therefore, checks with printed signatures are scrutinized carefully by bank personnel.

Printed check and altered check samples used in the experiments were created based on information obtained from experts and in the supporting literature [1]. The sample checks were scanned at 600 dpi resolution using a Canon 9000F Mark II flat-bed scanner. Two printed check samples were generated for each genuine check using an HP Color LaserJet

*Table 1.* Check features and regions of interest.

| Features | Regions |
|----------|---------|
| Pantograph | 1 |
| Microline | 3 |
| Alteration | 4 |
| Signature | 1 |

Pro MFP M177 laser printer and a Brothers DCP-T500W inkjet printer. The 600 dpi resolution was selected for scanning because it is the industry standard (all the banks whose checks were used in this study process checks at this resolution). Additionally, the 600 dpi resolution provides all the feature values that can be processed in a reasonable time. The legacy 300 dpi resolution produces scanned checks with poor or missing features while the higher 1200 dpi resolution requires significant scanning time and processing cost. Nevertheless, experiments were also conducted on scanned check samples at 300 and 1200 dpi resolutions. Altered check samples were created by writing information on the checks using a magic pen, erasing some of the information and writing new information using the same pen.

Table 1 lists the four primary features of checks examined in this research: (i) pantograph; (ii) microline; (iii) alteration; and (iv) signature. Each feature has one or more regions of interest (ROIs), yielding a total of nine regions of interest.

*Table 2.* Check samples and scanned images examined in this study.

| Bank | Genuine | Printed | | Altered | Printed Signature | | Total | Sub-Images per Sample | Total Processed |
|------|---------|---------|---------|---------|---------|---------|-------|-----------------------|-----------------|
| | | Laser | Inkjet | | Bank | Self | | | |
| SBI | 10 | 10 | 10 | 10 | 3 | 10 | 53 | 9 | 477 |
| PNB | 10 | 10 | 10 | 10 | 1 | 10 | 51 | 9 | 459 |
| AXIS | 10 | 10 | 10 | 10 | 0 | 10 | 50 | 9 | 450 |
| HDFC | 10 | 10 | 10 | 10 | 1 | 10 | 51 | 9 | 459 |
| Total | | | | | | | | | 1,845 |

Table 2 provides information about the check samples and scanned images examined in this study.

## 4. Fraud Detection Methodology Overview

Checks were scanned at 600 dpi resolution (Figure 1). Each check was aligned horizontally in order to be accepted as input. The Canon

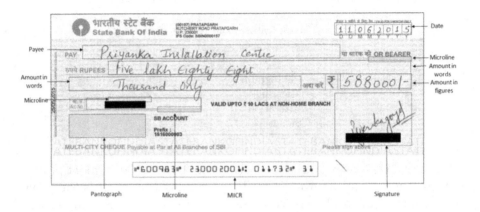

*Figure 1.* SBI bank check image showing sub-regions.

9000F Mark II scanner used in the experiments automatically corrects the alignment of a check image. However, bank personnel typically use software tools that ensure the proper alignment of check images before they are processed.

The first step involved the extraction of the regions of interest for localizing features such as the pantograph, microline, payee name, amount in words, amount in figures and signature (Figure 1). Predefined margins were created for checks from each bank so that the required features could be extracted in a convenient manner.

After the regions of interest were extracted, the check fraud detection workflow presented in Figure 2 was applied to the scanned images. The workflow comprises three parallel blocks.

The first block in the workflow is designed to identify whether or not a check has been printed. The processing focuses on one region for the pantograph and three regions for the microline. Three regions are used for the microline in order to deal with checks that have been handled roughly (i.e., old checks and folded checks).

The second block is designed to identify whether or not a check has been altered. The identification of alterations focuses on four regions of interest, payee name, amount in words (line 1), amount in words (line 2) and amount in figures.

The third block is designed to determine whether or not the signature on a check has been printed. It focuses on a single region of interest corresponding to the signature.

The outputs of the three blocks may be presented to bank security personnel to verify whether or not a check is genuine. In the case of

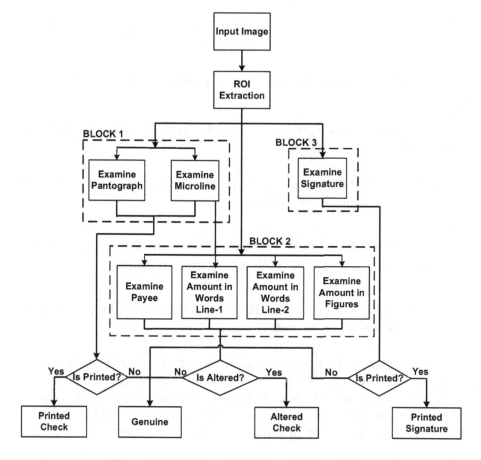

*Figure 2.* Check fraud detection system workflow.

an altered check, the fraud detection workflow also identifies the check regions that were modified.

## 5. Details of the Fraud Detection Methodology

This section presents the details of the check fraud detection methodology, including the underlying theory.

## 5.1 Check Pantographs

A pantograph is an anti-copying security feature printed on a bank check. It contains the word VOID that is hidden by artwork. The word VOID becomes visible when a scanned bank check is printed or a check is photocopied, indicating that the check is not genuine.

*Figure 3.*   Pantographs on genuine (left) and printed checks (right).

The following observations were made upon studying genuine and printed checks.

- The word VOID is much more visible on a printed check compared with a genuine check (Figure 3).

- Some broken lines are seen on a printed check because standard printers are unable to print at very fine resolutions.

- The noise induced by a printer (especially an inkjet printer) is clearly visible to the naked eye.

Based on these observations, two sub-features, surface roughness and unique color count (UNCC), were selected to distinguish between genuine and printed pantographs. Significant increases in surface roughness and unique color count occur due to the colored dots (noise) that are typically generated when printing with a laser or inkjet.

**Surface Roughness Sub-Feature.**  This sub-feature captures the roughness of a pantograph by taking the sum of the absolute gradients of the grayscale image $I_G$ of the pantograph along the horizontal axis. The sum is then divided by the size of the image:

$$Roughness = \frac{\sum abs(G_x)}{Image\ Size} \qquad (1)$$

where $G_x$ is the gradient of the grayscale image and Image Size = image rows × image columns.

**Unique Color Count Sub-Feature.**  This sub-feature expresses the total number of unique colors present in an image. Let $S_{xy} = f(x, y)$ be the intensity value at location $(x, y)$ where $S_{xy} = [R_{xy}\ G_{xy}\ B_{xy}]$ is a row vector. Then, the matrix $M$ is created by placing each intensity value in a separate row:

*Figure 4.* Microlines on genuine (top) and printed checks (bottom).

$$M = \begin{bmatrix} S_{11} \\ S_{12} \\ \cdot \\ \cdot \\ S_{1n} \\ \cdot \\ \cdot \\ S_{mn} \end{bmatrix} \qquad (2)$$

The unique color count is the number of unique rows (each representing a unique color) in matrix $M$.

## 5.2 Check Microlines

The microline security feature is a micro-printed line of text on a check. The micro-print is miniaturized to the extent that the text cannot be read with the naked eye; instead, it appears as a complete or broken line. The font size of microline text is too small for it to be printed clearly by normal printers available in the market.

Figure 4 shows a genuine microline (top) and a printed microline (bottom).

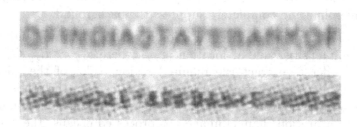

*Figure 5.* Zoomed views of microlines on genuine (top) and printed checks (bottom).

Figure 5 shows the zoomed views of the genuine and printed microlines shown in Figure 4.

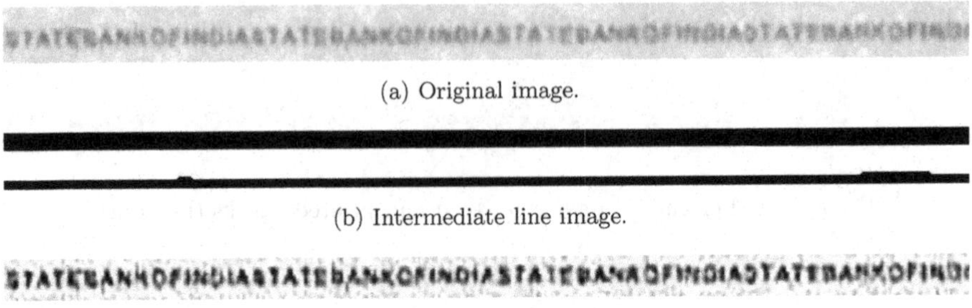

(a) Original image.

(b) Intermediate line image.

(c) Final sharpened image.

*Figure 6.*    Original, intermediate and image-sharpened microlines.

The following observations were made upon studying microlines on genuine and printed checks.

- The microline in a printed check appears as a complete line.

- The characters in the original microline are deformed in the microline of a printed check, where the letters merge with each other.

Optical character recognition (OCR) was performed on the check microlines using a Tesseract OCR engine (version 3.02) [5]. The hypothesis was that the number of consecutive pairs of characters obtained by optical character recognition of a printed microline is very small compared with that of the genuine microline. The reason is that multiple character deformities occur when printing a microline. The detection method involved the following steps:

- **Pre-Processing:** The microline was segmented and programmatically enhanced before the Tesseract OCR engine could process it. Since the segmentation process is highly dependent on the color of the microline, the goal of pre-processing was to highlight the microline and completely suppress the background.

  Let $F(x, y)$ be the original colored image (Figure 4) and $S_{xy}$ be the intensity value at location $(x, y)$ where $S_{xy} = [R_{xy} \ G_{xy} \ B_{xy}]$. In order to extract the required region (color of the microline, dark blue in this example) in the image $F(x, y)$, the original RGB image was converted to an HSV (hue, saturation, value) image and the saturation-channel image was processed because the microline region had a high saturation.

  The saturation-channel image (Figure 6(a)) was converted to a binary image using the Otsu threshold $T$ (Figure 6(b)), which was then processed by applying dilation to merge the characters and create a line image (Figure 6(c)). The sum of each row of the line image was then computed. The rows with sum values greater than 90% of the column of the line image were indexed. The indexed rows were then identified in the original image to produce an image containing only the microline text. Image sharpening was applied to enhance the microline and make the characters in the extracted line more recognizable by the Tesseract OCR engine (Figure 6(c)).

- **Feature Extraction:** Thirty images of the text in the microlines of checks from the four banks (e.g., STATE BANK OF INDIA on an SBI check) were provided to the Tesseract OCR engine. The engine processed each enhanced microline image and stored the output in a text file. Next, successive windows of three consecutive characters of the microline text were selected and matched against the optically-recognized characters stored in the text file. A "hit" occurred if all three characters matched correctly (i.e., they were recognized correctly by the engine); otherwise, a "miss" was recorded. Note that the windows started from the beginning of the microline and terminated at the end of the microline.

The experiments revealed that a genuine microline had on average more than six hits per 100 optically-recognized characters. In contrast, a printed microline check had almost no hits. It is anticipated that the accuracy of the microline feature could be improved with rigorous training of the Tesseract OCR engine for bank-specific check samples.

## 5.3 Check Alterations

A check alteration involves adding and/or replacing information on a check for malicious purposes. Altering bank checks is one of the easiest ways to perpetrate check fraud. This work focuses on the detection of erasable ink or removable ink used to alter bank checks. A fraudster often uses a magic pen with erasable ink; the ink is easily removed using the eraser attached to the end of the pen. The fraudster then offers the magic pen to the check writer to fill out the check; following this, certain information (e.g., payee name) is erased and replaced, and the resulting fraudulent check is submitted for clearance.

The following observations were made upon studying altered checks:

- Alteration of a check using a magic pen eraser affects the texture of the region of the check.

- The luminance and contrast of the check region are also affected and can be distinguished from the rest of the check.

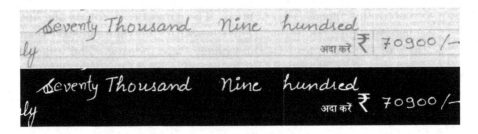

*Figure 7.* Original image (top) and text masked image $I_M$ (bottom).

The following detection method based on gamma correction identifies the regions where an eraser was used:

- **Pre-Processing:** The four regions of interest – payee name, amount in words (line 1), amount in words (line 2) and amount in figures – were segmented based on the bank-specific margins.

  Let $f(x, y)$ be the original RGB image (top of Figure 7) and $B_{xy}$ be the blue channel of image $f(x, y)$. The grayscale image $G(x, y)$ must be subtracted from $B_{xy}$ in order to extract the dominant blue color region image $I_B$. This enables the extraction of the luminance from the normalized blue channel image $B_{xy}$ (note that negative values are truncated). The dominant blue color region image $I_B$ is given by:

$$I_B = B_{xy} - G(x, y) \qquad (3)$$

  The highlighted image $I_B$ was converted to the text masked binary image $I_M$ (bottom of Figure 7) using the Otsu threshold $T$. The masked image $I_M$ was used to remove the text region in further processing. Note that, although the experiments were only conducted for the most commonly used blue and black inks, the feature extraction method used in this work is applicable to any color of ink.

- **Feature Extraction:** Identification of the altered region involves the application of the gamma correction method followed by post-processing. Let $S_{xy} = f(x, y)$ be the intensity of an image at location $(x, y)$ where $S_{xy} = [R_{xy} \ G_{xy} \ B_{xy}]$. Then, the gamma-corrected image is given by:

$$I_G = cS^\gamma \qquad (4)$$

*Figure 8.* Gamma-corrected image $I_G$.

*Figure 9.* Gamma-corrected binary image $I_{GB}$.

*Figure 10.* Image showing the erased region.

where $c$ and $\gamma$ ($\gamma > 1$) are positive constants.

Figure 8 shows the gamma-corrected image $I_G$. Since the background of the image belongs to a brighter region, the value of $\gamma$ must be greater than one to increase the contrast. The experiments used $\gamma = 9$.

The blue channel of the gamma-corrected image $I_G$ was converted to a binary image, primarily because the background was blue. The noise from the binary image was then removed to obtain the gamma-corrected binary image $I_{GB}$.

Figure 9 shows the gamma-corrected binary image $I_{GB}$ containing only the text and the erased region.

Finally, the masked image $I_M$ was subtracted from $I_{GB}$ to obtain the erased region. Figure 10 shows the image of the erased region.

## 5.4    Printed vs. Handwritten Signatures

A signature is a common feature in bank checks, certificates and other legal documents. When clearing a check, a bank attempts to match the signature on the check against a pre-stored scanned signature of the account holder. Several researchers have focused on the problem

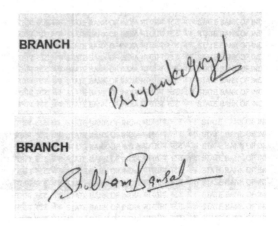

*Figure 11.*   Handwritten signature (top) and printed signature (bottom).

of distinguishing between genuine and forged handwritten signatures. However, little, if any, research has attempted to distinguish printed signatures from handwritten signatures.

Figure 11 shows images of a handwritten signature (top) and printed signature (bottom). In order to distinguish between the two types of signatures, ideas were drawn from research that attempts to differentiate between printed characters and handwritten characters [2]. In particular, the research revealed that high-density black and dark colored dots are present in printed characters whereas handwritten characters have no such dots.

In a bank check clearance system, scanned copies of the printed signature and genuine signature are compared. Thus, noise from the scanner is present in both scanned samples.

In the case of a check with a genuine signature, the check is scanned to produce the "original" scanned signature for verification. However, in the case of a check with a printed signature, a genuine signature is first scanned and the scanned image is then printed on the check. When the check with the printed signature is to be verified, it is scanned to produce the "candidate" signature for verification. This leads to three distinct noise sources: (i) noise generated when scanning the signature $N_S$; (ii) noise generated when printing the signature $N_P$; and (iii) noise generated when scanning the signature for verification $N_V$.

In the case of a handwritten signature, only the scanner noise $N_V$ (dark colored dots) is present. However, in the case of a printed signature, the noise introduced is amplified, corresponding to $N_S + N_P + N_V$.

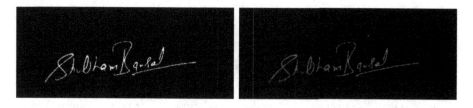

*Figure 12.* Mask image (left) and signature region image (right).

Therefore, the correlation of the RGB channel pixels in a printed signature is much less than that for a genuine signature.

The following correlation-based method was used to distinguish printed signatures from handwritten signatures:

- **Pre-Processing:** The first step was to segment the signature text region. Only the blue color channel was considered in the experiment, but the approach is applicable to the other channels. Note that the method for segmenting the blue color text in the signature region was the same as that used for check alteration detection.

  The mask image $I_M$ (Figure 12 (left)) was superimposed over the original image to obtain the signature region image $I_S$ (Figure 12 (right)).

- **Noise Removal:** The scanner introduces noise in a scanned image due to minute imperfections and dirt on the scanner lens and/or camera. A noise removal filtering function (discrete wavelet transform) was used to remove the noise from the image. Applying the discrete wavelet transform to the signature region image $I_S$ yielded the discrete wavelet transform coefficients for the four sub-bands (approximate, vertical, horizontal and diagonal). The image generated through the approximate sub-band $I_A$ was selected; this image contains low-frequency components indicating that the unwanted noise was removed.

- **Feature Extraction:** After obtaining the approximate sub-band image $I_A$, its RGB planes ($I_{R\_A}$, $I_{G\_A}$, $I_{B\_A}$) were converted to separate column vectors and stored in a matrix $M$. The zero rows in $M$ were removed because they belong to the background. Next, the cross-correlation $C_{xy}$ was calculated for $I_{R\_A}$-$I_{G\_A}$, $I_{R\_A}$-$I_{B\_A}$

*Table 3.* Pantograph results for SBI checks.

| ID | Genuine | | Printed | | | |
| | | | Laser | | Inkjet | |
| | UNCC | Roughness | UNCC | Roughness | UNCC | Roughness |
|---|---|---|---|---|---|---|
| 1 | 21402 | 14.56680 | 40309 | 31.15814 | 53481 | 46.73548 |
| 2 | 17828 | 16.77730 | 41026 | 34.95251 | 55845 | 47.81659 |
| 3 | 19808 | 17.27510 | 42947 | 30.54739 | 52846 | 44.30893 |
| 4 | 23949 | 19.92390 | 46798 | 31.84794 | 57262 | 47.74739 |
| 5 | 18905 | 18.23660 | 39749 | 30.84759 | 54736 | 42.93744 |
| 6 | 24237 | 16.41492 | 41449 | 32.85495 | 52846 | 48.47393 |
| 7 | 21415 | 19.62349 | 42137 | 31.95751 | 50746 | 45.17336 |
| 8 | 20757 | 17.06158 | 46583 | 33.84748 | 51746 | 43.58479 |
| 9 | 17030 | 17.63441 | 38596 | 30.85754 | 48364 | 41.28025 |
| 10 | 24511 | 18.47682 | 43957 | 35.75568 | 59791 | 48.85941 |

and $I_{G\_A}$-$I_{B\_A}$ using the equation:

$$C_{xy} = \frac{\sum_{i=1}^{n}(x_i - \bar{x})(y_i - \bar{y})}{\sqrt{\sum_{i=1}^{n}(x_i - \bar{x})^2}\sqrt{\sum_{i=1}^{n}(y_i - \bar{y})^2}} \tag{5}$$

This yielded three correlation values, $C_{RG}$, $C_{RB}$ and $C_{GB}$, corresponding to the R-G, R-B and G-B channels, respectively. The high noise $N_S + N_P + N_V$ in a printed signature resulted in low correlation values between the channels. On the other hand, a handwritten signature with low noise $N_V$ yielded high correlation values between the channels.

## 6.    Experimental Results

This section describes the experimental results obtained by applying the methods proposed for detecting printed checks, altered checks and printed signatures.

## 6.1    Check Pantograph Results

Table 3 shows the pantograph results for SBI checks. The results clearly show that the unique color count (UNCC) and surface roughness values are high for printed checks. Since inkjet printers produce more noise than laser printers, the inkjet printer results have very high unique color counts and surface roughness values.

*Table 4.* Microline results for SBI checks.

| ID | OCRed Characters | Matched Three Consec. Letters | OCRed Characters | Matched Three Consec. Letters |
|----|----|----|----|----|
| 1 | 100 | 9 | 100 | 0 |
| 2 | 100 | 7 | 100 | 0 |
| 3 | 100 | 12 | 100 | 0 |
| 4 | 100 | 8 | 100 | 0 |
| 5 | 100 | 11 | 100 | 0 |
| 6 | 100 | 14 | 100 | 0 |
| 7 | 100 | 9 | 100 | 0 |
| 8 | 100 | 20 | 100 | 0 |
| 9 | 100 | 7 | 100 | 0 |
| 10 | 100 | 9 | 100 | 0 |

## 6.2    Check Microline Results

Table 4 shows the microline results for SBI checks. Note that the optical character recognition output corresponding to the printed microline text in the fifth (last) column has no matches in all ten test cases (i.e., no consecutive three letters from the original microlines matched the optical character recognition outputs). This is because the shapes of characters in the microline text were deformed during the printing process.

## 6.3    Check Alteration Results

The process for identifying check alterations is described in Section 5.3. A check is determined to be altered when an altered segment is present in the check. The threshold value used to classify alterations was a 200-pixel cluster (Figure 10). If the cluster size in a suspect check image is greater than the threshold, then the check is classified as an altered check. Note that the threshold depends on the handwriting of an individual. Since compact handwriting requires less space for alteration, a lower threshold would be needed.

## 6.4    Printed vs. Handwritten Signature Results

The results in Table 5 clearly indicate that printed signatures have low correlation values $C_{RG}$ and $C_{RB}$ for the R-G and R-B channels, respectively. The reason is the high noise density introduced by the scanner and printer.

*Table 5.*   Signature results for synthetic SBI checks.

| ID | Handwritten | | | Printed (Generated) | | |
|----|-------------|---------|---------|---------|---------|---------|
|    | $C_{RG}$ | $C_{RB}$ | $C_{GB}$ | $C_{RG}$ | $C_{RB}$ | $C_{GB}$ |
| 1 | 0.948287 | 0.883214 | 0.838135 | 0.461677 | 0.192432 | 0.941885 |
| 2 | 0.993438 | 0.892849 | 0.947063 | 0.471177 | 0.361397 | 0.981709 |
| 3 | 0.936733 | 0.811338 | 0.825890 | 0.322946 | 0.217322 | 0.983191 |
| 4 | 0.992668 | 0.909226 | 0.874532 | 0.778200 | 0.444900 | 0.868800 |
| 5 | 0.956653 | 0.853285 | 0.827092 | 0.876000 | 0.499600 | 0.861900 |
| 6 | 0.972817 | 0.977369 | 0.922073 | 0.769200 | 0.466300 | 0.927000 |
| 7 | 0.986645 | 0.825093 | 0.794458 | 0.437484 | 0.351723 | 0.937494 |
| 8 | 0.985777 | 0.816379 | 0.763721 | 0.539573 | 0.289031 | 0.967497 |

*Table 6.*   Signature results for real SBI checks.

| ID | Handwritten (Bank Samples) | | | Printed (Bank Samples) | | |
|----|-------------|---------|---------|---------|---------|---------|
|    | $C_{RG}$ | $C_{RB}$ | $C_{GB}$ | $C_{RG}$ | $C_{RB}$ | $C_{GB}$ |
| 1 | 0.968258 | 0.892728 | 0.825478 | 0.253335 | 0.165359 | 0.982213 |
| 2 | 0.987253 | 0.927229 | 0.676692 | 0.884461 | 0.315626 | 0.703555 |
| 3 | 0.935719 | 0.815278 | 0.861325 | 0.627446 | 0.464848 | 0.849006 |

Table 6 shows the signature results for real check samples obtained from SBI. Note that the results are very similar to those in Table 5 for the synthetic check samples created by the authors of this chapter.

*Table 7.*   Pantograph results for SBI, AXIS, PNB and HDFC checks.

| Bank | Genuine | | Printed | | | |
|------|---------|-----------|---------|---------|---------|---------|
|      |         |           | Laser | | Inkjet | |
|      | UNCC Range | Roughness Range | UNCC Range | Roughness Range | UNCC Range | Roughness Range |
| SBI | 17,000–25,000 | 14–20 | 38,000–47,000 | 30–35 | 48,000–60,000 | 41–48 |
| AXIS | 18,000–24,000 | 18–22 | 37,000–45,000 | 41–45 | 51,000–63,000 | 55–60 |
| PNB | 21,000–30,000 | 27–30 | 41,000–52,000 | 47–54 | 57,000–70,000 | 67–75 |
| HDFC | 9,000–15,000 | 14–17 | 33,000–39,000 | 23–27 | 70,000–88,000 | 57–65 |

## 6.5   Results for Checks from Multiple Banks

Tables 7, 8 and 9 show the results obtained for pantographs, microlines and signatures in checks from the four banks considered in this study. The range of each feature was calculated by applying each detection method to all the check samples from each bank. The detection

*Table 8.* Microline results for SBI, AXIS, PNB, HDFC checks.

| Bank | OCRed Characters | Matched Three Consec. Letters Range | OCRed Characters | Matched Three Consec. Letters Range |
|------|------------------|--------------------------------------|------------------|--------------------------------------|
| SBI  | 100 | 7–20 | 100 | 0   |
| AXIS | 100 | 8–17 | 100 | 0–2 |
| PNB  | 100 | 6–18 | 100 | 0   |
| HDFC | 100 | 8–22 | 100 | 0   |

*Table 9.* Signature results for SBI, AXIS, PNB and HDFC checks.

| Bank | Handwritten | | | Printed (Generated) | | |
|------|-------------|---|---|---------------------|---|---|
| | $C_{RG}$ Range | $C_{RB}$ Range | $C_{GB}$ Range | $C_{RG}$ Range | $C_{RB}$ Range | $C_{GB}$ Range |
| SBI  | 0.90–0.99 | 0.70–0.99 | 0.65–0.95 | 0.39–0.88 | 0.19–0.70 | 0.70–0.98 |
| AXIS | 0.86–0.99 | 0.71–0.98 | 0.63–0.94 | 0.27–0.85 | 0.16–0.50 | 0.73–0.97 |
| PNB  | 0.85–0.98 | 0.72–0.99 | 0.65–0.91 | 0.30–0.89 | 0.23–0.48 | 0.78–0.98 |
| HDFC | 0.89–0.99 | 0.74–0.99 | 0.66–0.89 | 0.42–0.90 | 0.27–0.45 | 0.71–0.95 |

methods work very well at 600 dpi resolution. The detection methods were also tested at 300 and 1200 dpi resolutions for each feature. At the 300 dpi resolution, the microline feature fails because all the characters in the microline text merge with each other. The pantograph and printed signature results are same; however, in the case of check alteration, the accuracy drops slightly. At the 1200 dpi resolution, all the features provide very good results compared with the 600 and 300 dpi samples, but the computation time is higher for the 1200 dpi resolution. The 1200 dpi resolution should become more feasible as powerful computer systems become cheaper and easily available.

## 7. Integrated Check Fraud Detection Tool

An integrated scanner-based tool that implements all the methods described above has been developed to assist bank personnel in detecting check fraud. The algorithms, which were written using Matlab 2013a, execute on a Dell Inspiron 14R N4010 workstation with 4 GB RAM and an Intel Core i3 M 380 2.53 GHz processor. The fraud detection tool, which can process a check within two seconds, is efficient, inexpensive and works on low-magnification devices. Moreover, it is easily scaled to handle images with 600 dpi resolution taken by smartphones.

## 8.    Conclusions

Counterfeit documents are typically detected by human experts who manually analyze suspect documents using a microscope and video spectral comparator. This process is time-consuming, inefficient and non-scalable; indeed, it is infeasible for deployment at large banks. In contrast, the proposed check fraud detection methods are automated, low-cost, efficient and scalable. One method effectively determines whether or not a check is genuine or printed. Another method detects erasable ink alterations on checks by localizing the erased regions in the visible light spectrum. A third method distinguishes printed signatures from handwritten signatures based on the high-density noise introduced by scanners and printers.

The proposed check fraud detection methods have certain limitations. The principal limitation is that the methods have to be tuned to specific bank check designs, including the color schemes. Other limitations, which will be addressed in future research, include processing torn and damaged checks, signatures in colors other than blue and checks with information written in inks of multiple colors.

## References

[1] M. Abd-ElZaher, Different types of inks having certain medicolegal importance: Deciphering faded and physically erased handwriting, *Egyptian Journal of Forensic Sciences*, vol. 4(2), pp. 39–44, 2014.

[2] Australian Payments Clearing Association, Australian Payments Fraud: Details and Data – 2016, ABN 12 055 136 519, Sydney, Australia (www.apca.com.au/docs/default-source/fraud-stat istics/australian_payments_fraud_details_and_data_2016.pdf), 2016.

[3] P. Deng, L. Jaw, J. Wang and C. Tung, Trace copy forgery detection for handwritten signature verification, *Proceedings of the Thirty-Seventh Annual IEEE International Carnahan Conference on Security Technology*, pp. 450–455, 2003.

[4] U. Garain and B. Halder, On automatic authenticity verification of printed security documents, *Proceedings of the Sixth Indian Conference on Computer Vision, Graphics and Image Processing*, pp. 706–713, 2008.

[5] GitHub, Tesseract OCR (`github.com/tesseract-ocr/tesseract/wiki`), 2017.

[6] G. Gupta, C. Mazumdar, M. Rao and R. Bhosale, Paradigm shift in document related frauds: Characteristics identification for development of a non-destructive automated system for printed documents, *Digital Investigation*, vol. 3(1), pp. 43–55, 2006.

[7] G. Gupta, S. Saha, S. Chakraborty and C. Mazumdar, Document frauds: Identification and linking fake documents to scanners and printers, *Proceedings of the International Conference on Computing: Theory and Applications*, pp. 497–501, 2007.

[8] D. Kennard, W. Barrett and T. Sederberg, Offline signature verification and forgery detection using a 2-D geometric warping approach, *Proceedings of the Twenty-First International Conference on Pattern Recognition*, pp. 3733–3736, 2012.

[9] R. Kumar and G. Gupta, Forensic authentication of bank checks, in *Advances in Digital Forensics XII*, G. Peterson and S. Shenoi (Eds.), Springer, Heidelberg, Germany, pp. 311–322, 2016.

[10] C. Lampert, L. Mei and T. Breuel, Printing technique classification for document counterfeit detection, *Proceedings of the International Conference on Computational Intelligence and Security*, vol. 1, pp. 639–644, 2006.

[11] R. Patil and S. Takale, Signature verification by distance matrix method for bank check process, *Proceedings of the International Conference on Electrical, Electronics, Signals, Communication and Optimization*, 2015.

[12] G. Prakash and S. Sharma, Computer vision and fuzzy logic based offline signature verification and forgery detection, *Proceedings of the IEEE International Conference on Computational Intelligence and Computing Research*, 2014.

[13] M. Rajendar and R. Pal, Detection of manipulated check images in a check truncation system using mismatch in pixels, *Proceedings of the Second International Conference on Business and Information Management*, pp. 28–33, 2014.

[14] Rediff on the Net, In a year, bank fraud doubles – Maharashtra and West Bengal lead the way in bank fraud, November 18, 2015.

[15] Reserve Bank of India, Handbook of Statistics on the Indian Economy, 2014-15, Mumbai, India (`rbidocs.rbi.org.in/rdocs/Publications/PDFs/00HC398B27C6AFF47039ABE93049886B494.PDF`), 2015.

[16] A. Sarkar, R. Verma and G. Gupta, Detecting counterfeit currency and identifying its source, in *Advances in Digital Forensics IX*, G. Peterson and S. Shenoi (Eds.), Springer, Heidelberg, Germany, pp. 367–384, 2013.

[17] J. Xie, C. Qin, T. Liu, Y. He and M. Xu, A new method to identify the authenticity of banknotes based on texture roughness, *Proceedings of the IEEE International Conference on Robotics and Biomimetics*, pp. 1268–1271, 2009.

[18] M. Yusof and V. Madasu, Signature verification and forgery detection system, *Proceedings of the Student Conference on Research and Development*, pp. 9–14, 2003.

VII

# FORENSIC TECHNIQUES

Chapter 15

# AUTOMATED COLLECTION AND CORRELATION OF FILE PROVENANCE INFORMATION

Ryan Good and Gilbert Peterson

**Abstract**     The provenance of a file is a detailing of its origins and activities. Tools have been developed that help maintain the provenance of files. However, these tools require prior installation on a computer of interest before and while provenance-generating events occur. The automated tool described in this chapter can reconstruct the provenance of a file from a variety of artifacts. It identifies relevant temporal and user correlations between the artifacts and presents them to an investigator. Results from six use cases demonstrate that these correlations are reliable and valuable in digital forensic investigations.

**Keywords:** File provenance, Windows operating systems, forensic timelines

## 1.     Introduction

Computer forensics, which involves analyzing a digital medium for evidence of a crime, requires the tracking and digesting myriad files and their relationships. Parsing this information can be a daunting task and the time requirement to conduct an analysis can prevent an investigator from obtaining the information needed to prosecute a crime. The automated extraction of the relationships between files and their origins, along with the number of times and ways in which they have been modified and accessed, can greatly speed up this process.

The provenance of a data object (e.g., file) is the "ownership and the actions performed on [the] data object" [7]. Ownership describes the creator of the file or the user responsible for the file arriving on the system, while the actions describe how the file was interacted with post arrival. In many cases, it is important to discover the responsible party for the arrival of a file on a system in order to determine attribution.

© IFIP International Federation for Information Processing 2017

Published by Springer International Publishing AG 2017. All Rights Reserved

G. Peterson and S. Shenoi (Eds.): Advances in Digital Forensics XIII, IFIP AICT 511, pp. 269–284, 2017.

DOI: 10.1007/978-3-319-67208-3_15

Incorrectly arriving at the heredity of a file or not providing enough evidence can derail a case.

The automated tool presented in this chapter enables a digital forensic investigator to quickly identify correlations that can determine the source and activity of a file in a system image. This is accomplished by extracting common sources of provenance information from a storage media image. The automated tool then processes and compares the extracted information to determine the correlations that exist. The correlations are provided to the digital forensic investigator to assist with the case.

Six use cases demonstrate the efficacy of provenance information extraction and correlation. The use cases cover a range of file sources as well as common file activities. The correlations that are discovered are listed within certain categories. A short explanation is provided for each use case along with the results, demonstrating how the automated tool can help a digital forensic investigator identify the provenance of files.

## 2.     Related Work

This section discusses methods for gathering file provenance information. It also provides an overview of the locations that may contain temporal and ownership artifacts in a Windows operating system. Finally, it discusses research in the area of automated provenance creation.

Provenance refers to the earliest known history of an object [7]. It can also refer to the record of ownership of an object. In the context of a computer system or network, provenance pertains to the origins of a piece of data, its relationship to other pieces of data and the processes that created and modified it. One use of provenance is as metadata, which enables a user to search for a file based on past interactions or the original source. A user may forget the document that he/she was working on, but may remember that email was exchanged with someone about pertinent data. This information can help reduce the search space of possible documents, enabling the user to quickly identify the object of interest.

## 2.1     File Provenance Maintenance Systems

A file provenance maintenance system tracks and gathers file provenance information. The system runs in the background and monitors and records all file actions performed on the system. For example, the Provenance Aware Storage System (PASS) [10] collects and maintains provenance information comprising references between files and memory

*Table 1.* Temporal Granularity.

| Target | Source | Granularity |
|---|---|---|
| Registry Last Modified Times | NTUSER.dat | Microseconds |
| File MAC Times | File of Interest | Seconds |
| History Entries | Browser History Files | Seconds |
| Recent Documents | NTUSER.dat | Days |
| USB Key | SYSTEM | Seconds |
| User/Group Information | SAM | Seconds |
| CurrentVersion Subkey | SOFTWARE | Seconds |

elements such as pipes and sockets in order to create the provenance of files.

The File Provenance System (FiPS) [14] enables the recreation of files. This system improves on the significant overhead required by PASS. However, it still suffers from overhead due to its use of a stackable filesystem. Stackable filesystems are much easier to develop than kernel-level filesystems. Unfortunately, this ease of use comes at the cost of performance [15].

## 2.2 Sources of Provenance Data

Sources of file provenance information in Windows operating systems running the NT Filesystem (NTFS) include the modified, accessed and created (MAC) times, file metadata, Windows registry hives and application history, and log files. Table 1 lists the sources of provenance data and their temporal granularities.

**NTFS MAC Times and File Metadata.** NTFS stores the modified, accessed and created (MAC) times for each file in the Master File Table (MFT) [8]. The mtime is the time of a file's last modification; it updates whenever the file contents change. The ctime updates whenever a file's content changes; it also updates whenever the file attributes change. A file's attributes can change for many reasons, including file movement and ownership changes. The atime is the last interaction time of a file and updates after any type of interaction, including simply opening the file.

To summarize, if a file is simply opened and viewed, only its atime changes. If the file is opened, viewed and edited, the atime and mtime change. If the file is opened, edited and placed in another directory, then all three values change. It is also important to note that all three values change when the file is copied and pasted. This is because copying and pasting creates a new file. This does not occur if the file is simply moved because it is still the same file. When a file is copied or moved, the MAC times of the containing folders reflect similar changes.

Many file formats contain metadata, which is data about data. File metadata may comprise the file creator, the subject that last modified the file and when actions on the file occurred. It may be tempting to simply accept these values and assume that the origins of the file are known. Unfortunately, values may be missing and are easily modified. Therefore, a digital forensic investigator should either fill in the missing information or validate the available data. Metadata can be acquired in a number of ways; the ExifTool [6] was used to extract metadata in this work.

**Registry Hives.** The registry is also a source of provenance for a filesystem. The registry contains a number of hive files that have responsibilities ranging from tracking user activities to holding system configuration information. Whenever an event occurs in a filesystem, it can be expected to impact the registry in some way. Every registry key has a value known as the "last write time," which is modified when a relevant event occurs. This value is extracted by timeline generators such as `log2timeline` [4] when they collect temporal artifacts from storage media. RegRipper [13] is also a useful tool for searching the registry and collecting items of interest.

The registry has two types of hives: (i) user hives; and (ii) system hives [2]. User hives focus on specific users and contain data that can be used to trace user activity. User hives include `NTUSER.dat` and `USRCLASS.dat`. System hives include the Security, SAM, System, Software and AmCache hives. System hives contain information about the overall functioning of the computer system. Information about external storage connections, user login dates and times, account permissions, program executions, etc. are easily obtained from the hives using tools such as RegRipper.

**Application History Files.** Web browser applications serve as entry points to a file. Browser application history files exist for each user on a system as well as for each browser employed by a user. Each file contains the recent history of a user's activities involving a specific browser. Internet Explorer, Google Chrome and Mozilla Firefox have separate history files that are viewable with the right tools. The history files can be parsed to discern activities that occurred in close temporal proximity to the file's arrival on the system. This can help determine if the file arrived on the system via download from a website.

Each browser requires a separate tool to parse its history. NirSoft provides a suite of tools that includes Internet Explorer History View (IEHV) [11] for viewing Internet Explorer history folders, ChromeHistoryView [12] for the Google Chrome browser and MZHistory View, a Firefox history viewer.

## 2.3 Evidence Correlation

Image analysis tools such as EnCase, Sleuth Kit and Forensic ToolKit can be used to gather event information, but they do not present it in a form that facilitates the comparison of timestamps. Timelines are a visualization aid that assist forensic investigators in understanding the events that occurred on a system. Zeitline [1] allows for enhanced visualization of the data in a storage media image in the form of timelines. An investigator may import events that are grouped, filtered and presented in a manner that is more indicative of a timeline or sequence. The `log2timeline` tool expands on this functionality by incorporating additional sources of timeline data such as artifacts and log files. Timeline tools facilitate information presentation, but still require effort on the part of a human to parse the events and determine correlations. PyDFT [5] improves on the basic timeline functionality by analyzing low-level events to determine when high-level interactions (e.g., USB device connections) occur. The functionality provided by these timeline tools is valuable, but they do not provide summarized information about a file of interest.

A clear and concise view of relevant data makes it easier for digital forensic professionals to quickly parse through information that can aid in their investigations. The FACE tool [3] enhances data presentation and automates forensic data correlation; it primarily focuses on data in system memory and network traffic captures. Ramparser, a tool for Linux memory analysis, gathers information from running processes, open files and socket/netstat information. This data is provided by Ramparser to FACE, which then discovers correlations. Unfortunately, none of this is viable for storage media images.

Forensic automation is also valuable for determining the attributes of a file. The approach leverages machine learning techniques to sift through large amounts of data. For example, a machine learning algorithm can use provenance data to determine a file's extension [9]. This data includes the relationships between files and processes, their locations relative to each other and the frequency with which they are accessed.

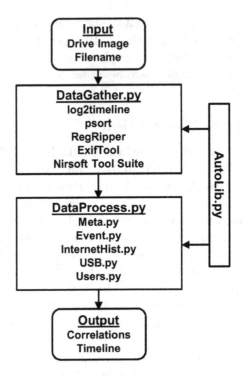

*Figure 1.*    Provenance Collection Tool.

## 3.        Provenance Collection

The Provenance Collection Tool developed as part of this research constructs the provenance of a file of interest and its logical path in a storage media image. The tool runs several external programs to collect temporal and association artifacts related to the file. It then parses the information to discover correlations that can help determine the origin of the file and activities involving the file.

Figure 1 shows the provenance extraction and correlation process. Data is collected by DataGather.py, which invokes the RegRipper, log2-timeline, psort, ExifTool, ChromeHistoryView, MZHistory View and IEHV tools. Next, DataProcess.py attempts to determine the origins of the file in the image. It accomplishes this by searching for indicators that a forensic investigator often leverages to determine file origin. The two Python scripts use functions in AutoLib.py, a library created as part of this research. The Provenance Collection Tool considers indicators related to local file creation, web browsers, USB devices, etc. The indicators are passed to the user, who can draw conclusions and determine how to best tailor the forensic analysis to the investigation.

## 3.1 Data Gathering

DataGather.py requires the file of interest to be specified by its name and logical path, along with the location of the image in which it is contained. In order to mount the image, DataGather.py needs to know the start block of the image of interest. It obtains this information by running mmls on the image and routing the output to a text file, which is parsed to find the start block of the image. The block size is assumed to be 512 because this is almost always the case. After the information has been gathered, the mount command is invoked to locally mount the image as read only. The find command is then invoked to find the file of interest. Following this, DataGather.py checks for a file with the same name that has a .torrent extension, as this can be an indicator of a torrent source.

File metadata is extracted using ExifTool. This tool collects information about the file creator, editor and creation/editing dates/times, if they are available. The state command is then invoked to obtain the NTFS MAC times of the file.

After capturing the metadata, DataGather.py obtains the last write times from the NTUSER.dat hive, along with any pertinent values. The NTUSER.dat hive is examined because it contains most of the information relevant to file provenance, including user activities and program execution. This is accomplished using the log2timeline tool, along with filters that prevent it from analyzing the entire image.

For user attribution, DataGather.py checks the Users folder in Windows to determine the users that are present in the system. The default users that are present in all systems are filtered along with unrelated directories. These include All Users, desktop.ini, Default, Default User and Public.

DataGather.py obtains the USB connection history from the system hive. This information includes the first date/time that the system interfaced with the USB device, most recent time that the system interfaced with the USB device and serial number of the device. Following this, the RegRipper samparse plugin collects all the relevant information in the SAM hive. Since log2timeline gathers information in the GMT/UCT format while other sources are relative to the system time, the system timezone is parsed from the SYSTEM registry hive to obtain the data.

The next item of interest is the user web history. The IEHV tool is used to obtain a user's Internet Explorer history by examining the corresponding history folder. Following this, a similar process occurs with ChromeHistoryView. Finally, the MZHistoryView tool obtains the user's Firefox history.

## 3.2    Data Processing

A digital forensic investigator typically has to manually parse the collected data in order to determine where relevant correlations may exist. DataProcess.py automates many of the correlation checks that are relevant to file provenance by parsing the data and modifying it so that all the data is in the same format and comparable. It then searches for correlations and sets the relevant Boolean flags based on its findings.

DataProcess.py facilitates the comparisons by organizing all the data sources into class structures. All timestamps are modified to be in UTC 24-hour time, the names of months are replaced by their numerical equivalents, etc., in order to enable value comparisons.

Five categories of provenance correlations are considered. The categories are: (i) local factors; (ii) browser factors; (iii) USB factors; (iv) Skype factors; and (v) torrent factors.

**Local Factors.**    The following Boolean flags are indicators of local file creation or interactions:

- **recentuser:** The file of interest appears in the user's recent document registry key list.

- **localuser:** A reference to the file exists in the user's recent documents or any recent documents iterations in the history (found using log2timeline).

- **date_check:** Relevant timeline entries exist in NTUSER.dat, which refer to the file of interest on the day of its creation. The creation date is determined from the metadata, if available. If no metadata is available, the flag is set to false.

- **time_check:** Relevant timeline entries exist in NTUSER.dat, which refer to the file of interest within 30 minutes of its creation. The creation time is determined from the metadata, if available. If no metadata is available, the flag is set to false.

- **systemuser:** The file creator has the same user name as another system user. The creating user is determined from the metadata, if available. If no metadata is available, the flag is set to false.

- **word_create_day:** Microsoft Word was used on the creation date of the file. The flag is only set to true if the file type is a Microsoft Word document.

- **word_appear_day:** Microsoft Word was used on the first day that the file was seen on the system. This flag is mostly a fail-safe if the file metadata is not available. It is also useful to reinforce the validity of the metadata and to indicate the possibility of editing, but not creation. The flag is set to true if Microsoft Word ran on the same day that the file first appeared in the log created by log2timeline based on NTUSER.dat.

- **impossiblelocal:** The operating system was installed on the system after the file was created. Therefore, the file could not have been created on the system. The creation date/time is determined from the metadata. Therefore, if metadata is unavailable, the flag is set to false.

- **movement:** The file was likely moved within the system file structure. This is determined based on the file's MAC times. If mtime is much different from ctime, then the file was likely moved because there are few other reasons for this difference in the timestamps.

- **editing:** This indicates possible file editing while the file was on the system of interest. This is based on the file's MAC times as well as NTUSER.dat timestamps. If mtime is not relatively close to the first date/time the file was seen on the system, then the file has likely been edited. Note that this could also occur if the user had copied and pasted the file of interest and then deleted the original file. This is because the system would consider the copied file as a new file and reset the MAC times to the time when the file was copied while the same arrival date/time would be in NTUSER.dat.

- **difmod:** The file was modified by someone other than the creator.

- **samedaylogin:** This flag is set to true if the last login date of a system user is the same as the date that the file arrived on the system. All the users with the matching last login date are listed.

**Browser Factors.** The following Boolean flags are indicators of browser source:

- **relevant_chrome_visits:** This flag is set to true if Chrome websites were visited within ±2 hours of the file's arrival on the system. If this is the case, all the relevant visits are recorded. For each visit, the user who visited the site, the site that was visited and the date and time of the visit are listed.

- **relevant_ie_visits:** This flag is the same as that for Chrome, except that it is for Internet Explorer.

- **relevant_firefox_visits:** This flag is the same as that for Chrome, except that it is for Firefox.

**USB Factors.** The following Boolean flags are indicators of USB source:

- **timelinerelevant_removable_disk_usage:** This flag is set to true if a timeline entry references the file of interest and a USB device. This usually occurs when the recently used documents contain references to both items at any point in time.

- **usbdatematch:** A removable disk was used on the same day that the file first arrived on the system. This is determined based on the output of RegRipper's `USBdevices` plugin, which examines the system hive to determine when USB devices were last used. This flag assumes that, if a user decides to transfer a malicious or inappropriate file to a computer using a USB device, the USB device will most likely not be used again. For this reason, the USB device's last write times are compared against the first sighting of the file in the `log2timeline` logs.

**Skype Factors.** The following Boolean flags are indicators of Skype source:

- **skypedatematch:** Skype was used on the same day that the file first arrived on the system. This is determined by searching for references to `Skype.exe` under the `UserAssist` key in the registry. An entry is created whenever Skype is used. All updates to this key can be seen in the timeline created by running `log2timeline` on the `NTUSER.dat` hive.

- **skype30min:** Skype was used within 30 minutes of the file first being seen on the system. This is the same check as `skypedatemach` except that the granularity of the check is narrower.

**Torrent Factors.** The following Boolean flags are indicators of torrent source:

- **torrentfile:** A torrent file exists that has the same name as the file of interest. This file is found by searching the system for the file of interest with `.torrent` appended to the end of the filename. If a file with this extension is found, it is highly likely that the source of the file of interest is a torrent file.

- **fwiredatematch:** FrostWire was used on the day that the file first arrived on the system. This is determined by searching for references to `FrostWire.exe` under the `UserAssist` key in the registry. An entry is created whenever FrostWire is used. All updates to this key can be seen in the timeline created by running `log2timeline` on the `NTUSER.dat` hive.

## 4.     Experimental Results

The effectiveness of the tool in constructing the provenance of files is demonstrated via six use cases. For each use case, a user conducted a different interaction with a file of interest. After the interaction, the computer media was imaged and analyzed.

Each use case was performed on a computer running Windows 7 Service Pack 2 with Google Chrome, Firefox, FrostWire and Skype installed. The following six use cases were evaluated:

- **Use Case 1:** A user logged on, created a Word document and then logged off. Another user then logged in and edited the Word document.

- **Use Case 2:** A Word document was transferred to the system via USB. A user then edited the Word document.

- **Use Case 3:** A user called someone using Skype and received a Word document from the called party. The file was then moved.

- **Use Case 4:** A user torrented a Word document using FrostWire and then edited the Word document.

- **Use Case 5:** A user downloaded a Word document using Chrome and then edited the Word document.

- **Use Case 6:** A user downloaded a Word document using Internet Explorer and then edited the Word document.

The following flags were set in Use Case 1:

- **difmod:** The file creator and modifier are different.

- **localuser:** The file is in one or more users' recent documents.

- **time_check:** Relevant timeline entries exist that refer to the file within 30 minutes of its creation.

- **systemuser:** The file creator has the same username as a user on the system.

- **word_create_day:** Microsoft Word was used on the system on the creation date of the file.

- **word_appear_day:** Microsoft Word was used on the first day that the file was seen on the system.

- **editing:** The file was possibly edited on the system.

From these flags, a digital forensic investigator can determine that the file was edited and that the editing most likely occurred locally. This is based on the `editing` and `difmod` flags and supported by the `localuser` flag. In addition, the `time_check`, `systemuser`, `localuser` and `word_create_day` flags show that the file was created locally.

The following flags were identified in Use Case 2:

- **usbdatematch:** A removable disk was used on the same day that the file first arrived on the system.

- **timelinerelevant_removable_disk_usage:** A timeline entry references the file of interest as well as a USB device.

- **word_appear_day:** Microsoft Word was used on the first day that the file was seen on the system.

- **difmod:** The file creator and modifier are different.

- **samedaylogin:** The users who last logged in on the same day that the file first arrived on the system are listed.

- **time_check:** Relevant timeline entries exist that refer to the file within 30 minutes of its creation.

The `usbdatematch` and `timelinerelevant_removable_disk_usage` flags indicate that the file could have originated from a USB device. The `word_appear_day` and `difmod` flags show that the file was most likely modified using Microsoft Word after its arrival. The `samedaylogin` flag implies that all the users who logged in that day would be listed, helping narrow down the user who connected the USB device to the system. The `time_check` flag was active due to testing, because the file was quickly transferred after creation for the purposes of this use case; therefore, the presence of this flag can be ignored.

The following flags were identified in Use Case 3:

- **skypedatematch:** Skype was used on the same day that the file first arrived on the system.

- **skype30min:** Skype was used within 30 minutes of the file first being seen on the system.

- **samedaylogin:** The users who last logged in on the same day that the file first arrived on the system are listed.

- **movement:** The file was likely moved in the system file structure.

The `skypedatematch` and `skype30min` flags indicate that Skype was used within 30 minutes of the file's arrival. The `samedaylogin` lists the users who were logged in on the date the file arrived, helping narrow down the user who allowed the file to arrive on the system. The `movement` flag shows that the file may have been moved because the `ctime` and `mtime` are different. The `ctime` and `mtime` values are reported for verification.

The following flags were identified in Use Case 4:

- **torrentfile:** A torrent file exists that has the same name as the file of interest.

- **fwiredatematch:** FrostWire was used on the day that the file was first seen on the system.

- **difmod:** The file creator and modifier are different.

- **editing:** The file was possibly edited on the system.

- **samedaylogin:** The users who last logged in on the same day that the file first arrived on system are listed.

- **impossiblelocal:** The operating system was installed on the system after the file was created.

- **time_check:** Relevant timeline entries exist that refer to the file within 30 minutes of its creation.

- **word_appear_day:** Microsoft Word was used on the first day that the file was seen on the system.

The `torrentfile` and `fwiredatematch` flags indicate a possible torrent source. The combination of the `difmod`, `editing`, `time_check` and `word_appear_day` flags indicate that the file was edited locally with high likelihood. It is unlikely that any of these flags was activated by file creation because of the `impossiblelocal` flag. The `impossiblelocal` flag also indicates the creation date of the file is earlier than that of the operating system. This dramatically decreases the likelihood of local file creation.

The following flags were identified in Use Case 5 and Use Case 6:

- **relevant_chrome_visits:** Chrome was used within ±2 hours of the file's arrival.

- **relevant_ie_visits:** Internet Explorer was used within ±2 hours of the file's arrival.

- **difmod:** The file creator and modifier are different.

- **editing:** The file was possibly edited on the system.

- **samedaylogin:** The users who last logged in on the same day that the file first arrived on system are listed.

- **impossiblelocal:** The operating system was installed on the system after the file was created.

- **time_check:** Relevant timeline entries exist that refer to the file of interest within 30 minutes of its creation.

Use Cases 5 and 6 have similar results because they both involve browser history parsing. The `relevant_chrome_visits` and `relevant_ie_visits` flags are both set, which means the tool lists all the web pages visited within a four-hour period. This provides insight into the source of the file, especially because the file's source web page contains the name of the file in the download mirror. The tool presents information in a readable single-line format, enabling a digital forensic investigator to parse the results easily. The usual login (`samedaylogin`) and editing (`difmod` and `editing`) flags are also active, showing that the file was modified locally.

## 5.      Conclusions

This research demonstrates that it is possible to automatically correlate factors related to file provenance. The factors are of great value to digital forensic investigators who seek to determine the origins and activities of files of interest. Typically, an investigator would have to manually mount the image, run various tools and analyze the results in order to determine file provenance. The Provenance Collection Tool presented in this chapter could shave hours off investigations by revealing correlations that would enable digital forensic investigators to quickly focus their attention on more relevant factors.

There are many other checks that, if incorporated, could greatly enhance the functionality and utility of the tool. For example, many different torrent sources exist apart from FrostWire. While the Provenance Collection Tool focuses on FrostWire to show how torrent detection can occur, it is important that it should account for other torrent tools. The same is true for browsers, starting with the implementation of Firefox history checks. The timespans used by the tool to determine correlations are often arbitrary; therefore, the approach can benefit from a large-scale analysis of user activity that would enable the timespans to be narrowed or broadened to render them more effective.

# References

[1] F. Buchholz and C. Falk, Design and implementation of Zeitline: A forensic timeline, *Digital Investigation*, vol. 6(S), pp. S78–S87, 2005.

[2] H. Carvey, *Windows Registry Forensics: Advanced Digital Forensic Analysis of the Windows Registry*, Syngress, Cambridge, Massachusetts, 2016.

[3] A. Case, A. Cristina, L. Marziale, G. Richard and V. Roussev, FACE: Automated digital evidence discovery and correlation, *Digital Investigation*, vol. 5(S), pp. S65–S75, 2008.

[4] K. Gudjonsson, Mastering the super timeline with log2timeline, InfoSec Reading Room, SANS Institute, Bethesda, Maryland (www.sans.org/reading-room/whitepapers/logging/mastering-super-timeline-log2timeline-33438), 2010.

[5] C. Hargreaves and J. Patterson, An automated timeline reconstruction approach for digital forensic investigations, *Digital Investigations*, vol. 9(S), pp. S69–S79, 2012.

[6] P. Harvey, ExifTool (www.sno.phy.queensu.ca/~phil/exiftool), 2017.

[7] C. Jensen, H. Lonsdale, E. Wynn, J. Cao, M. Slater and T. Dietterich, The life and times of files and information: A study of desktop provenance, *Proceedings of the SIGCHI Conference on Human Factors in Computing Systems*, pp. 767–776, 2010.

[8] G. Lenik, I'm your MAC(b) daddy, presented at *DEF CON 19*, 2011.

[9] D. Margo and R. Smogor, Using provenance to extract semantic file attributes, *Proceedings of the Second Conference on Theory and Practice of Provenance*, 2010.

[10] K. Muniswamy-Reddy, D. Holland, U. Braun and M. Seltzer, Provenance-aware storage systems, *Proceedings of the USENIX Annual Technical Conference*, 2006.

[11] NirSoft, IEHistoryView v1.70 (www.nirsoft.net/utils/iehv.html), 2011.

[12] NirSoft, ChromeHistoryView v1.30 (www.nirsoft.net/utils/chrome_history_view.html), 2017.

[13] B. Shavers, RegRipper (brettshavers.cc/index.php/brettsblog/entry/regripper), 2015.

[14] S. Sultana and E. Bertino, A file provenance system, *Proceedings of the Third ACM Conference on Data and Application Security and Privacy*, pp. 153–156, 2013.

[15] E. Zadok and I. Badulescu, A stackable filesystem interface for Linux, *Proceedings of the LinuxExpo Conference*, pp. 141–151, 1999.

# Chapter 16

# USING PERSONAL INFORMATION IN TARGETED GRAMMAR-BASED PROBABILISTIC PASSWORD ATTACKS

Shiva Houshmand and Sudhir Aggarwal

**Abstract**     Passwords are the primary means of authentication and security for online accounts and are commonly used to encrypt files and disks. This research demonstrates how personal information about users can be added systematically to enhance password cracking. Specifically, a dictionary-based probabilistic context-free grammar approach is proposed that effectively incorporates personal information about a targeted user into component grammars and dictionaries used for password cracking. The component grammars model various types of personal information such as family names and dates, previous password information and possible information about sequential passwords. A mathematical model for merging multiple grammars that combines the characteristics of the component grammars is presented. The resulting merged target grammar, which is also merged with a standard grammar, is used along with various dictionaries to generate guesses that quickly match target passwords. The experimental results demonstrate that the approach significantly improves password cracking performance.

**Keywords:** Password cracking, context-free grammars, personal information

## 1.    Introduction

The use of passwords for authentication is almost universal and the quality of passwords continues to be important despite mechanisms such as two-factor authentication and biometrics. A recent survey [15] reports that a typical user has around 26 online accounts, but only five different passwords. To ensure quality passwords, policies are used by many websites to ensure that users employ strong passwords; however, there are no clear indications about the efficacy of these policies.

© IFIP International Federation for Information Processing 2017

Published by Springer International Publishing AG 2017. All Rights Reserved

G. Peterson and S. Shenoi (Eds.): Advances in Digital Forensics XIII, IFIP AICT 511, pp. 285–303, 2017.

DOI: 10.1007/978-3-319-67208-3_16

Research has demonstrated that many passwords from revealed datasets [13] can be broken via improved password cracking techniques. However, in a real-world situation, a substantial number of passwords are not easily broken because users may employ different forms of passwords for "high value" sites.

During forensic investigations of seized hard drives, law enforcement professionals frequently encounter encrypted volumes or disks. Encryption techniques such as the one used by TrueCrypt are specifically designed to take a long time to compute the hashes, rendering it impractical to try millions of guesses; in such situations, additional resources – beyond more computing power – must be brought to bear.

A promising solution is to leverage personal information about users in cracking their passwords. This research explores how knowledge about a user (target) can be used to enhance the ability of law enforcement to attack passwords belonging to the target. The attacker might leverage specific information about the target such as names of family members, important dates, addresses and numbers, as well as possibly some of the target's previous passwords for the same account or from sister accounts. The approach employs the dictionary-based probabilistic context-free grammar (PCFG) approach to password cracking [6, 16, 17], which trains a grammar on revealed password sets and uses the learned grammar – called the attack grammar – to generate guesses in optimal probability order. Personal information about a target can be incorporated in PCFG-based password cracking in a very straightforward manner. The experimental results demonstrate that the approach augmented with information about a target significantly improves password cracking performance.

## 2. Background and Related Work

A probabilistic context-free grammar is derived via training on a large set of revealed passwords. This grammar is then used to generate guesses in probability order. If no other information is known, this is referred to as an optimal off-line or on-line password attack. Interested readers are referred to [6, 17] for details about PCFG-based password cracking.

PCFG-based password cracking has two major phases (and code components):

- **Training:** In this phase, first-level production rules of the grammar are learned. These rules generate base structures from a start symbol $S$. A base structure comprises grammar variables that abstract the class and length of password components. For example, class types can be $L$ denoting alphabet strings, $D$ denoting digits and $S$ denoting special characters. Additionally, $K$ is used for keyboard patterns and $M$ for multi-word patterns. Capitalization is represented by the class type $U/N$ (uppercase/lowercase), but they are treated slightly differently. The length of a substring is indicated as a part of a variable. For example, $S \rightarrow M_8 D_4 S_2$ is a rule that derives a base structure of three variables of the indicated lengths.

Second-level grammar rules derive terminal substrings from base structure variables such as $D_4 \rightarrow 2001$. For example, the derivation of the password *iloveyou2001##* is:

$$
\begin{aligned}
S &\Rightarrow M_8 D_4 S_2 \\
&\Rightarrow iloveyou D_4 S_2 \\
&\Rightarrow iloveyou2001\, S_2 \\
&\Rightarrow iloveyou2001\, \#\#
\end{aligned}
$$

The probabilities of most of these secondary rules are also learned from the training set. Probability smoothing can be used to give appropriate probability values to rules that are not found in the training set. To calculate the probability of a string derived from the start symbol, the probabilities of the rules used in the various steps are multiplied together. Additional information used for cracking is incorporated in dictionaries, which contain words that can replace the $L$ and $M$ structures when generating guesses.

- **Guess Generation:** In this phase, the learned probabilistic context-free grammar and a set of multiple (attack) dictionaries are used to generate password guesses in decreasing probability order. Probabilities are associated with each dictionary. A dictionary can be generated by learning from the training set or via other means. The probabilities of the actual words used during guess generation depend on the dictionaries and their probabilities.

Little research has focused on using personal information, including previous passwords, to improve password cracking. One reason is that very few revealed password datasets with personal information were available. A second reason is ethical concerns about using email and personal information about users, even if they were leaked by hackers and posted on public websites. For example, if one has a revealed email and password, the ethical dilemma is whether it is appropriate to look online to find additional personal information about the user even if the new information is not made public. Several authors [1, 7, 14] have recently used leaked information to explore how users create passwords using personal information and how this information may be used to crack passwords.

Castelluccia et al. [1] have attempted to leverage personal information to improve password cracking using a Markov model [10]. Their OMEN+ system integrates personal information with normal training based on revealed passwords. The fundamental difficulty with the Markov approach [4, 10] is that it is computationally expensive to generate passwords in probability order because the training typically uses the learned probabilities of n-grams to determine the probability of a password string. Thus, it is first necessary to create various discretized probability levels assigned to buckets in which strings are placed based on the 3-gram probabilities of strings in the training set. The strings in the buckets are attempted in the highest probability order of the buckets.

Castelluccia et al. [1] have also explored the use of personal information such as email, birthdays and usernames, but did not use previous passwords or cross-site passwords. Their OMEN+ system attempts to determine if a password set containing personal information has any overlap with a password with personal information. If an overlap exists, then the corresponding probabilities of the overlapping 3-grams are increased based on a parameter. For some reason, instead of targeting a specific individual, Castelluccia et al. modify the 3-gram probabilities such that better results can be obtained for a complete test set. In contrast, the proposed approach uses a highly efficient PCFG-based training system without the problems of the Markov approach. Moreover, it does not require changes to the training or cracking components; instead, only additional grammars and dictionaries have to be created.

Li et al. [7] have explored the use of personal information in password cracking using the 12306 dataset that was leaked from a Chinese railway ticket website. The dataset contains approximately 130,000 Chinese passwords as well as personal information such as email address, username, cell phone number and the user's Chinese name. Additional information that can be extracted includes the birthday and gender of a user. Li et al. extended the probabilistic context-free grammar approach of Weir et al. [17] to develop the Personal-PCFG system. The extension adds a new grammar variable for each type of personal information such as $B$ for birthday, $N$ for name and $E$ for email address; additionally, as in other probabilistic context-free grammars, subscripts are used to indicate lengths. During the preprocessing phase, a password such as *helloalice816!* is converted to the structure *hello$N_5 B_3$!* if the personal information (name and birthday) match.

The problem with this approach is that Li et al. do not appreciate the grammar ambiguity that arises when several base structures yield the same terminal string. Generating guesses in the order of highest probability when using a context-free grammar relies on the grammar being unambiguous. This ensures that there is a well-defined probability for a guess that depends on a single unique derivation.

The ambiguity problem is discussed by Houshmand et al. [6], where several new variables such as $K$ for keyboard combinations and $M$ for multiword combinations are introduced to minimize or eliminate grammar ambiguity. Note that the training and cracking components have to be modified to accommodate the new variables. Furthermore, the highest probability order of guesses generated cannot be maintained unless an effort is made during training to eliminate ambiguity. Otherwise, the PCFG-based approach would still generate guesses for all the base structures, but the probability order of guesses would not be preserved.

Wang et al. [14] also extend probabilistic context-free grammars [17] to accommodate personal information and explore the use of previous passwords. They follow the approach of Li et al. [7], except that instead of using a new variable $B$ for personal information such as birthday with the subscript indicating length, they incorporate a tagged variable system where specific subscripted variables reflect different formats for a birthday. Thus, for each type of personal information, they have to predefine different formats for the particular variable; these become the only formats that are learned during the training process.

The approach of Wang et al. has exactly the same, if not worse, ambiguity problems as that of Li et al. when generating guesses because many different base structures can yield identical passwords, leading to incorrect assignments of probabilities to the guesses. For example, the password string *120982* can be derived from various variables represented as $B_1$, $B_2$, ... , $B_{10}$ or even $D_6$, which would then give incorrect probabilities to terminal strings during guessing because all possible probabilities of the string derivations have to be added. When using previous password information, Wang et al. also introduce new variables to the grammar that represent various transformations of passwords. But this causes similar problems as discussed above. In contrast, the approach for accommodating previous passwords presented in this chapter does not require changes to probabilistic context-free grammar training or guess generation.

Das et al. [3] have used publicly-available leaked password sets with user identifiers and have analyzed the data to find passwords for the users. In particular, they were able to find 6,077 unique users with at most two passwords for each user; 43% were identical passwords and the remaining were non-identical. However, Das et al. do not consider the changes that a user might make when using similar passwords for the same or other accounts.

Zhang et al. [18] have conducted a large-scale study focusing on password changes necessitated by password expiration. They were able to access a dataset of more than 7,700 accounts containing a known password and a subsequently changed password for each account. They model a password change as a sequence of transforms (based on various criteria) and organize the transforms as a tree with the old password as the root. A path in the tree is a sequence of transforms that yields the new password with common subsequences being the same from the root. A search starts at the root with an input password and, upon visiting each node in the tree, the corresponding transform is applied to the output of the parent node. Then, each output is tested as a password guess against the target password hash. The primary limitation of this algorithm is its time complexity; thus, the depth of the tree is restricted to three levels. Furthermore, the algorithm does not incorporate information about a user. In contrast, the approach proposed in this chapter derives a new grammar that precisely incorporates user information to enhance PCFG-based password cracking. The approach enables the use of specific information about a previous password instead of generic transformations that a number of users may employ. Additionally, the approach can simultaneously incorporate personal information about the targeted user.

## 3.    Building a Targeted Attack

This section discusses the proposed approach for creating a probabilistic context-free grammar designed to crack a password for a targeted user. It is assumed that there is a single target and that some personal information about the target and the password hash are available. The goal is to create an attack grammar that specifically generates guesses for the target. Note that multiple hashes are not targeted simultaneously. This is not really a limitation because, if the hashes are salted, attacks have to be re-executed for each hash. Also, this is a common situation that holds true for online attacks on the target; this is because there is no notion of trying multiple users simultaneously. If no personal information is available, the same grammar would most likely be used for all targets. Of course, some general information could guide the use of different training datasets (e.g., Chinese vs. English targets). The added complexity of the proposed approach is simply that a grammar is developed for each target. As will be discussed later, grammars can be combined to handle a situation where the personal information was used to create the password as well as a situation where it was not (e.g., the user simply created some other password).

The available personal information can be as simple as the username or the first and last names of the user or it can be more detailed such as the names of family members, their dates of birth and addresses. Password policies often do not allow users to use their login ids or even their real names when creating passwords. However, human beings tend to use phrases, names and numbers that are familiar to them for easy memorization. Thus, personal information gathered about a target can be very useful in password cracking. The proposed approach can leverage any type of personal information about a target with only minor categorization.

The next section discusses the combination of multiple grammars to create a new grammar that models the use of the component grammars in a precise way. Following this, the use of the combined grammar in cracking passwords belonging to a specific target is described.

## 3.1 Merging Context-Free Grammars

Generating a probabilistic context-free grammar from a training set of disclosed user passwords can be time consuming depending on the size of the training set. Merging two or more grammars gives the advantage of combining two training sets without having to repeat the training phase.

Suppose it is desired to concatenate two training sets to create a grammar. One way is to merge the training sets and produce a context-free grammar from the entire set. On the other hand, assume that two grammars have been generated, each using a different training set. Then, the two grammars can be merged to create a new grammar that is the result of training using both the sets. This technique also permits the specification of a weight for each grammar to control how much it is affected by each training set.

A probabilistic context free grammar has a set of production rules $R_j$ ($j = 1..n$) where $n$ is the number of rules. Each rule has a single variable (or non-terminal) on the left-hand side with a sequence of variables or terminals on the right-hand side. Each rule $R_j$ has an associated probability $p_j$ with the requirement that the probabilities of all the rules with the same left-hand side must sum to one.

**Definition:** Let $G_1$ and $G_2$ be two probabilistic context-free grammars with base structures and component structures as defined in [6, 17].

Then, the new grammar $G$, which is called the "merge" of $G_1$ and $G_2$, is given by:

$$G = \alpha G_1 + (1 - \alpha)G_2 \quad where \quad 0 \le \alpha \le 1$$

Note that this is only representational because grammars are actually complex abstract tuples. It is assumed that the variables and terminals in the two grammars are chosen from the same possible sets. The parameter $\alpha$ is used to give an appropriate weight to grammar $G_1$ versus grammar $G_2$.

Next, it is necessary to define the new set of rules and their probabilities for the merged grammar $G$.

**Definition:** Let $R$ be a grammar rule that is in $G_1$ or $G_2$. Let the probability of $R$ in $G_1$ be $p_1$ and the probability of $R$ in $G_2$ be $p_2$ (if $R$ is not in a grammar, then its probability is zero). Then, the probability $p$ of $R$ in the merged grammar $G$ is given by:

$$p = \alpha p_1 + (1 - \alpha)p_2$$

It is easily shown that $G$ is a well-defined probabilistic context-free grammar. This is because the probability values of all rules with the same left-hand side variable in the merged grammar sum to one. Furthermore, the combination of the two grammars can be viewed as an affine transformation with the points being grammars in an abstract space. Intuitively, it is possible to combine any number of grammars by simply ensuring that the sum of their component weights is equal to one and the resulting grammar is the same regardless of the ordering of the combinations.

Table 1 shows a simple example involving the merging of two grammars. The following sections discuss how merged grammars can be used to crack passwords belonging to a target.

## 3.2    Integrating Personal Information

The approach enables a user to input almost any available personal information about a target. Law enforcement personnel often encounter cases in which they have to break the passwords of suspects about whom they have significant personal information. Examples include the names of family members and friends, usernames, relevant numbers (social security and phone numbers), addresses (street name, city, state and zip code), important dates, favorite sports teams and players. Personal information is entered in a structured way such that the entries can be massaged as needed.

*Table 1.* Merging grammars $G_1$ and $G_2$ with $\alpha = 0.8$.

| Grammar $G_1$ Rule | Probability |
| --- | --- |
| $S \rightarrow L_5D_3 \mid L_5S_1$ | 0.6 \| 0.4 |
| $D_3 \rightarrow 999 \mid 124$ | 0.8 \| 0.2 |
| $S_1 \rightarrow ! \mid @$ | 0.63 \| 0.37 |

| Grammar $G_2$ Rule | Probability |
| --- | --- |
| $S \rightarrow L_5S_1 \mid L_4S_1$ | 0.7 \| 0.3 |
| $D_3 \rightarrow 123 \mid 124$ | 0.6 \| 0.4 |
| $S_1 \rightarrow \# \mid \&$ | 0.72 \| 0.28 |

| Merged Grammar Rule | Probability |
| --- | --- |
| $S \rightarrow L_5D_3 \mid L_5S_1 \mid L_4S_1$ | 0.48 \| 0.46 \| 0.06 |
| $D_3 \rightarrow 999 \mid 124 \mid 123$ | 0.64 \| 0.24 \| 0.12 |
| $S_1 \rightarrow ! \mid @ \mid \# \mid \&$ | 0.504 \| 0.296 \| 0.144 \| 0.056 |

Based on the personal information (PI), a PI-grammar and PI-dictionary are constructed for password cracking. Numbers are added to the digit variables of the PI-grammar. Names, words and alphabet character strings are added directly to the PI-dictionary. Multiple dictionaries can be used during the attack phase (guess generation). For example, a basic dictionary would be a fairly large standard dictionary of words; these words are not learned via the training process because the training set would be too sparse to accurately account for or reflect word usage. Additional specialized dictionaries could be used; examples include a "top words" dictionary that contains the most frequently-occurring words in the training set and the PI-dictionary that contains words based on personal information for use in a targeted attack. The use of the PI-dictionary during guess generation ensures that the strings in the dictionary will be used with higher probabilities in the guesses.

Dates are broken down into month, day and year components, and most variations of dates are similarly added to the PI-grammar. For example, when *02/10/2016* is entered, the following numbers are added to the digit components of the PI-grammar: *02, 10, 2016, 16, 02102016, 021016, 10022016, 100216, 0210, 1002*, etc. The name of the month and its variations are also added to the PI-dictionary (e.g., *February* and *Feb*). Note that the PI-grammar alone is not very useful in password cracking because it has very few base structures and components. The proposed approach merges this grammar with a general grammar in order to generate guesses.

## 3.3    Using Old Password Information

As the number of accounts per user increases, users are more likely to reuse their passwords or change their passwords slightly to avoid memorizing new passwords. This is particularly true when a security policy forces users to change their passwords frequently. A survey by Shay et al. [12] conducted on 470 university students, staff and faculty revealed that 60% of the individuals used one password with slight changes for different accounts. Moreover, a study of leaked password sets by Durmuth et al. [4] demonstrated that users often apply simple tricks to make slight changes to their old passwords.

Old passwords contain vital information such as important numbers, dates and names of family members. The goal is to specify a grammar that can generate guesses similar to an old password. Since users often change their passwords with slight modifications, the AMP edit distance [5] is used to define a metric for similar passwords and to determine a grammar that can generate such passwords. AMP uses a distance function to create strengthened passwords within an edit distance of one of a user-chosen password based on the Damerau-Levenshtein edit distance [2]. The Damerau-Levenshtein edit distance measures the minimum number of operations needed to transform one string into another. The AMP version of this distance function includes insertion, deletion, substitution and transposition of components of the base structure as well as similar operations within a component. The AMP distance function is improved by adding operations on keyboard patterns and multiword patterns. These patterns were originally incorporated in probabilistic context-free grammars by Houshmand et al. [6]. For multiwords, the revised AMP edit distance has the unit operations:

- **Insertion:** Insert a $D_1$ or $S_1$ in between two words in a multiword. For example, for a password containing *starwars* ($M_8$), *star5wars* or *star!wars* are created.

- **Transposition of Components:** Transpose two adjacent words as well as the first and last word in a multiword. For example, *mysweetbaby* can be changed to *sweetmybaby*, *mybabysweet* and *babysweetmy*.

- **Deletion:** Delete a word from a multiword, which results in a new base structure as well as a new multiword in the grammar. For example, given the password *mysweetbaby12* with base structure $M_{11}D_2$, it is possible to create other base structures such as $M_9D_2$, $M_6D_2$, $M_7D_2$ as well as *mysweet, mybaby* and *sweetbaby* as multiwords in the grammar.

This approach produces an ED-grammar (edit distance grammar) that, by itself, generates all the guesses within a revised AMP edit distance of one from an old password. Note that every possible change is considered to be equally probable.

## 3.4    Predicting New Passwords

This section assumes that the attacker has even more information about the target. The focus is on the knowledge about the target's password habits and it is assumed that the attacker has access to at least two similar subsequent old passwords. The first approach can be leveraged to use the passwords to generate an ED-grammar. However, it is also possible to gather information about the changes made to the previous passwords of the target and use this information to predict the new password. In the following paragraphs, an algorithm for determining changes between two subsequent known passwords is presented. Following this, a new password based on the information is predicted.

In order to determine the changes between two passwords, a function is implemented that finds the minimum edit distance by creating a distance matrix. The function also incorporates a backtracking algorithm that determines the operations made between the two strings. The edit distance function is based on the Damerau-Levenshtein algorithm. The algorithm starts by filling a (distance) matrix $D$ of size $n_1 \times n_2$, where $n_1$ is the length of the first string $s$ and $n_2$ is the length of the second string $t$. The $D[i,j]$ value measures the distance between the initial substring of $s$ of length $i$ and the initial substring of $t$ of length $j$. At the time of creating the matrix, the operations associated with each step are captured and stored in another matrix $O$ (using i: insertion, d: deletion, t: transposition). This is used to create the transformation algorithm that backtracks using the matrix and finds the exact operations made when transforming one string to another.

**Hierarchical Transformation Algorithm.**   Note that the AMP edit distance function [5] is different from the regular Damerau-Levenshtein edit distance. The main difference is in the transposition operation. The Damerau-Levenshtein edit distance considers a transposition of two adjacent characters as one edit distance. While this can be useful to model string similarities, it is not appropriate for password changes. For example, when two passwords such as *iloveyou123* and *123iloveyou* are compared, the Damerau-Levenshtein edit distance between the two strings is computed as 6 (the algorithm finds that there are three insertions in the beginning and three deletions at the end of the string). However, when considering these two strings as passwords with different components, it is clear that the target has only made one change by transposing the multiword component $M_8$ with the digit component $D_3$.

This is modeled using a hierarchical transformation algorithm that first finds the edit distance between the simple base structures. A simple base structure is the base structure of the password without considering the length of each component. For example, the simple base structure of *love456!* is *LSD*.

Given two old subsequent passwords, in the first level, both passwords are parsed to their simple base structures. Then, the edit distance algorithm is invoked for these two simple base structures to determine the differences in the base structures. Using the backtracking algorithm, the operations that caused the change in the simple base structure are determined.

The backtracking algorithm starts from the bottom-right corner of the matrix and travels back to the upper-left corner of the matrix and, in each step, determines the operation that was performed to calculate the edit distance. It then creates a string of the operations along the path that shows how one string has been transformed to the other. If a transposition has been made within the simple base structure, the algorithm checks the values of each component and then reverses the transposition such that it neutralizes the initial transposition effect and recreates one of the passwords similar to the other by applying the transposition.

The second level of the hierarchical algorithm proceeds to find the edit distance between the changed password along with the second password to identify the edit distance and the operations between the two strings. For example, the backtracking function returns nndnnnnnt (n: no change, d: deletion, t: transposition) given *123alice!$* and *12alice$!*. This hierarchical transformation algorithm is used in the next section to predict the changes that the target has made to create the new password.

**Creating the Grammar.** The transformations between two old passwords can be used to generate guesses of the most recent password of the target. Some of the most common and important changes based on the available data and the results of other studies [3, 18] are used to create the PM-grammar (password modifications grammar). The following functions add appropriate structures to the PM-grammar:

- **Increment/Decrement the Digit Component:** An increment or decrement of one in the digit component in the old passwords is identified. Upon finding such a change, the next predictable change is added to the grammar. For example, if the old passwords are *bluemoon22* and *bluemoon23*, the number *24* is added to the $D_2$ component of the grammar. The same base structure $L_8D_2$ also has to be added to the grammar to increase the likelihood of using the same structure again.

- **Insertion of the Same Digit:** Algorithms have been developed to recognize if a digit has been inserted into a password and if it has been added repeatedly. Examples are *bluemoon* → *bluemoon5* → *bluemoon55* → *bluemoon555*. In this case, if the old passwords are *bluemoon3* and *bluemoon33*, *333* is added to $D_3$ in the grammar as well as $L_8D_3$ to the base structures of the grammar.

- **Capitalization of Alpha Strings:** If the old passwords both have the same alpha sequence with different capitalizations, both the capitalizations are added to the grammar because the chances of using the masks are higher.

## 3.5    Merging Grammars and Generating Guesses

After the PI-grammar, ED-grammar and PM-grammar have been constructed based on the kind of information available, the grammars are merged with a more comprehensive general grammar that is used for password cracking when no personal information is known. By assigning appropriate weights to the grammars, the generated guesses can be balanced such that guesses with personal information are typically generated earlier with higher probability values and guesses that are more general are typically generated later in the guessing process.

This approach, unlike other methods [7, 14], does not require changing the training code or the cracking code of the probabilistic context-free grammar that implements training and guessing. In fact, it can be viewed as an add-on intermediate step that requires no changes to training and guessing.

After training on a large password set (general grammar), the PI-grammar, ED-grammar and PM-grammar are created based on the available personal information. These grammars are merged with the general grammar. The resulting final target grammar can be used as before in offline or online attacks and can generate a wide variety of guesses (in highest probability order) while giving higher probabilities to passwords similar to those used by the target.

The advantage is that no matter which version of a probabilistic context-free grammar is used, the approach still holds. Note that the attacker uses personal information in the hope that the target has used personal information to create the password. Clearly, the merging of grammars is a powerful mechanism.

A key aspect of the merging technique is that, if the target has not used personal information in passwords, the password cracking system will still work appropriately. For example, merging a general grammar and a special targeted grammar based on a seed password can be used to generate passwords that favor the seed password, but it is not stuck with a limited number of guesses and generates guesses based on the general grammar as well. Furthermore, by adjusting the weights when merging the grammars, it is possible to favor one approach (general) versus the other (seed).

## 4.    Experiments

This section discusses the experimental results on the effectiveness of targeted password attacks. It can be proven that, if personal information (excluding previous passwords) was used in a password such as a name or date, the password cracking approach would automatically use such passwords earlier in guess generation because the probabilities of these passwords are higher due to the grammar merging operation. Unfortunately, obtaining a validated personal information password set or simulating one through user studies is problematic. Therefore, no tests were performed on the PI-grammar. Instead, the experiments focused on a situation where previous passwords are available.

The first experiment compared attacks with and without the ED-grammar. These attacks are referred to as targeted and general attacks, respectively. The (extended) probabilistic context-free grammar of Houshmand et al. [6] was used for training. In the general attack, training was performed using a large dataset of real user passwords and the (general) grammar was used to generate guesses. In the targeted attack, the old password was used to create the ED-grammar, which was then combined with the same general grammar produced for the general attack while also using the same dictionary.

A total of 300,000 passwords were randomly selected from the Yahoo! set of real user passwords that was leaked in 2012 [9]. This training set was used to produce the general grammar. The training approach requires a training dictionary to determine multiwords [6]. EOWL [8] augmented with common proper names and top words from movie scripts was used as in [5]. Additionally, dict-0294 [11] was used as the primary attack dictionary. The test set contained 56 pairs of old and new passwords obtained through a survey of how users change passwords. The survey study was approved by the Florida State University Institutional Review Board (IRB).

## 4.1     Password Survey

About 2,000 randomly-selected students from Florida State University were invited to participate in the password survey. The participants were asked to create an account with a password on the survey website. The only password policy requirement was to use at least eight characters. The participants were asked to log in once a day for a total of four times during a period of one week. At each login, the participants were asked a few survey questions. On the third website visit, the participants were asked to change their passwords. On the fourth visit, the participants logged in with their changed passwords and completed the survey.

Multiple logins enabled the participants to gain familiarity and become comfortable with the passwords they had created before they were asked to change their passwords. A total of 144 participants created accounts and 56 of them proceeded to change their passwords; 53% of the participants were female and 47% male. About 40% said that they did not create new passwords for the survey, but simply used their old passwords. Only 14% said that they created new passwords for each account. When creating their passwords, 30% of the participants said they modified their existing passwords, about 24% reused their old passwords and only 14% created new passwords. These percentages are consistent with other studies.

## 4.2     Testing and Cracking Results

After the participants had changed their passwords, they were asked how they changed their passwords and whether they changed them by modifying their previous passwords. This question was important because it revealed which passwords were changed intentionally by modifying the old passwords. Otherwise, it would not have been possible to divine the intentions of the user although the passwords appeared to be similar. Of the 56 passwords, 23 were claimed to be created based on the previous password. Therefore, the analysis only focused on these passwords to check if the passwords could be guessed effectively.

During each cracking session, the old password was used as input to generate the ED-grammar. This grammar was then combined with the general grammar. Guesses were generated for the targeted and general attacks. Table 2 shows the old password used as input, the new password that was attacked and the number of guesses required to find the new password using the targeted and general attacks.

*Table 2.*    Test Result of Targeted Attack.

| Old Password | New Password | Guesses in the Targeted Attack | Guesses in the General Attack |
|---|---|---|---|
| *tharaborithor* | *thorborithara* | – | – |
| *Simba144!* | *@Simba2523* | 734,505,973 | – |
| *$unGl@$$220* | *$unGl@$$110* | 4,070 | – |
| *research!* | *Research!* | 554 | 5,059,949,503 |
| *starWars@123* | *star#Ecit@123* | 2,227,558 | – |
| *thebigblackdogjumps* | *blackdogmoretime* | – | – |
| *Ahk@1453* | *Ahk#1453* | 12,026 | – |
| *qpalzm73* | *qpalzm73\** | 1,810 | – |
| *pluto1995* | *boonepluto* | – | – |
| *caramba10* | *caramba12* | 14 | 11,424,542 |
| *Elvis1993!* | *Professional1993!2* | – | – |
| *pepper88* | *peppergator88* | 128,197,109 | 2,563,504,751 |
| *ganxiedajiA1!!* | *1ganxiedajiA* | 7,794 | – |
| *88dolphins!* | *55dolphins!* | 38,503 | – |
| *kannj2013!* | *Kannj2013* | 97 | – |
| *!FSU$qr335* | *!FSU$qr335mcddt* | – | – |
| *vballgrl77* | *schatzimae* | – | – |
| *nickc1007* | *corkn1007* | – | – |
| *sunflower12* | *sunflower13* | 202 | 119,336,969 |
| *meg51899* | *Meg51899\** | 5,381 | – |
| *Research1* | *research11* | 206 | 23,728,452 |
| *Gleek1993* | *Gleek1985* | 9,661 | 1,994,709,669 |
| *Oaklea0441* | *Oaklea0112* | 91,014 | – |

Since this work seeks to demonstrate that passwords are cracked faster using personal information (e.g., old passwords), the number of guesses was limited to 10 billion in the password cracking session. The idea was to verify that passwords can be cracked in much shorter sessions than in a regular offline password cracking session.

The results in Table 2 reveal that it was possible to guess most of the passwords that were changed slightly. However, a few of the passwords could not be guessed (shown as –) primarily because there were no relevant alpha strings in the dictionaries. For example, the password *tharaborithor* is not in English and the password *vballgrl77* was not actually modified, although the user claimed it was. The results show that only a few of the passwords were broken during a general password cracking attack and it took much longer for the others compared with the targeted attack. Indeed, the targeted attack was more efficient when information about the old passwords of users was incorporated.

To explore the proposed approach further, a small list of 30 sets of previous passwords from a private entity was used. This list contained no other information. All but two of the passwords were pairs and only two comprised three sequential passwords. The PM-grammar could be used on the two sequential sets and the third password in the sequence could be cracked on the first guess. Furthermore, 78% of the passwords in the list could be cracked, with 66% of the passwords cracked in less than 20 guesses.

## 5. Conclusions

This research has demonstrated that personal information belonging to targeted users can be systematically incorporated in probabilistic context-free grammars to efficiently generate password guesses. Three grammars, PI-grammar, ED-grammar and PM-grammar, are created based on various pieces of information such as names, dates, numbers and previous passwords. Multiple grammars are merged using a parameter that appropriately weights each grammar and the new merged grammar maintains its probabilistic properties. The proposed approach is an add-on intermediate step between the training and cracking phases of probabilistic context-free grammars, enabling it to be used very easily with all the probabilistic context-free grammar variations.

Experimental results demonstrate that many of the passwords can be guessed using a targeted grammar; however, a general grammar is not as successful. Passwords are also guessed at a much faster rate (many fewer guesses) using a targeted grammar compared with a general grammar. Future research will attempt to evaluate and refine the proposed research by conducting surveys with much larger numbers of participants and, therefore, more password pairs.

## References

[1] C. Castelluccia, A. Chaabane, M. Durmuth and D. Perito, When privacy meets security: Leveraging personal information for password cracking, *Computing Research Repository*, abs/1304.6584, 2013.

[2] F. Damerau, A technique for computer detection and correction of spelling errors, *Communications of the ACM*, vol. 7(3), pp. 171–176, 1964.

[3] A. Das, J. Bonneau, M. Caesar, N. Borisov and X. Wang, The tangled web of password reuse, *Proceedings of the Network and Distributed Systems Security Symposium*, 2014.

[4]  M. Durmuth, F. Angelstorf, C. Castelluccia, D. Perito and A. Chaa-
     bane, OMEN: Faster password guessing using an ordered Markov
     enumerator, *Proceedings of the Seventh International Symposium
     on Engineering Secure Software and Systems*, pp. 119–132, 2015.

[5]  S. Houshmand and S. Aggarwal, Building better passwords using
     probabilistic techniques, *Proceedings of the Twenty-Eighth Annual
     Computer Security Applications Conference*, pp. 109–118, 2012.

[6]  S. Houshmand, S. Aggarwal and R. Flood, Next Gen PCFG pass-
     word cracking, *IEEE Transactions on Information Forensics and
     Security*, vol. 10(8), pp. 1776–1791, 2015.

[7]  Y. Li, H. Wang and K. Sun, A study of personal information in
     human-chosen passwords and their security implications, *Proceed-
     ings of the Thirty-Fifth Annual IEEE International Conference on
     Computer Communications*, 2016.

[8]  K. Loge, The English Open Word List, Dreamsteep (dreamsteep.
     com/projects/the-english-open-word-list.html), 2017.

[9]  S. Musil, Hackers post 450K credentials pilfered from Yahoo, *CNET*,
     July 11, 2012.

[10] A. Narayanan and V. Shmatikov, Fast dictionary attacks on pass-
     words using time-space tradeoff, *Proceedings of the Twelfth ACM
     Conference on Computer and Communications Security*, pp. 364–
     372, 2005.

[11] Outpost9.com, Word Lists..., (www.outpost9.com/files/WordLis
     ts.html), 2004.

[12] R. Shay, S. Komanduri, P. Kelley, P. Leon, M. Mazurek, L. Bauer,
     N. Christin and L. Cranor, Encountering stronger password require-
     ments: User attitudes and behaviors, *Proceedings of the Sixth Sym-
     posium on Usable Privacy and Security*, article no. 2, 2010.

[13] A. Vance, If your password is 123456, just make it hackme, *The
     New York Times*, January 20, 2010.

[14] D. Wang, Z. Zhang, P. Wang, J. Yan and X. Huang, Targeted on-
     line password guessing: An underestimated threat, *Proceedings of
     the ACM SIGSAC Conference on Computer and Communications
     Security*, pp. 1242–1254, 2016.

[15] R. Waugh, No wonder hackers have it easy: Most of us now have
     26 different online accounts – but only five passwords, *Daily Mail*,
     July 16, 2102.

[16] M. Weir, S. Aggarwal, M. Collins and H. Stern, Testing metrics for password creation policies by attacking large sets of revealed passwords, *Proceedings of the Seventeenth ACM Conference on Computer and Communications Security*, pp. 162–175, 2010.

[17] M. Weir, S. Aggarwal, B. de Medeiros and B. Glodek, Password cracking using probabilistic context-free grammars, *Proceedings of the IEEE Symposium on Security and Privacy*, pp. 391–405, 2009.

[18] Y. Zhang, F. Monrose and M. Reiter, The security of modern password expiration: An algorithmic framework and empirical analysis, *Proceedings of the Seventeenth ACM Conference on Computer and Communications Security*, pp. 176–186, 2010.

Printed in the United States
By Bookmasters